China's Belt and Road Initiatives and Its Neighboring Diplomacy

China's Belt and Road Initiatives and Its Neighboring Diplomacy

Editor

ZHANG Jie

Chinese Academy of Social Sciences, China

Translator

XU Mengqi

People's Public Security University, China

社会科学文献出版社
SOCIAL SCIENCES ACADEMIC PRESS (CHINA)

World Scientific

Published by

World Scientific Publishing Co. Pte. Ltd.

5 Toh Tuck Link, Singapore 596224

USA office: 27 Warren Street, Suite 401-402, Hackensack, NJ 07601

UK office: 57 Shelton Street, Covent Garden, London WC2H 9HE

Library of Congress Cataloging-in-Publication Data
Names: Zhang, Jie, 1973–   editor.
Title: China's belt and road initiatives and its neighboring diplomacy /
    [edited by] Jie Zhang (Chinese Academy of Social Sciences, China).
Description: New Jersey : World Scientific, [2016]
Identifiers: LCCN 2016015691 | ISBN 9789813140202 (hc : alk. paper)
Subjects: LCSH: China--Foreign economic relations. | China--Commerce. |
    Economic development--China. | Trade routes--China. | Infrastructure
    (Economics)--China. | China--Economic policy--2000–
Classification: LCC HF1604 .C4525 2016 | DDC 337.51--dc23
LC record available at https://lccn.loc.gov/2016015691

British Library Cataloguing-in-Publication Data
A catalogue record for this book is available from the British Library.

《中国周边安全形势评估2015》
Originally published in Chinese by Social Sciences Academic Press (China)
Copyright © 2015 Social Sciences Academic Press (China)

Desk Editors: Anthony Alexander/Dong Lixi

Typeset by Stallion Press
Email: enquiries@stallionpress.com

Contents

About the Editor-in-Chief

Ms. Zhang Jie is a Research Fellow of National Institute of International Strategy of Chinese Academy of Social Sciences. Her research has been focusing on China–ASEAN relations in both security and diplomacy, and the issue of South China Sea. She had her monograph, *Ethnic Separatism and National Identity: A Case Study on Ethnic Conflict in Aceh*, published in 2012 by Social Sciences Academic Press in China. At the same time, she is the editor-in-chief of *China's Regional Security Review* for five consecutive years from 2011 to 2015, and writer of dozens of articles in journals such as *The Journal of International Studies*, *Journal of International Security Studies*, *Journal of Contemporary Asia-Pacific Studies*, *Southeast Asian Studies*, and *Pacific Journal*, etc.

About the Translator

Ms. Xu Mengqi graduated from Beijing Foreign Studies University where she obtained Master Degree in translation studies. Having been engaging in international affairs for two years, she is now with the International Cooperation Office of People's Public Security University of China in Beijing. She has a five-year experience of translating and interpreting in a variety of fields including finance, culture, international relations, and manufacturing industry. She is the translator of such books as *China–Africa Relations: Review and Analysis*, *China's Quantitative Economics in the Past 30 Years*, *Chinese National Cultural Security in the Age of Globalization*, and *China's Financial Stability: Inherent Logic and Basic Framework*.

Preface

National power of neighboring countries has waxed and waned ever since the U.S. engaged in its rebalance to Asia-Pacific region in 2010. What is worth noticing is that China's strength growth stimulates immense changes to safety situations of its neighborhood. In face of new challenges, China begins to design and shape its peripheral environment.

Against such background, "Silk Road Economic Belt" and "21st Century Maritime Silk Road" (Belt and Road Initiative) came into being successively in 2013. In the year after, China delivered to the world its commitment to and resolution in realizing its proposal through ways of leaders' oversea visits, regional dialogue, dialogue on partnership of connectivity, construction of Asian Infrastructure Investment Bank and Silk Road Foundation, and so on.

The Belt and Road Initiative extends to the whole world by and through China's neighboring countries and regions. In this case, peripheral region should be given top priority in a country's strategic practice. At the same time, Belt and Road Initiative values openness and cooperation, which calls for interaction between China and its neighbors rather than one-way advancement of the proposer. Thus an observation of the attitude of China's neighbors towards the initiative, be it positive or negative, is necessary for China to forge ahead with its national strategy. That's also where the idea of writing this book came from.

This book selects four countries, the U.S., Japan, Russia, and India, and four regions, Northeast Asia, Southeast Asia, South Asia, and Middle Asia, as objects of observation. It addresses questions such as what the reasons behind their different attitude towards the Belt and Road Initiative are, what influence their attitude is going to exert to the progress of realizing the initiative, and whether or not their attitude will change some day.

At the time when the Belt and Road Initiative was born, disputes on the sea have affected China's safety environment for a while with a tendency of escalation. Some of the disputes are about territory and interests in attached sea areas; some are in relation to the shaping of new maritime order; and some involves the division and grouping in security order of Asia-Pacific region. Under such circumstances, can the Belt and Road Initiative, especially the 21st Century Maritime Silk Road, which aims at building a new sea order of free voyage, common security on the sea, and joint exploitation of marine resources, act as a key propeller in solving maritime disputes and in completing China's strategy on its neighborhood? Answering this question is where the book ends up with despite the fact that the initiative is still a new-born.

In closing, I want to mention that this book is a result of collective efforts made for many years. Previously, the research group made up mainly by researchers from the Department of Asia-Pacific Security and Diplomatic Studies of National Institute of International Strategy, CASS has published annual reports on China's safety environment for four consecutive years. In essence, the research is a long-term observation, through which descriptive analysis of situations can be abstracted as regularities, and concerns on single cases ignite the thoughts of trend study. Hopefully, this academic endeavor can contribute to the shaping of China's strategy on its neighborhood.

Introduction

Chinese President Xi Jinping proposed that China and Central Asia join hands to build a Silk Road Economic Belt when he visited Kazakhstan in September 2013 and the 21st Century Maritime Silk Road during his visit in ASEAN countries in October of the same year.

Being an externally grand strategy, the Belt and Road Initiative is no longer just a proposal but what China is promoting by concrete actions. The initiative started from economic cooperation with neighboring countries, such as establishing Asian Infrastructure Investment Bank (AIIB) and Silk Road Fund. Some neighbors of China welcomed such move and got themselves involved willingly, while others had doubts so they waited and saw.

In light of development in both security and economy, we see 2014 a year when China's grand strategy towards neighbors has basically taken shape. It is the foremost feature of China's regional security situation that year. Specifically speaking, China gained increasing willingness and capacity to lead and shape the region and thus brought forth a dual track of strategies, the Belt and Road Initiative-centered economic strategy and the security strategy focusing on control over sea issues.

This book consists of four parts, including the Overview, the Belt and Road Initiative and Big Powers, the Belt and Road Initiative and Regions, and the Belt and Road Initiative and Hot Issues. The Overview is made up of two sections, one explicating the strategic orientations, connotations and approaches of implementation of the initiative from a theoretical perspective and the other being the general report. This book compares four pairs of big power relations in terms of changes and features, and reveals new trends in the South China Sea issue and non-traditional security. Besides, it summarizes current situations of promoting the Belt and Road Initiative, responses of major powers and sub-regions to the initiative, and strategic docking and main challenges in the near future.

The second part is the Belt and Road Initiative and Big Powers. The report chooses four great powers, namely the US, Russia, Japan and India, and analyzes their Asia-Pacific strategies, their relations with China, and responses to the Belt and Road Initiative.

The third part discusses the Belt and Road Initiative and four regions, namely Northeast Asia, Southeast Asia, South Asia, and Central Asia. It not only reveals the security situation in those regions in 2014, but as well evaluates their attitude and response towards the Belt and Road Initiative, strategic docking and major challenges in this regard.

The fourth part touches upon the initiative and current hot issues like non-traditional security, the South China Sea dispute, and venture analysis on investment environment renovation. This part observes main security challenges which the Belt and Road is faced with from different aspects and how China copes with them.

Overview

Chapter 1

Belt and Road Initiative as a Grand Strategy

Zhang Yunling

Academic Division of International Studies,
Chinese Academy of Social Sciences
ylzhang@cass.org.cn

President Xi Jinping proposed that China and Central Asia join hands to build a Silk Road Economic Belt when he visited Kazakhstan in September 2013 and the 21ˢᵗ Century Maritime Silk Road during his visit in ASEAN countries in October of the same year. Thereby the Belt and Road Initiative came out of water as a grand strategy at a new phase of development of China. Not long ago, the Chinese government held a meeting to discuss how to put the initiative into practice. At the meeting, President Xi pointed out that the Belt and Road Initiative is "the call of the time" and "a huge and inclusive platform for development", "gearing the rocketing Chinese economy to the interests of countries along the Belt and the Road". He demanded that "Efforts should be concentrated to grasp key projects so as to yield positive results as soon as possible". This marked that the Belt and Road strategy was put on the table and into action.

Why does China pay much attention to the construction of the Belt and the Road? How to recognize the meanings embodied in the strategy? Final realization of the strategy calls for deeper acknowledgment of it, especially, the understanding and support of relevant nations and their collaborative work with China.

1. Connotations Endowed by the Times

The Belt and Road strategy is the requirement of the times as peace and development are two most prominent natures of the era we are in, or in other words, to develop is what people in every nation value most.

The world is always keeping an eye on China's rapid growth and is wondering what and how China is to do as it becomes stronger and stronger. In the light of world history, great powers always contend with each other and the strongest one usually seeks hegemony. China keeps assuring that it will insist on the principle of peaceful development, but its promise has not been considered persuasive enough by other countries. It is quite understandable. Actions speak louder than words after all. People are worrying that the world will fall into the Thucydides's trap, conflicts among big powers arise, and that larger wars will be triggered once China adopts expansionary strategy and starts to vie with the USA for global influence.

To live up to its promise of not rising up in traditional way, China pledges a new model of China–US relations based on non-confrontation, dialogue, and cooperation. At the same time, China tries to resolve people's suspicion of its adopting expansionary strategies by advocating the Belt and Road Initiative. In this way, it tells the world that it is forging ahead with its promise of peaceful development and its commitment to win–win cooperation.

The era we are living in is themed by the growth of developing countries up to the level of economic takeoff and the appearance of emerging economies. It requires us to figure out how to constantly develop, and to provide developing countries with the conditions for their continuous development. Although China is a world economic giant, it is still a developing country which demands a long-lasting course of development in the first place. Given that, China is the second largest economy in the globe and is the owner of the largest amount of foreign exchange reserves, China is committed to contribute to world development and to improve the circumstances for world economic growth. In this regard, the Belt and Road Initiative act as a big platform where China ties its economic development up with other countries' development. On that platform, China takes the lead and gathers the efforts of all parties in their endeavor of enlarging the space and creating new engines for development.

The Belt and Road strategy is a stage open to collaborative projects between China and relevant countries. Financing, especially in fields of infrastructure construction and long-term projects, is rather hard to developing countries. The development of infrastructure lags behind and the circumstances for its development improve slowly due to limited capacity of prevailing international financial organizations and little investment willingness of private financial institutions. In this respect, the Belt and Road Initiative can break the bottleneck of financing by founding cooperative financing organizations and financial institutions in other forms. Here, China plays a bigger role. It advocated the foundation of the New Development Bank BRICS (NDB BRICS), Asian Infrastructure Investment Bank (AIIB), and SCO Development Bank and sponsored the Silk Road Fund. Some denounce that what China is doing is the "New Marshall Plan". Actually it is mistaken. The Marshall Plan was set up by the United States for aiding post-war economic renewal of Europe, while the idea of building new financing instructions values full participation, joint management, and the sharing of resources. There are also harsh words criticizing that China is to undermine the existing framework of international financial organizations. Obviously it is a misunderstanding or even slander. These newly founded organizations are to supplement and fortify insufficient functions of current ones rather than disrupting them.

Institutional innovation is the demand of the new age, so is the promotion of new organizations. China, being in the current international system, is summoned by the times to propel the adjustment and changes to the system and to build new institutions so as to satisfy newly emerging needs of development. Evidently, instead of being a strategy to stand against the current system, the Belt and Road Initiative is a strategy open to cooperation. Only by recognizing the strategy by an open mind and the concept of collaboration can we identify its quality of being the demand of the times.

2. Born to be a Grand Strategy

The Belt and Road Initiative is originally designed as a grand strategy based on not only the development of China, but also the growth of the region and the world. So it is not a short-term project. Some drew a map or a timetable for it, which is necessary because we need steps and plans to remind us when a step shall be accomplished. Nevertheless, the map or timetable is by no means a once for all plan.

The Belt which specifically refers to the Silk Road Economic Belt, is a strategy pursuing balanced regional development and structure equilibrium of external relations. For the past decades, coastal areas of China benefited from the reform and opening up policy and rose up to be the economic growth center of the country. That leads to imbalance in two aspects. On the one hand, there is a gap as to the level of growth between eastern and western China, the latter being left far behind. On the other hand, China has attached greater importance to its relations with eastern world than with the western one. Now the Silk Road Economic Belt offers more opportunities for the development of western China and acts as a new channel for China to foster friendly and cooperative relations with Central Asia and Western Asia, which is significant to both China's overall development and its national security.

The ancient Silk Road started from Chang'an (now referred to as Xi'an), an ancient Chinese capital, which went through countries in Central Asia like Afghanistan, Iran, Iraq, Syria to reach the Mediterranean, and ends in Rome. The road ran 6,440 km. It is regarded as a channel of trade that connects western and eastern civilizations across the Eurasia. However, instead of simply restoring the ancient passage, the Belt initiative was built for a new economic development belt that upholds openness and cooperation and abides by the spirit of mutually beneficial exchanges embodied by the old Silk Road, and to link China with countries along the belt in aspects of economy, politics, security, and humanity so as to form an interest-based community of shared destiny.

As part of China's grand strategy, the Road, the 21st Century Maritime Silk Road to be specific, targets at advocating and constructing new sea order for the new era. Western great powers have been pursuing Sea Power Theory on the basis of sea control since their rise. Will China follow the pattern if it wants to become a maritime big power? The Road Initiative gives a clear answer. China is to be committed to the new order based on open and free sea voyage, common maritime security, and mutual exploration of maritime resources, and to a coastal economic belt for cooperation and development.

Maritime Silk Road emerged during Qin and Han dynasties in around 200 BC and gradually grew to be a golden route of transport and trade along with time. The road started from the Southeast coastal region in China, went through South China Sea to reach the Indian Ocean and the Persian Gulf, and even stretched far to East Africa and Europe. It was an important corridor that linked up world civilizations. Nowadays, China proposes the Road Initiative to not only facilitate an open and safe sea lane, but to also build a coastal economic belt with concerted efforts of relevant countries, so as to incubate new space for development through port linkage, port economy, and coastal economy.

Connectivity are pillars of the Belt and Road strategy. Specifically, they refer to a multi-facet, three-dimensional and network shape linking that makes possible for the communication of policies, facilities, trades, funds, and feelings of people. To realize that, the construction of an all-round linkage of infrastructure, regulations and personnel communication is required, and an infrastructure network that extends in all directions. The concept of connectivity was initially coined by the Association of Southeast Asian Nations (ASEAN) and later applied to East Asian and Asia-Pacific cooperation mechanisms. Now it is also an important part of the Belt and Road Initiative. Recent years have seen a trend in forming Free Trade Areas (FTA) which increases the openness of markets whereby element resources circulate faster and trade and investment develops further. Moreover, when it comes to developing countries, the bottlenecks for their development are poor infrastructure and numerous restrictions between nations that block the exchanges of logistics, investment, service and personnel. In this case, to construct an interconnected and intercommunicating network calls for developing the network of infrastructure on one hand, and on the other removing obstacles that hamper communication and resetting united or mutually recognized rules. The foundation of AIIB and Silk Road Fund is a key solution to resolve the financing bottleneck in infrastructure construction.

Apparently, from the perspective of opening up to the outside world, the Belt and Road Initiative aims at an environment of comprehensive development rather than the FTA or the multilateral trading system. The initiative surpasses beyond the self-centered outlook of interests. Instead, they treasure concerted endeavor for construction and development. Therefore, the cooperative projects of the Belt and Road Initiative are not to be implemented by negotiation but by consultation, a brand new manner of collaboration and development.

3. Neighboring Countries Come First

China neighbors more than 20 countries, connecting with them by land or sea. For all this time China has been laying its diplomatic priority to fostering friendship with its neighbors. A conference on the diplomatic work on neighboring countries in Beijing in 2013 emphasized that "neighboring regions has major strategic significance with respect to geography, the environment, and intertwined relations",[1] so China should plan and manage its diplomacy and pay special attention to neighboring countries. At the same time, the conference put forward the basic tenet of diplomacy with

---

[1] "Xi Jinping: China to further friendly relations with neighboring countries". Retrieved from http://news.xinhuanet.com/english/china/2013-10/26/c_125601680.htm. July 12, 2015.

neighbors, which is "to treat them as friends and partners, to make them feel safe and to help them develop".[2] At the historic moment, the Belt and Road Initiative arises as a hallmark of the major strategic transition in China's recognition of relations with neighboring countries. Consequently, the new national strategy comes up, that is to forge ahead with building mutual development-oriented communities of interests and of shared destiny between China and its neighbors.

As the second largest economic power, China develops itself by reforms domestically and opening up exteriorly. The contemporary open economy, totally different from the economic pattern long time ago, is characterized by close relations between world and regional markets and linear featured peripheral economic circles. The Belt and Road Initiative will create closer interrelations within the circle around China. Economy is fundamental to a country. A tight economic connection will harvest closely related profits, acting as a basis for building the community of shared destiny. With respect to this, the Belt and Road Initiative will greatly change the traditional structure of economic relationships that were dominated by trade and resources. They take achieving connectivity as the primary step, gradually pursuing an open development-oriented economic zone, and building an economic belt where manufacturing, service, financial industries, and cultures interact and integrate with each other.

At the first stage after China initiated the policy of reform and opening up, development of the country, mainly depended on attracting foreign investment and expanding exports. China entered into the second stage upon its ranking as the second in the world in terms of economic aggregate. The stage required a transition from being big to being strong and a shift and upgrade of models for economic growth. Although Chinese economy is open to global market, neighboring region is still the most direct and most convenient potential space for China's future development. Besides, except for several developed countries, the northwestern,

---

[2] *Ibid.*

southern, and southeastern neighboring areas including South Asia, ASEAN, and Central Asia are developing and eager to develop. The Belt and Road Initiative gives them a chance to benefit from China's growth and take a free ride to their economic boost. In return, China will capture more opportunities from the achievements of its neighbors to extend its development.

4. An Open and Broad Vision is Necessary

The Belt and Road strategy is a transregional and open framework that is based and focused on peripheral areas and is able to include a broader sphere, like the whole Asia, Europe, Africa and even further regions. In this sense, it is a grand strategic plan, being dynamic and inclusive and it is a more proactive rather than decisive strategy. Resting upon the development of China's neighboring region, the strategy explores the rest of the world, seeking for secure, mutually dependent, and joint development communities of interests and of shared destiny.

It takes time to see the results and effects of the Belt and Road strategy. It requires both a coolheaded and solid baby step and looking ahead to the days to come. It is necessary to start from the easy ones to the hard ones and from peripheral regions to distant ones, and to concentrate on crucial points with priorities. In this regard, economy comes first and foremost and should commence from surrounding areas. Besides, political relations, cooperation in security and cultural construction are of great importance. Not only China, but also other countries should gain a clear knowledge of the Belt and Road strategy, as it is a cause that calls for collective endeavor and full participation. In particular, it is crucial to let relevant countries recognize the benefits and the initiative that can bring along for them and their obligations in the cause.

However, there are not a few challenges that hinder the course of making the initiative true and effective.

Firstly, there exist doubt about the strategic intention of the initiative. Some neighboring countries suspect that China is taking this chance to expand outwards, hesitant to accept the proposal of building a network of infrastructure, opposing China's participation in the Great Passageway, and politicizing economic issues. Some NGOs, agitated by other forces, distribute public opinions against China joining the construction of the Great Passageway. Some big powers, concerned about their own interests, exert pressure on their partner countries and even persuade them straightforwardly to disperse the rumors of China's dominance over the world. For example, the United States publicly expressed objection to the foundation of AIIB, and Japan refused to be a part of the bank, and allies of the US like Australia and South Korea appeared to be unsupportive. India and Myanmar questioned the construction of networks of highways and railways. Offshore and port collaborations with countries like Pakistan and Sri Lanka were mistaken as of political or military aims.

The second challenge is how to solve or defuse conflicts properly. For example, the first problem we will meet during the construction of the 21st Century Maritime Silk Road is to solve conflicts over South China Sea by creating an environment for laying aside disputes and developing together and replacing fights with cooperation. On the one hand, negotiation with nations in the disputes shall be carried on to expand the consensus of enhanced collaboration; on the other hand, China should keep communicating with ASEAN to reach full consensus on the Code of Conduct in South China Sea as soon as possible, sign it and get down to practice. Besides, given that 2015 is the Year of China–ASEAN Maritime Cooperation, we should make full use of this opportunity and set up a project about the construction of the Maritime Silk Road. Achieving this will facilitate more relevant projects in a broader scope.

The third challenge is how to create a new sustainable development mode. Take the construction of the Silk Road Economic Belt as an example. The economic and trade relations between China and Central Asia is mainly centered on energy, or in other words, on building an energy transport pipeline to China by exploiting the resources in Central Asia. To develop the Belt requires alterations of simple energy relations and establishment of industries of resources processing, manufacturing and services to boost the economy of that region. Only by doing so, can there be greater space for the growth of both China and Central Asia. President Xi Jinping emphasized at the latest conference on foreign affairs that China should push on the Belt and Road Initiative actively, looking for shared benefits with its partners, and realize win–win cooperation through practical effort. He also remarked that the first station of the Belt is Central Asia and a good start makes further steps possible.

Along with China's growth in its strength, there generate more interest demands, greater influence, and power. Inevitably comments of various kinds come too. Now that the Belt and Road Initiative is taken as a grand strategy with firm directions, China should take it seriously and practically. Moreover, China should cooperate in accordance with the core concept of the initiative, advocate shoulder to shoulder construction, full participation, mutual development and shared interests, and invite powers from all aspects, such as international and regional organizations, to come into play so that the Belt and Road Initiative can turn into commonly shared goals.

Chapter 2

Security Environment around China: Changes, Construction, and Challenges

Zhang Jie

National Institute of International Strategy
Chinese Academy of Social Sciences
zhang_jie@cass.org.cn

In 2014, China grew to be stronger and more willing to take the lead and shape its relations with neighboring countries. It adopted dual strategies, one being the Belt and Road Initiative that focuses on economy and the other a security strategy that pursues control over maritime issues. Attitudes and responses of neighboring countries to the strategies varied. US–Japan alliance pins down China; Russia sought for cooperation with China; India wavered and applied a seesaw policy. Thus, security environment of China was characterized as overall stability, partial improvement, and coexistence of game and cooperation.

The regional security environment of China has been pushed forward by two major forces, one being that the US strengthened Rebalance Strategy to add pressure on China and the other being that China was actively dedicated to building a new type

Asia-Pacific security framework based on its new outlook of security and to foster closer economic ties with Southeast Asia, South Asia, and Central Asia. Accordingly, the predicted that China's surrounding situations would enter into a complicated transitional period. The prediction was verified throughout the following year. But what is out of expectation is the strength and speed of China in shaping its environment. The most prominent moves are its practical promotion of the Belt and Road Initiative and vigorous measures to tackle with issues regarding the South China Sea.

There are mainly four features as to big power relations in 2014. Firstly, China and the US contended against each other. Secondly, China and Japan gave each other cold shoulders and the structural contradictions could barely be solved in a short-term regardless of the signs of improvement at year end. Thirdly, Russia, influenced by the Ukraine crisis, offered an olive branch to Asia-Pacific region and accelerated its strategic coordination and cooperation with China. Fourthly, the new Indian government collaborated with China economically and at the same time aimed at strategic balance with China, so the China–India relation was stable with limits.

Moreover, maritime security remained highlighted when it comes to regional security. Dispute between China and Japan over Diaoyu Islands reached a deadlock; conflicts in the South China Sea broke out in many aspects; low-intensity disputes over fisheries enforcement between China and South Korea occurred. As to the South China Sea issue, the US stepped in by taking advantage of those maritime disputes. The US enhanced its military presence in the Philippines and Australia and exerted pressure on government in Taiwan of China to hinder the settlement of South China Sea issue. Japan, as the ally of US, colluded with countries like the Philippines and Vietnam to play off against China. Given these, it is foreseeable that the Four Seas[1] Comovement Policy will continue to function but with newly emerging changes and features. Besides the new situations, worth noticing are the new concepts, newly signed agreements and newly reached consensuses in

---

[1] Four seas refer to the South China Sea, the East China Sea, the Yellow Sea, and the Sea of Japan.

relation to regional security, particularly maritime security, for these trends will lay a solid foundation for China to build a new sea order.

As a grand strategy, the Belt and Road Initiative is no longer just a proposal but what China is promoting by concrete moves. The initiative commenced from economic cooperation with neighboring countries, such as establishing the Asian Infrastructure Investment Bank (AIIB) and the Silk Road Fund. Some neighbors of China welcomed such moves and were willing to be a part of it, while others doubted about it and held a "wait-and-see" attitude, and even resisted and undermined it.

There are at least three main challenges that China's regional security will face within 2015. The first challenge is the strategic squeezing against the rise of China by the United States and Japan, together with their allies. Second is the goal of reshaping sea order and controlling upon maritime safety. The third is to advance the Belt and Road Initiative and to cope with external pressure. The smooth process for realizing the initiative depends on building trust and clearing up doubts between China and its neighbors, on finding out mutual interests and concordant strategies, and on game and collaboration between big powers.

1. Changes

China enjoyed overall stable regional security situations in 2014. Some chronic hot issues like the issue of Korean Peninsula and the issue of Afghanistan did not present surges. Its regional security is characterized by prominent adjustments to big power relations, coexistence of maritime confrontations and collaboration, and the rebound of non-traditional security challenges.

1.1. Obvious adjustments to big power relations and strengthened multipolarization

Firstly, Sino-US relation was dominated by competition. Obama and high officials in Washington appeared non-committal about the new model of major country relations between China and the United States mainly for two reasons. On the one hand, the US government worried that a direct rejection would negatively affect its cooperation with China. On the other hand, since the US government has been emphasizing "differences" to its counterpart and declared that it would challenge China when necessary to protect its rights, the acceptance of China's new idea would send a wrong signal to its allies in Asia and therefore weaken its power in the region.

China became a bigger target of the Asia-Pacific Rebalance Strategy. In 2014, despite that the US government invested much diplomatic efforts on Ukraine Issue, ISIS terrorism, and the Ebola epidemic, it still attached great importance to the deepening of its Asia-Pacific Rebalance Strategy as an established state policy. US Secretary Kerry remarked that "the US–China relationship is the most consequential in the world today, and it will do much to determine the shape of the 21st century".[2] He also expressed the dissatisfaction over China's ways of coping with the issues of East and South China Seas, and of Ukraine, claiming that China was undermining the stability of East Asia. And what is for sure is that "the United States will never shy away from articulating our deeply held values or defending our interests, our allies, and our partners throughout the region".[3]

The US lavished its endeavor on fostering friendly relations with allies when it came to security. The US government showed support to Japan's lifting the ban on the right of collective self-defense and regarded it as a measure of backing up the US defense system instead of a step towards militarism. US signed new contracts with Australia and the Philippines, respectively, gaining access to Cocos Islands of Australia, HMAS Stirling, a Royal Australian Navy's base, and military bases of the Philippines, and increased the size of US shift crews and preset arms in the Philippines. All these moves were aimed at a more convenient projection of military

---

[2] "Kerry on US–China Relations". Retrieved from http://chinese.usembassy-china.org.cn/2014ir/kerry-on-u.s.-china-relations.html, November 4, 2014.
[3] *Ibid.*

power upon Asia-Pacific, and especially at longer, wider, and higher-frequency spying of the US warships and warcrafts on the South China Sea. In return, the US government mounted its military aid to the Philippines to strengthen maritime domain awareness and maritime security capacity of the latter. In addition, the US established a closer military cooperation with Vietnam by making use of the issue of South China Sea.

When it comes to economy, the year of 2014 did not witness significant achievements made to the Trans-Pacific Partnership Agreement (TPP) except for "substantial progress". But given that, Japan took part in TPP because of the US–Japan alliance, it is expected that Japan will make concessions and the TPP is expected to be accomplished in 2015. The new strategy dominated by the United States is stretching its influence over the progress of Asia-Pacific economic integration. TPP and Free Trade Area of the Asia-Pacific (FTAPP) identically appear to be about free trade, but deep down they represent a match between China and the US over the economic impact on the Pacific region.

Nevertheless, China and the US acknowledge that they share common interests in global issues. They reached 27 consensuses during Asia-Pacific Economic Cooperation (APEC) in Beijing, including collaborating in emission reduction, enhancing military communication, accelerating the establishment of bilateral investment treaty, joining hands in fighting against terrorism and corruption, and making reciprocal arrangements for visa application. For example, the *US–China Joint Announcement on Climate Change* ascertains goals of emission reduction of both parties and makes political promises in terms of cooperation in clean energy and environment protection. They also signed a Memorandum of Understanding (MOU) on notifying each other of important military activities and a code of conduct for close encounters between military vessels and aircraft in international waters and airspace, whereby both learn about each other's strategic intent, strengthen strategic mutual trust, gain stronger ability of crisis control, and prevent potential risks. It is out of question that these positive results will promote China–US military relations.

Secondly, cooperation accelerated China–Russia relations. The spreading Ukraine crisis and the pressure from Europe and the US compelled Russia to shift its focus of Eurasian Union to Asia-Pacific and to reinforce and reconstruct cooperation with China, Mongolia and Central Asia in all aspects, in hope of vying against the West by the power of the East.

As a result, China and Russia achieved a stronger friendship in 2014. The two countries issued a joint declaration announcing that China–Russia relations have climbed up to a new stage in their comprehensive strategic partnership. Russia adopted a new diplomatic policy towards Asia, which was trading natural resources for funds, whereby China and Russia signed a natural gas supply contract worth 400 billion USD. In a word, both countries supported and depended on each other in international affairs under the framework of the UN Security Council.

Moreover, the most meaningful watching point may be that Russia started to loosen its restriction against the Belt initiative and against China's so-called "infiltration" into its "traditional sphere of influence" for Moscow expected that China would be helpful in hindering the interference of Europe and the US in Central Asia and Mongolia. Besides, China–Russia cooperative intention regarding Central Asia and Mongolia went up.

For a very long time, Russia has held the five Central Asian countries and Mongolia together and restrained them to assure that they were geopolitically neutral so as to disrupt the strategic space besiege by Europe and the US and to prevent China's influence from going into that region. The Ukraine crisis stimulated the establishment of Eurasian Economic Union between Russia and Central Asia. At the same time, cooperation agreements involving multiple domains were signed between Russia and Mongolia. Visa Exemption Agreement, in particular, is a mark of highly mutual trust between them. The Moscow's olive branch to Mongolia indicates Russia's consideration more in geopolitics and national security than in economic profits. Besides, in the China–Mongolia–Russia Summit held in September 2014, the three nations discussed the proposal of building a

China–Mongolia–Russia Economic Corridor, "dovetailing the Silk Road Economic Belt initiative with Russia's transcontinental rail plan and Mongolia's Prairie Road program".[4]

Still and all, China is keeping a clear head on China–Russia relations. Responding to the questions holding that a long-term China–Russia security cooperation aims at "NATO of the East", China firmly claims that "the Chinese side always opposes the establishment and expansion of military blocs, objects to the forming of spheres of influence and rival camps… The China–Russia relationship is based on equality, trust, mutual support, common prosperity and generations of friendship, following the principle of non-alliance, non-confrontation and not targeting any third party. This is where the vigor and vitality of the constant growth of China–Russia relationship comes from".[5]

Thirdly, China–Japan relations remained in "Ice Age". Shinzo Abe has advocated getting rid of post-war system, breaking the ban on the right of collective self-defense, and amending constitution across Japan since he returned to power. Externally, Abe's government sought for more influence and capacity of military interference in Asia-Pacific in virtue of Japan–US alliance, paving the way to dispatch its army outwards to the world. Moreover, guided by its "value oriented diplomacy", Abe's government sharply augmented its investment in and aids for Southeast Asia, South Asia and Central Asian countries. Especially in security domain, Japan strengthened dialogue and institutional construction regarding maritime security with Southeast Asia. It can be recognized that Abe's internal and external strategies are to achieve the international position of a political giant by helping countries in Asia-Pacific with their institutional construction and process of

---

[4] "Xi proposes to build China–Mongolia Russia economic corridor". Retrieved from http://eng.mod.gov.cn/TopNews/2014-09/12/content_4536947.htm. July 10, 2015.
[5] "Foreign Ministry Spokesperson Hua Chunying's Regular Press Conference on November 27, 2014". Retrieved from http://www.fmprc.gov.cn/mfa_eng/xwfw_665399/s2510_665401/2511_665403/t1215099.shtml. July 10, 2015.

democratization, and to force those countries to stay away from China to form a united force against China.

Abe showed obvious intention of containment and vigilant attitude towards China, resulting in the "Ice Age" of China–Japan relations. The issue of Diaoyu Islands and Abe's homage to the Yasukuni Shrine and other issues are hard to be addressed in a short time. What is worse is that Abe's new move on lifting up the ban on the right of collective self-defense encouraged political right deviation and Japan's ambition of being a military power. China expressed firm objection to it. By the end of the year in 2014, China and Japan reached four principled consensuses, aiming at a continuous development of a strategically reciprocal relation. Nevertheless, due to various contradictions and obstacles which Abe's government does not intend to address by adjusting its strategy towards China in a fundamental manner, China–Japan relations can hardly be improved in the near future. Moreover, China has accumulated its economic power to 61.2% of Japan's from the end of the Cold War to the year 2013. The economic accumulation is expected to reach 70% by the end of 2014, which is likely to be the critical point for the shift of comprehensive national power of the two countries. This will be a big turnover in the history of China and Japan, so current period and that follows will witness the historic reconstruction of Japan–China relations. The shift might take longer time than expected. Anyhow, the two countries are in a strategic rivalry where China gains the upper hand.

Fourthly, China–India relations are characterized by balance strategy. China established a strategic partnership for peace and prosperity with India in 2005. In 2014, China recognized India as its development partner, a closer and more practical relation with clearer objectives. 2014 is the Year of China–India Friendly Exchanges and also the 60th anniversary of the release of the "Five Principles of Peaceful Coexistence". And it is also in 2014 that the leader of the Chinese government has for the first time regarded the promotion of China–India relations as a historical mission, demonstrating China's resolve in developing partnership with India.

To realize the linking of Chinese market with that of India and create new economic growth point for Asia, China has been dedicating to inviting India to the regional cooperative framework that aims at regional prosperity, advocating the Bangladesh–China–India–Myanmar (BCIM) Economic Corridor, asking India to join in Asia Infrastructure Investment Bank (AIIB), promoting the establishment of NDB BRICS where an Indian is taking up the post of the Chief President.

India entered into the time of Modi in May 2014. Modi's new government adopts a dual track relation with China, namely economic cooperation and strategic balance. As to economy, India hopes to extend collaborations in trade and investment with China so as to further bridging India's trade deficit to China. Therefore, India supported China's building industrial parks in India, welcomed China to invest on Indian infrastructure construction, and responded positively to China's proposal of BCIM subregional cooperation that could benefit the development of Northeast India.

Strategically, India was devoted to balancing China's influence regionally, even globally. First of all, India pursued to play a dominant role in the South Asian Association for Regional Cooperation (SAARC) and Modi visited Bhutan and Nepal after assuming his new post to intensify India's impact on those countries. Secondly, India is to enhance strategic interaction with Association of Southeast Asian Nations (ASEAN) countries, Japan and US to create a favorable environment to achieve strategic balance. During Modi's visit to Washington in September 2014, India and US issued a joint declaration. Modi stressed that India would give priority to its relations with US to realize India's rise. Obama reaffirmed that US would support India to become a permanent member of the Security Council. Both parties agreed to collaborate in counterterrorism, intelligence and coping with climate change, and to reinforce security dialogue and defense relations.

Both India and China want to control border issues. Modi's government, being eager to resolve border problems, has dialogued with China through current multiple border-related mechanisms, while in the meantime the government has taken several steps to become more powerful in border management and thus to bridge the gap of strength with China. Given that, India made its policy towards China by considering both needs of cooperation and strategic balance, it is unlikely that big changes or retrograde standpoint will occur to border-related policy of the Indian government.

1.2. Maritime security: A hot-spot issue as ever

Conflicts on the sea have long been one of the main sources of tension situations around China since 2010. Clashes relevant to sovereignty of islands and maritime rights and interests constantly occurred. The deep involvement of the US in security issues of Asia-Pacific by virtue of the power of its military allies sophisticated maritime disputes. Thus, how to cope with conflicts on the sea has become a question that is critical to rebuild regional security order.

In 2014, the issue of Diaoyu Islands remained in a normalcy of moderate tension while the issue of South China Sea was on the upswing, demonstrating several features as follows. Firstly, the Philippines and Vietnam were still the major trouble makers. The Philippines arrested Chinese fishermen after seizing their boat near Half Moon Shoal and conflicts of Second Thomas Shoal occurred more often than not; Vietnam gave a great shock to Chinese drilling rigs and exercised oil and gas exploration in disputed sea area. Secondly, jurisprudential struggle and negotiation are a major part. On the one hand, the Philippines initiated and kept pushing forward the arbitral proceeding on the South China Sea issue and Vietnam showed stronger tendency of resorting to international arbitration after HD-981 Incident. On the other hand, consultations on the Code of Conduct in the South China Sea gained "early harvest". Thirdly, parties in disputes were faced with "cold politics and hot economy". In other words, the value of trade and investment volume of China with the Philippines and Vietnam kept increasing and *vice versa* regardless of the intensified contradictions between them. Fourthly, Chinese policy of the South China Sea has been changed dramatically and "active" is the most salient feature.

The HD-981 Incident was undoubtedly one of the (most sensational events that occurred to the South China Sea in 2014 and was likely to become the hallmark event of the year. China National Petroleum Corporation (CNPC) has initiated the exploration of two prospecting wells in Paracel Islands (Xisha Islands) in May 2014, taking a solid first step towards petroleum and natural gas exploration in the area of the Paracel Islands and even the whole South China Sea area. However, ASEAN countries were prone to coming together to constrain China and solving South China Sea issue by resorting to a third party. Vietnam even threatened China with international arbitration. Nonetheless, China is still going to consolidate its presence in South China Sea, Spratly Islands (Nansha Islands) in particular, through oil and gas development.

External countries intervened in South China Sea issue and tended to hold an identical standing. The US had following responses. Firstly, the US has officially questioned for the first time the legitimacy of the dotted line marking the South China Sea. Secondly, as to the HD-981 Incident, the US criticized that China adopted a unilateral destructive action in order to further assert its ownership of the South China Sea. In this regard, the US claimed that it would remove its embargo on Vietnam's lethal weapon to strengthen Vietnam's defense at sea. Thirdly, the US reinforced its influence on the opinions of its allies and partners. In August 2014, when Tony Abbott, the then Prime Minister of Australia, visited America, the two governments reconfirmed their consistent attitude towards the issues of East and South China Seas. The US and India issued a joint announcement that touched upon the South China Sea issue and remarked that both would safeguard a free navigation and the issue should be resolved in accordance with the United Nations Convention on the Law of the Sea (UNCLOS). Fourthly, the US put forth so-called "three-halts" proposal to prevent China from claiming its presence in the South China Sea. Thus, maritime disputes are keys for the US to fortify and expand its military presence in Asia-Pacific region, and main reasons to cause tensions in China–US relations.

Japan follows the US. First of all, Japan condemned in its *Annual White Paper: Defense of Japan 2014* that China rapidly expanded its activities in East and South China Seas and airspace by "coercive measures".[6] It holds that the establishment of East China Sea Air Defense Identification Zone by China is likely to result in upgrade of tensions and "unintended consequences",[7] and that "China has not set out a clear, specific future vision of its military strengthening. The transparency of its decision-making process in relation to military and security affairs is not enough either".[8] This is virtually a re-rendering of China Threat theory. Moreover, Japan was committed to making use of ODA to help the Philippines, Vietnam and others to raise maritime capacity in a highly efficient manner and with strategic purposes. In addition, on Japan–ASEAN Defense Ministers' Meeting, Japan expressed its resolve in offering more aids to countries of Southeast Asia, which would center on the personnel training in fields of maritime security and disaster relief.

Another eye-attracting trend as to maritime security is that parties were seeking for more dialogues and collaboration in terms of conflict prevention and crisis management. Although the Pacific Ocean is vast, vessels and aircrafts of countries like China and the US are practicing activities with increasing frequency and in wider and wider sphere, which urgently calls for the prevention and management of potential crises. Twenty one countries, including China, the US and Japan passed the *Code for Unplanned Encounters at Sea* on the 14th Western Pacific Naval Symposium in April 2014. At the China–US summit meeting held in November of the same year, two MOUs about military security were signed. And the presidential statement of the 17th China–ASEAN Leaders' Meeting announced that the Code of Conduct in South China Sea had achieved early harvest.

---

[6] *Defense of Japan 2014*. Retrieved from http://www.mod.go.jp/e/publ/w_paper/2014.html. July 12, 2015.

[7] *Ibid*.

[8] *Ibid*.

We can see from the above that as maritime issues are taking an increasingly greater proportion in regional security and diplomacy with neighboring countries, the previous sea order can no longer cater to the needs of the times. All nations and regions are setting up new rules and regulations through conflicts and dialogues. Thus, it is unavoidable that a new order will replace the old one, during which process China is expected to play a leading role. But of course, China has to be faced with the challenges of dealing with the old US-dominated sea order in a proper manner.

1.3. New challenges to non-traditional security

Non-traditional security is a long-lasting challenge. The year of 2014 witnessed some new changes to terrorism, sea disasters, security of water resources, and environment security in neighboring region.

The upswing in terrorism is closely related to subregional security. South Asia and Central Asia have long been suffering from terrorist issues aroused by traditional ethnic and ideological conflicts. Afghanistan entered into an "era of post anti-terrorism war" upon the reign of its new president and upon the announcement of withdrawing the last combat troops by the US and the UK. It is likely that terrorism, there will deteriorate. Besides, terrorist forces have launched several attacks on Pakistan since 2014. The Pakistani government commenced Sword Action to clean up the forces, but the results failed to be satisfied. At the same time, the ISIS and al-Qaeda were contending for the leadership of global jihad. The fiercer their competition, the weaker the security environment of South Asia will be.[9]

The most prominent feature of terrorism upswing in Southeast Asia is that number of followers after ISIS climbed due to the influence of jihad in Iraq and Syria. On the one hand, not a few Muslims in Southeast Asia joined the jihad plotted by the ISIS in

---

[9] Li Wei: "South Asia and Southeast Asia: Terrorism may get worse", *World Affairs*. 2014 (22), p. 24.

Iraq and Syria. On the other hand, the ISIS kept enlarging its influential power over Southeast Asia. Moreover, several Islamic clergies in Indonesia pledged loyalty to the ISIS after the latter announced its "foundation" in June 2014. What is directly related to China's national security is that Southeast Asia has become a critical transfer passage for international terrorists, especially those in Xinjiang autonomous region of China. Previously, those extremists fled away through borders of China with countries in South Asia and Central Asia. But China has reinforced its border control in recent years. Some of the extremists in Xinjiang were caught up in Vietnam, Indonesia, and so on when they were attempting to get trained there or to head for jihad in Iraq or Syria.

Pacific and Indian regions are areas where sea disasters are prone to occur. In March 2014, the flight MH370 from Malaysia to Beijing got lost. Twenty six countries including China and Malaysia joined hands in the search and rescue (SAR), arousing global concerns on issues of maritime SAR and aids. In August, the ASEAN Regional Forum Statement on Strengthening Coordination and Cooperation on Maritime and Aeronautical SAR called for regional countries to further strengthen SAR coordination and cooperation at bilateral, regional and multilateral levels, including through dialogue and cooperation in ARF.[10] At present, there are two big challenges to maritime rescue coordination and cooperation, one being the financial support to the rescue and the other coordination when taking rescue actions at sea. Collaborations of China with other countries and the building of cooperative mechanism are still insufficient in those aspects.[11]

Affected by climate change, South, Southeast, and Central Asia are faced with shortage of water supply and environment pollution

---

[10] "ASEAN Regional Forum Statement on Strengthening Coordination and Cooperation on Maritime and Aeronautical Search and Rescue". Retrieved from http://world.people.com.cn/n/2014/0811/c157278-25438226.html. July 10, 2015.
[11] "International Maritime SAR Cooperative Mechanism should be Established". *Beijing Daily*. March 19, 2014.

to different degrees. Take marine pollution as an example, the Vietnam oil spilt over in the South China Sea in 2011, resulting in contamination in a large area and the gravity of marine litter pollution was exposed during the SAR of flight MH370. Marine litter not only poses a threat to the safety of sea voyage, but also affects the virtuous circle of marine ecosystem and undermines the healthy development of maritime economy. Thus, to dispose marine litter properly is a critical subject that countries involved need attaching importance to.

Non-traditional security is a public and transnational issue, which can be tackled only through bilateral and regional cooperation. China is supposed to deal with challenges to non-traditional security from three aspects. Firstly, promptly provide necessary public goods. Secondly, promote the construction of network-based supportive mechanism for security cooperation. Lastly, build a mechanism for smooth domestic coordination and cooperation and practice efficient public diplomacy.

2. Geopolitical Strategy of China: To Build the Belt and the Road

China has been remolding its relations with neighboring countries since 2010. As its national strength grows, China has become the most important independent variable that affects surrounding situations. Adjusting the previous passive way of dealing with challenges, China began to proactively design and manage its grand neighboring strategy.

After the Belt and Road Initiative was put forward within 2013, President Xi Jinping visited the countries in 2014 most of which are along the Belt and the Road. What is more, the orientations, concrete configurations, and implementation route map of the Initiative was gradually deciphered along with the foundation of AIIB and the Silk Road Funds, the Dialogue on Strengthening Connectivity Partnership, and platforms like APEC and ASEAN Leaders' summits. At the same time, China showed to the rest of the world its resolve to realize the initiative.

2.1. Orientations and connotations of the Belt and Road Initiative

As a grand strategy, the Belt and Road Initiative is of inclusive feature as it was designed for not only the good of China's growth, but as well needs of the region and the world. The initiative aims at gearing Chinese economic growth to the development of other countries and creating new spaces and engine for future development by leading and mobilizing neighboring partners. Obviously the strategy is open and cooperation-oriented instead of being aggressive. China hopes to deliver a message to the world that it will keep its promise of peaceful development and achieve win–win cooperation by concrete actions.

Connectivity is the core of the initiative and also the fundamental step for infrastructure construction. For developing countries, financing, especially in areas of infrastructure and long-term projects, is always hard. Regarding this, the initiative can function as the key to this financing bottleneck.

Some denounce that what China is applying is a "New Marshall Plan". Actually, the Marshall Plan was set up by the US to help with the post-war economic reconstruction of Europe, while the current idea of building new financing instructions upholds full participation, joint management, and the sharing of resources. There also exist harsh words criticizing that China is damaging the existing framework of international financial organizations. Obviously it is a misunderstanding or even slander. These newly founded organizations are to supplement and fortify insufficient functions of current ones rather than disrupting them.

The implementation of the Belt and Road strategy is a long process. Priorities should be managed. And it requires that concrete actions start from the easy ones to the hard ones and from close regions to distant ones, and to concentrate on crucial points with priorities. In this regard, economy comes first. Besides, political relations, cooperation in security and cultural construction should be given equal importance. From the perspective of grand strategy of China, the Road initiative, or to build the

21ˢᵗ Century Maritime Silk Road, aims at advocating and constructing a new sea order for the times. Western great powers have been pursuing Sea Power Theory on the basis of sea control since their rise. Will China follow the same pattern if it wants to become a maritime big power? The Road initiative gives a clear answer. China is committed to the new order based on open and free navigation, common maritime security, and joint development of marine resources, and to a coastal economic belt for cooperation and development.

2.2. Responses of neighboring countries

The Belt and Road Initiatives is supported by the development of the neighboring region and countries whereby it stretches out to the rest of the world. It is also a strategy that targets at establishing secure, interdependent, and mutually developing communities of interests and of shared destiny. It provides an open stage where China would like to plan and carry out projects with its partners.

The pivot of building the community of shared destiny is "one country, one policy". During his visit in Tajikistan, Maldives, Sri Lanka, and India in mid-September 2014, President Xi Jinping emphasized that it is necessary to inosculate the Belt and Road Initiative with, development strategies of the four countries and to gear, competitive Chinese industries to regional features and demands of development of the host countries.

Nonetheless, countries have responded differently to the Belt and Road Initiative for they regarded this issue more political than economic. It appears that Singapore is the most supportive neighbor in Southeast Asia, mainly for three reasons. Firstly, Singapore has established a close economic tie with China and their economic and trade contacts become more and more frequent. Secondly, Singapore is rather positive towards the economic prospect of China. Thirdly, Singapore is expecting China to drive regional economic growth and it believes that China can make it. Besides, former and incumbent high officials in Laos, Thailand, Indonesia, and

Malaysia show welcome to the initiative.[12] Of course, their responses are barely verbal and the recognition to China's real strategic intention remains limited. So their standpoints will gradually become clear as the Road initiative is put into practice and concrete projects are carried out.

China's initiative has gained the support of the bulk of South Asian countries. The Road initiative, BCIM Economic Corridor, China–Pakistan Economic Corridor (CPEC) dominated by China dock with their policies for development, such as India's Connect Central Asia Policy (CCAP), International North–South Transport Corridor (INSTC), the plan to develop its northeastern region and the project to connect with its neighbors, and Pakistan's National Trade Corridor Programme (NTCP) and National Trade Corridor Improvement Programme (NTCIP), etc. As a result, Pakistan holds a supportive attitude towards China's proposal and works actively with China to promote the CPEC. Sri Lanka formulates a medium and long-term development program aiming at building an interconnected country by 2020, which was stated in *Sri Lanka: The Emerging Wonder of Asia: Mahinda Chintana Vision for the Future.*[13] As to the Road initiative, Maldives and Sri Lanka respond favorably, both considering it as an opportunity for their development. Bangladesh is willing to join in the BCIM Economic Corridor, while it holds a wait-and-see attitude towards the Belt and Road Initiative. Nepal indicates that it will grasp the opportunities created by BCIM Economic Corridor and the Silk Road, in hope of improving the well-being of its countrymen. India welcomes researches and cooperation in BCIM Economic Corridor, but appears prudent and contradictory over the Belt and Road Initiative, the Road initiative in particular. Given the impact of India on South Asia, its standpoint will more or less influence the depth and the range of collaboration between China and South Asian countries.

[12] http://gb.cri.cn/42071/2014/09/17/5931s4695379.htm.
[13] Department of National Planning, Ministry of Finance and Planning, Government of Sri Lanka, "Sri Lanka: The Emerging Wonder of Asia: Mahinda Chintana-Vision for the Future", Retrieved from http://203.94.72.22/publications/npd/mahindaChintanaVision-2010full-eng.pdf. July 10, 2015.

The president of Mongolia proposed the Prairie Road program in August 2014, hoping to recover the trade channel that was once popular in its history. The Prairie Road includes the road of prairie that connects Ienghiz Khan's empire to the Atlantic and Pacific Oceans, and the road of tea that went through the prairie region of Mongolia to Europe during Ming and Qing dynasties. This program is to restore the road of exchanges and communication across Northeast Asia and even the Eurasia. The China–Mongolia–Russia Summit in September 2014 called on the three nations to build an economic corridor as the extending part of the Silk Road Economic Belt towards north. This conception of transregional cooperation integrates into the 21st Century Maritime Silk Road to the south, realizing the consistency between China's Belt and Road Initiative and Russia's Eurasian Union.

2.3. External challenges and risks of the Belt and Road Initiative

Uncertain challenges and risks to the construction of the Belt and Road Initiative derive from regional security issues that have long beset China, competitive attitudes of big powers like the US and Japan towards China, neighbors' suspicion of China's strategic intent, and insufficient capacity and experiences of investment abroad.

Firstly, the challenge comes from the doubts about the strategic intention of the initiative. Some neighboring countries suspect that China is taking this chance to expand outwards, hesitant to accept the proposal of building a network of infrastructure, opposing China's participation in the Great Passageway, and politicizing economic issues. India and Myanmar questioned the construction of networks of highways and railways. Offshore and port collaborations with countries like Pakistan and Sri Lanka were mistaken as of political or military aims. Besides, some NGOs, agitated by other forces, distribute public opinions against China.

Having a bias on China's economy and its immigration problem, Central Asia is concerned about unfavorable effects that the

Road initiative might bring along with to the society. Media in some countries pointed out that the Road initiative demonstrated China's diplomatic ambition and its attempt of "soft aggression". What is more, the Central Asia community, even holds that the closer the economic ties with China, the more dependent on China's economy, it will be, and if it goes on like this, the region worries that it will become the sales market for Chinese products or the base of energy and raw materials for China. This opinion reflects to some degrees the disagreement of Central Asian countries to China's pattern of economic development. Thus, they articulated reservations about China's proposal of free trade agreement (FTA) and believed that their own industries will stagnate once the FTA allows the inflow of large numbers of commodities.

The second challenge is the game of major powers. Some big countries fear that the Belt and Road strategy will weaken their impact on the regions, thus, they object to it while inciting their Asian allies and partners not to be a part of it. The US has been expressing disagreement to the AIIB for quite some time, asserting that the AIIB will hinder the operations of current multilateral organizations that are supporting infrastructure construction, such as the World Bank and the Asian Development Bank. In America's opinion, China is challenging the international financial order where the US takes the lead and also the ADB-based financial pattern in Asia, so the US is vigilant against China's proposal. Moreover, the US straightforwardly asked Australia to stay away from the founding of the AIIB. Washington denies it, but its strong alertness is apparent.

As to promote its Eurasian Union, Russia is strong in will but weak in power at present, especially when its shortage in funds becomes the biggest obstacle to making progress in its cooperation with Central Asia. Even though Russia wants to strategically cooperate and coordinate with China, it has to be alert and make sure that China's large investment on the Belt and Road Initiative will not penetrate into its "backyard". Thus, China should resort to the "traditional legacy" between Russia and Central Asia and to insist on the cooperative principles of "shared market, shared resources and energy, joint investment, mutual benefit, and win–win results" in some projects, hallmark ones in particular.

The third challenge is how to properly resolve disputes between China and its neighbors and among neighbors. The South China Sea dispute is the first problem that needs solving during the course of realizing the Road initiative. To show objections to China's building "981" Rig in Paracel Islands (Xisha Islands), a large-scale anti-China movement in Vietnam broke out, resulting in profit loss of Chinese enterprises and even injuries to Chinese people. According to the Economic and Commercial Counselor's Office of the Embassy of China in Vietnam, the Vietnam government has issued several rules to set limits to direct investment from China in the second half of 2014.[14] In this way, the government hopes to diversify foreign investment, ease its economic dependence upon China and Vietnam is not the only one in Southeast Asia to have such considerations.

Southeast Asia is an important region and the first choice for China to construct the Road, so it is critical for the success of the Belt and Road strategy. Given this, China is supposed to strengthen mutual trust in politics and security to create a favorable environment for regional economic collaboration, while insisting on maintaining the bottom line of the integrity of national sovereignty. It is indeed a challenging task that needs giving strategic priority. To realize that, China should make more consensus with countries in disputes through dialogue and consultation, as well as enhance dialogue and negotiations with ASEAN, make full use of suggestions supported by the Declaration of Conduct in South China Sea, and formulate action plans as to the Maritime Silk Road by taking the opportunity of the Year of China–ASEAN Maritime Cooperation in 2015. The Maritime Silk Road projects will be promoted to a wider range if this step is taken successfully.

---

[14] For example, Vietnam imposes anti-dumping duties on China's cold rolled stainless steel strips. There are occasions when Chinese enterprises' trademarks are maliciously registered.

The fourth challenge is how to guarantee the security of Chinese funds and enterprises. The Belt and Road Initiative relies heavily on "going out" of Chinese enterprises. Before Chinese companies stepped out of their motherland, they have to investigate the investment environment of the host countries with comprehensive and prudent considerations. The reason is that the factors of enterprises *per se*, of their motherland and of the host countries, especially economic and political situations and social stability of the host countries, are of great influence on the investment. There are three potential risks requires that special attention. The first risk comes from the stability of political situation in the host country. Political turbulence, ethnic and religious conflicts, and civil strife are prone to damage the interests of overseas-funded enterprises. Some Southeast Asian countries were troubled with unstable political and social instability, such as in Thailand, Myanmar and Vietnam. The second risk goes to corruption. The corruption of officials in host countries will raise unreasonable costs for investors. As a result, investors are forced to violate international practice based rules of markets during transaction and it will weaken government credibility of the host countries if things go on like that. The third risk roots in legal system of the host country, including strength on governing by laws and on supervision, and law enforcement regarding contracts of enterprise cooperation. For instance, Mongolia keeps adjusting its laws and policies in terms of mining industries to ensure its own rights, which causes loss of its credibility in the eyes of foreign direct investors. Statistics show that China's direct investment in Mongolia presented a sharp increase since 2010 but plummeted in 2013 with 57% decrease compared to the previous year. Mongolia's new Law on Regulation of Foreign Investment in Business Entities operating in sectors of strategic importance[15] developed in 2012

---

[15] Mongolian government lists mineral industry, financial and media industry, and information and communication industry as its three sectors of strategic importance. The Law says that foreign investors, when investing in the above industries, must ask for the approval of the Mongolian government and the parliament if they take up over 49% of shares and invest more than 76 million USD.

mainly account for the drop. Not a few investors worried that the Mongolian government would set limits on their operations through the Law and lessened their investment intentions. The Mongolian government passed a new Investment Law the following year, lifting some of the restrictions, although it appeared to be powerless to save the depressed foreign investment which kept reducing throughout the year. This shows that the changing investment policies have aroused cautiousness of investors and it will take some time to recover market confidence.

The initiative enters into the hard time of implementation when China is faced with multiple tasks. The Chinese government should specify cooperative projects, make the best use of the AIIB, the Silk Fund, and the SCO Development Bank, design the projects to meet the strategic needs of neighboring countries, and cope with competition and block of the TPP under the leadership of the US. All these require China to carefully observe its surroundings, determine diplomatic agenda, attach importance to details so as to take every step firm and solidly during building the Belt and the Road. At the same time, China should be devoted to realizing the dual targets of promoting economic strategy relevant to neighboring countries and forming a secure order, which requires China foster an amicable environment for better resolvement of maritime disputes by giving full play of its economic advantages and through win–win approaches.

The Belt and Road Initiative and Big Powers

Chapter 3

The US Asia-Pacific Rebalance Strategy versus China's Belt and Road Initiative

Cao Xiaoyang

National Institute of International Strategy,
Chinese Academy of Social Sciences
caoxy@cass.org.cn

Due to the slow progress in the Trans-Pacific Partnership Agreement (TPP), the Asia-Pacific Rebalance Strategy of the US remains to be focused on the military area. In the Asia-Pacific region, the US has been strengthening alliances and developing new partners, while criticizing China in a much harsher way, consequently, the competitive side of the Sino-American relation has become more prominent. Meanwhile, China has proposed the strategic ideas and initiatives like the "Belt and Road Initiative" and the plan of building the Asian Infrastructure Investment Bank, causing the vigilance of the US. As the contradiction in China and US strategies pricks up, it is an important task for both countries to manage and control the Sino-US differences and avoid the serious deterioration of the bilateral relation.

The year of 2014 has seen a series of incidents, the surge of rampant activities of the extremist force in the Middle East "Islamic State", the issue of Ukraine, the spread of the Ebola outbreak in West Africa, etc., drawing the attention of the US. Whereas, as a set national policy, the Asia-Pacific Rebalance Strategy of the Obama Administration was further continued and deepened in 2014. Especially, the issues, including deepening alliances, strengthening the cooperation with Asia-Pacific countries in the field of maritime security, restricting the development of China's sea power have become the important part of the Rebalance Strategy. In 2014, the US congressmen and officials criticized China in a much harsher way, making the competitive side of the Sino-American relation more prominent. How to manage and control the Sino-US differences and avoid the serious deterioration of the bilateral relation has become an important task for both countries.

1. US Actions in 2014 to Implement the Asia-Pacific Rebalance Strategy

As a set national policy, the Asia-Pacific Rebalance Strategy of the US showed a further continuation and new characteristics in 2014. The continuation is reflected in the following aspects: in the field of security, the US continued to strengthen its alliances, develop new partners and help the allies and partners to improve their power; in the economic field, the US continued to negotiate with the Asian-Pacific countries on the *TTP*, hoping to reach the agreement by the end of the year; the US actively develops its relationship with China to avoid the challenge of China to its dominant position in the Asia-Pacific region.

So overall, to return to the Asia-Pacific region militarily is still the emphasis of its Asia-Pacific Rebalance Strategy. The US actions to implement the Strategy mainly cover the following aspects.

1.1. In the economic field, the US actively pushes forward to reach the TPP by the end of the year

The TPP is an important step of the US Asia-Pacific Rebalance Strategy. The US hopes to dominate the trade pattern in the whole Asia-Pacific region by reaching high standard trade agreement.

Since 2013, TPP negotiation has entered a key stage. Up to now, there are two points exerting influence on the overall TPP negotiation: the first is whether the US and Japan could reach consensus on the issues relevant to automobiles, agriculture, beef, etc.; the second is, under the condition that the core members of the US Democratic Party were opposed to TPP and that the government failed to obtain the authorization of the *Trade Promotion Bill*, how would the US push forward the TPP negotiation. The TPP ministerial meeting, closed on October 27, 2014, did not achieve impressive results, only confirming that "there has been substantial progress". Japan participated in the TPP to strengthen the US–Japan alliance, so it is certain that Japan would make concession on the issue of TPP, so the TPP agreement is hopeful to be reached in the next year. The influence of this new strategy dominated by the US on the Asia-Pacific economic integration is expanding gradually. At the Asia-Pacific Economic Cooperation (APEC) meeting in November, China initiated to build the Free Trade Area of the Asia-Pacific (FTAAP). FTAAP and TPP are only relevant to free trade on the surface, actually, they could change the influence of China and US in the Asia-Pacific region.

1.2. In the field of security, the US continued to strengthen its alliances, develop new partners and help the allies and partners to improve their power

First, the US continued to strengthen its relation with its allies, including Japan, Republic of Korea, Australia, Philippines, etc. With the decline of the US power and the situation of fiscal restraint, to implement the Rebalance Strategy, the US has to rely on the power and cooperation of its alliances.

In October 2013, the US and Japan officially started the discussion to reevaluate the *US–Japan Defense Cooperation Guidelines*. On October 8, 2014, US–Japan Joint Defense Group meeting submitted the interim report on modifying the *Guidelines*. The report released by both sides showed that the two countries expected to build the alliance to be "an international cooperation platform making positive contributions to developing the two countries and other regions throughout the whole world". The emphasis of the future bilateral defense cooperation would be "seamless, intensive, flexible and highly efficient bilateral response, the global influence of the US–Japan alliance, as well as the cooperation with the partners in other regions". Once the new *Cooperation Guidelines* are concluded, the two countries would realize more efficient and closer cooperation in the field of security. For Japan, the rapid development of China has become a huge challenge and a threat. To deal with this threat, strengthening the US–Japan alliance would be the core of its diplomatic policy. In July 2014, the Prime Minister of Japan Shinzo Abe passed the cabinet resolution which lifted the ban on its collective self-defense right. Obviously, he thought that the US–Japan alliance cannot be strengthened if Japan could not achieve equally mutual defense for each other with the US. The US showed its welcome for this, in that the exercise of the collective self-defense right of Japan has long been regarded as the symbol that Japan equally supports the defense for the US, instead of the hint that Japan is heading for militarism.

The military relation between the US and the Philippines keeps developing gradually. In April 2014, during Obama's state visit to the Philippines, the two countries signed a 10-year *Enhanced Defense Cooperation Agreement.*[1] According to the Agreement, the US army obtains the admission to enter the military base of the Philippines army, increase the number of soldiers for rotational deployment in the Philippines and preset weapons in the Philippines. The US and the Philippines will enhance the military exercises and the US would help the Philippines to realize modernization of military power.

After the US military base had been closed for more than 20 years, the US military deployment in the Philippines is expanded for the first time. The reuse of the military base in the Philippines evidently increased the frequency and duration of the US ships and

---

[1] U.S. Embassy in the Philippines: "Signing of Enhanced Defense Cooperation Agreement". Retrieved from https://ph.usembassy.gov/signing-enhanced-defense-cooperation-agreement/. April 28, 2014.

airplanes in investigating the South China Sea, consequently, the US was able to offer a large quantity of information to the Philippines and Malaysia about the China's right defense activities in the South China Sea, making the situation of the South China Sea more complicated. When the two countries held the "Shoulder to Shoulder" joint military exercise in May, the foreign minister of the Philippines Rosario remarked that this joint military exercise is helpful to strengthen the sea power of the Philippines and in turn enable it to tackle with the challenge from "a hostile neighboring country". In June, the Pentagon announced that the anti-terrorism training specialists deployed on the Mindanao Island by the US would end their 10-year mission, and the US Special Forces would continue to help fight against the remnants of the Abu Sayyaf in the southern part of the Philippines, the size of which had shrunk from 320 to a dozen or so. The new defense cooperation agreement would bring some adjustments on the US army deployment in the Philippines in order to deal with the external threats. Since the heat up of the South China Sea dispute, the US has largely increased its military aid for the Philippines, mainly supporting the Philippines' situation awareness in the sea area and the maritime security ability.

The US–Australia cooperation has been further developed. In June 2014, Australian Premier Tony Abbott visited the US, stating that Australia would continue to maintain and strengthen the alliance relation with the US and to support the US Asia-Pacific Rebalance Strategy. Both countries reconfirmed the consistent attitude and proposition on the issue of the East and South China Sea. The leaders of the two countries later declared the conclusion of the *Military Power Situation Agreement*, the long-term defense cooperation of the two countries would be deepened. The US planned to build a taking off and landing base for the reconnaissance aircrafts on the Cocos-Keeling Islands, meanwhile Australia would build more docking points for the US Navy destroyers and other naval ships at the royal Navy base Sterling so as to facilitate the release ability of the US in this area. In August 2014, the US–Australia "Two & Two" (i.e. the foreign minister and the defense minister of the two countries, noted by the translator) Ministerial Meeting was held in Sydney, at which the two countries signed an agreement on expanding the US deployment of sea and air military power in the northern part of Australia. The Agreement reconfirmed that the US would send another 2,500 marines to Darwin before 2017. In addition, the two countries exchanged views on the cooperation in the field of missile defense, network security, maritime security, etc.

The US–Thai relation was affected by the coup in Thailand. After the military coup on May 22, the US criticized this and showed its expectation that the Thailand could resume democracy as soon as possible, warning that this might affect the US–Thai relation. It is during the US–Thai CARAT joint military exercise when the army was making political interference, the US immediately terminated the ongoing military exercise and the US fleet retreated to Thailand. At the end of June, the US stopped the military aid for Thailand worth 4.7 million dollars.

Second, the US paid special attention to developing its relation with the Association of Southeast Asian Nations (ASEAN), which strengthened the partnership with the countries including Vietnam, Malaysia and Mongolia, etc. and continued to improve its relation with Burma.

The US emphasized the central role of the ASEAN for many times. In April 2014, the US–ASEAN Defense Ministers' Meeting was held in Hawaii. The defense ministers of Burma and Laos made an official visit to the US for the first time. The US officials, on many occasions, affirmed the central role of the ASEAN, the crucial function of the ASEAN Regional Forum, as well as the importance of strengthening the maritime defense capabilities of the allies and partners. On November 13, the US President Barack Obama was present at the US–ASEAN Leaders Meeting in Burma's capital Naypyidaw and denoted that the US would strengthen the cooperation with the ASEAN countries in the field of security assurance.

Since the US and Vietnam declared to build the "comprehensive partnership" in 2013, the relation of the two countries has experienced rapid development. The heat up of the South China Sea dispute is the important background of the reinforcement of the US–Vietnam relation. Located in the western Pacific Ocean, the strategic position of Vietnam in the US "Two Ocean Strategy" keeps rising. The US also attempted to return to the Cam Ranh Bay, the excellent natural harbor originally built by the US. To enhance Vietnam's capability to monitor and defense its coastline and to maintain the maritime security, the US has been considering to lifting the ban to sell lethal weapons to Vietnam. In June 2014, the senior diplomat Ted Osius, also the next US ambassador to Vietnam nominated by the President Obama, remarked at the state senate hearing of approving his appointment, that it is time for the US to consider to lifting the ban to sell lethal weapons to Vietnam. In August 2014, Dempsey, the president of the US Joint Chiefs of Staff, visited Vietnam and denoted that the embargo of the lethal weapons to Vietnam could be soon lifted after the discussion of the two countries and the equipment Vietnam obtains would mostly be used for maritime monitoring. Dempsey is the first president of the US Joint Chiefs of Staff to have visited Vietnam since 1971, which shows that the military relationship of the two countries is rapidly developing. The two countries denoted to strengthen the military cooperation, with maritime security and training at the center.

On April 27, 2014, the US President Barack Obama visited Malaysia, being the first incumbent US president to visit Malaysia in the past 48 years. The leaders of the two countries declared to build the "comprehensive partnership".[2] Security and trade are the two issues for their cooperation. With the heat up of the South China Sea issue, Malaysia cautiously carried forward the military exercise with the US and the security cooperation in other forms, especially the cooperation in the field of maritime security. Among all the countries claiming the sovereignty of South China Sea, Malaysia is one of the countries keeping good relation with China, so the US hopes to get the Malaysian cooperation and support on the South China Sea issue. Malaysia will take the post of ASEAN

---

[2] Alexander Sullivan: "Advancing US–Malaysia Security Cooperation in a Changing Environment", September 2014, Center for a New American Security, p. 11.

Chairman in Office and will set the issues under discussion at the scheduled time. Considering this, the US hopes that Malaysia could exert influence on the ASEAN to form a unified voice on China's "intimidation" and other movements damaging the regional stability, and offer diplomatic support in reaching unified statement.

When present at the ASEAN Summit and the ASEAN–US Summit in November, the US President Obama met with the journalists with the opposition party leader Aung San Suu Kyi and requested the Thein Sein regime to accelerate the democratic process. In 2014, the US added another 150 million dollars to provide aid for Burma. The US government declared that it will let the worldwide deployed foreign aid organization "The Peace Corps" to carry out activities in Burma. The purpose of the US to provide such great aid to Burma is to contain China from behind. Currently, the US Congress still impose restriction on the military aid for Burma, in that the development of the US–Burma relation still depends on the political situation of Burma, especially the 2015 Burma Election.

On April 10, the US Defense Secretary Hagel visited Mongolia, the inland country of the Central Asia, drawing the attention of the whole world. He is the first US Defense Secretary to visit Mongolia since Rumsfeld (the former US Defense Secretary, period in office: January 1, 2001–December 18, 2006) visited Mongolia in 2005. During this visit, the defense ministers of the two countries signed the *Mongolia–US Security Cooperation Goal Joint Declaration*. The two countries decided to expand the cooperation relation of their armies by way of training and aids. Whereas, the Mongolian Defense Minister Bart Elden excluded the possibility of the US building military base in Mongolia. This visit of Hagel to Mongolia is also one part of the US power distribution around China, a kind of continuation and expression of the Asia-Pacific Rebalance Strategy. Mongolia is located between Russia and China, hence, once there is steady security cooperation established between the US and Mongolia, the US would have bigger geographic advantages while implementing its Asia-Pacific Strategy.

Last, the US keeps carrying forward the deepening of the US–India relation. In December 2013, the Indian female diplomat in the US was arrested and "roughed up", incurring strong interaction of the Indian people and making the relation of the two countries dropping to the low point in the past 10 years. This May, Modi, the candidate of the People's Party, won the election and India enters the "Modi Era". After Modi was elected, the US attitude to Modi changed greatly; before that, Modi was ever included in the US visa blacklist for almost 10 years. As a determined nationalist, where would Modi lead the US–India relation to? This question has drawn extensive attention of all. In Obama's Asia-Pacific Rebalance Strategy, India is one of the countries the US needs to rely on for support. After Modi won the election, Obama gave him a call at the first time to send his congratulations and invited him to visit the US. The US Secretary of State Kerry, the Commerce Minister Penny Pritzker and the Defense Secretary Hagel visited India in July and August successively, and held the fifth round of US–India strategic dialogue with India. In September 2014, when the Indian Premier Modi visited Washington, the US and India issued a joint declaration, in which Modi emphasized that India will regard the relation with the US as a priority so as to realize the rise of India; Obama restated that the US supports India to be one of the permanent members of the UN Security Council; both countries agree to strengthen the cooperation on the issues, including anti-terrorism, intelligence and dealing with the climate change, as well as enhancing the security dialogue and defense relation. In the joint declaration, the two countries mentioned the South China Sea for the first time, stating that it is necessary to maintain the maritime navigation freedom and India shall deal with the South China Sea dispute according to the *United Nations Convention on the Law of the Sea*. Both countries agree to strengthen the maritime security cooperation, upgrade the "Malabar" maritime joint exercise and enhance technological cooperation between the navy of the two countries. The US President Obama will visit India on the National Day of India in January 2015, showing that both countries hope to expand and deepen the cooperation relationship.

In addition to developing close military security cooperation through diplomatic visits, bilateral or multilateral negotiation, the US also reinforces the training of the allies and partners through military aids. Meanwhile, the US would continue to be devoted to strengthening the capability building of the allies and regional partners by way of as many as 130 military exercises every year. As part of the Rebalance Strategy, the US is planning to increase the foreign military funding costs of the whole Asia-Pacific area by 35%, the military education and training funding costs by 40%.

2. New Development of the Sino-US Relations and the US Views on the "Belt and Road Initiative"

2.1. New development of the Sino-US relations: Continue to cooperate, but the competitive side is becoming more prominent

In 2014, Obama visited Japan, the Republic of Korea, Malaysia and the Philippines, which made the US media think that the visits of President Obama highlighted the intention of "containing China". The US is dissatisfied with China's policy on the issues of East China Sea, South China Sea, Ukraine, etc. The US officials and members of congress criticized China on many occasions explicitly or implicitly. The US argues that the confidence of China is weakening the stability of the East Asia, and that China fails to play a constructive role on the issues like the Northern Korea, the Syria civil war, and Russia encroaching Crimea, etc; while China holds that the US Asia-Pacific Rebalance Strategy is to contain the rise of China and the US is strengthening the unjust international system unfavorable for the developing countries. Although China and the US continue to cooperate on a series of issues, with the agreements concluded by the two countries during the Asia-Pacific Economic Cooperation (APEC) meeting as the representative results; yet, the competitive side of the bilateral relation is becoming more prominent, with the South China Sea issue as the main conflict point.

2.1.1. *The US intervenes in the South China Sea dispute, criticizing China explicitly for many times*

On February 5, 2014, Russell, the assistant Secretary of State in charge of the East-Asia and Pacific affairs, stated at the congressional meeting that China's action of claiming the maritime rights and interests according to "nine-dotted line" in the South China Sea does not confirm to the international law.[3] He requested China to clearly clarify the legal meaning of "nine-dotted line".

This marks that the US has changed the obscure policy it has long been adopting, and intervenes in the South China Sea dispute from the legal, military and diplomatic perspectives. At the Shangri-La meeting held in June, the US Defense Secretary Hagel criticized China saying that China took unilateral and destructive actions to strengthen the territorial declaration in the South China Sea. Although the US takes no position in the aspect of competitive territorial claim, the US is strongly against any country that pursues the territorial proposition by intimidation or threat of force. The US is also against any country that imposes restrictions on the freedom of flight or navigation by any behavior. In the speech given in Brisbane on November 15, the President Obama stated that "the safety of Asia could not be built on the basis of deterrence or intimidation, in the way that big countries oppresses small countries, rather, it should be guaranteed by the international law and international norms. Although he did not say it explicitly, it is rather obvious that he is referring to China.

This July, in the US–China Strategic and Economic Dialogue held in Beijing, the two countries had evident opposition on the issues of network attack and unilateral maritime activities. In August, over the water area 135 miles to the east of the Hainan Island, a Chinese fighter was at a stalemate with a p-8 reconnaissance plane of the US Navy, with only 6 m between the two airplanes. With the enhancement of China's comprehensive strength

---

[3] Daniel R. Russel: "Maritime Disputes in East Asia", Testimony before the House Committee on Foreign Affairs Subcommittee on Asia and the Pacific. Retrieved from http://www.state.gov/p/eap/rls/rm/2014/02/221293.htm. March 1, 2014.

and the rise of China's position in the international configuration, the containing side of the US diplomacy to China has been further reinforced. Shen Dawei, the China expert of the George Washington University, states that the competitive elements of the Sino-US relations have a clear advantage, which will continue and turn to the new normal trend.

Since September 28, 2014, the "Occupying the Central Hong Kong" event continues to be heating up. This street protest is similar to the other activities overthrowing governments driven by the US worldwide, in which the US plays the role of pushing forward and supporting secretly. The initiator of the event Dai Yaoting was ever present at the forums and activities held by the National Endowment of Democracy (NED) and the National Democratic Institute for International Affairs (NDI) under the US Department of State. The NED sponsored many non-governmental organizations in Hong Kong and openly supported the "Occupying the Central Hong Kong" event. Under the guise of "democracy, freedom, human rights", the US attempted to interfere in China's internal affairs, which has aroused strong aversion of the Chinese people.

In February 2012, Xi Jinping put forward the concept of "new pattern of relationship between great powers" during his visit to the US. In October 2013, at the Obama-Xi Summit, President Obama showed his agreement to the "new Sino-US cooperation model based on mutual interest and mutual respect".[4] In November 2013, the US National Security Advisor Susan Rice, while giving speech at the George Washington University, noted that it is necessary to "put the new pattern of relationship between great powers into practice". Since then, although China has been making efforts to promote this idea, the US still feels reluctant to accept it out of many reasons. Some scholars think that despite that the "new pattern of relationship between great powers" emphasizes

---

[4] Ely Ratner: "The Obama-Xi Summit: Three Essential Messages from Washington", Policy Brief, November 2014, S. Rajaratnam School of International Studies.

expanding cooperation and control conflict, this concept perhaps harms the US interests in Asia. This concept makes the US allies and partners in Asia worry that China and the US would realize co-governance in Asia, not concerning with their interests. Some scholars even argue that the intention of Chinese officials by putting forward the concept of "new pattern of relationship between great powers" is to request the US to give up its profits in Asia and to tolerate the interests of China while, on the contrary China would not make any concession or compromise.

The US thinks that the "new pattern of relationship between great powers" is actually China's scheme to find solutions to all the global problems which is beneficial to China itself.

At the Conference on Interaction and Confidence-Building Measures in Asia (CICA), the Chairman Xi advocated new Asian security concept, emphasizing that "the affairs of Asia should be dealt with by the Asian people". Later, China proposed to build the "Silk Road Economic Belt" and the "21st Century Maritime Silk Road", as well as the strategic vision and initiative of building the Asian Infrastructure Investment Bank. Some officials of the US government and the think tank is concerned that China is accelerating its action to build new regional order, to exclude the US outside Asia so as to strengthen its dominant power in the Asia-Pacific affairs.

2.1.2. *The cooperation between the two countries continues to develop and the two countries have achieved several results during the APEC meeting*

China and the US have common interests in maintaining regional stability, strengthening economic cooperation, counter-terrorism, non-proliferation and other issues, and therefore cooperation is an important aspect of Sino-US relations. In 2014, the two countries continued to promote the cooperation on the bilateral and multilateral platforms and a series of major issues. At the 2014 APEC Summit, China and the US completed 27 achievements and consensus to reduce emission, to strengthen military exchanges, to accelerate the bilateral investment agreement negotiations, as well as joint anti-terrorism, joint anti-corruption, reciprocal visa arrangements, among which the emission reduction agreement has great significance. On November 12, the two sides jointly issued the *Sino-US Joint Statement on Climate Change*. Both sides confirmed their operational targets after 2020, and would jointly promote the conclusion of the international climate change negotiations at the Paris Meeting in 2015 as scheduled and strengthen the cooperation in the areas of clean energy, environmental protection, etc. Under the agreement, the US plans to achieve 26–28% of the economy-wide emission reduction targets by 2025 on the basis of 2005, and will make efforts to reduce emissions by 28%. China plans to reach the carbon dioxide emissions peak around 2030 and will try to reach the peak value as soon as possible, and plans to increase the proportion of non-fossil fuels in primary energy consumption to around 20% by 2030. As the world's largest and second largest carbon emitters, China and the US had been having disagreement on how to deal with the climate change. The agreement concluded this time was warmly welcomed by all countries. After the two countries announced the agreement, the US Republicans immediately expressed opposition to the agreement. Therefore, to implement, the statement still needs sustained efforts.

On November 12, China and the US also signed two files, namely *Decision to Establish Mutual notification Mechanism on Major Military Operations to Maintain Mutual trust* and *Code of Conduct to Maintain Security in the Case of Meeting at Sea or in the Air*, reaching agreements to prevent ships and aircraft sporadic conflict of the two sides. The establishment of mutual trust mechanism of two sides is an important measure to enhance the understanding of the strategic intent of each other, to enhance strategic mutual trust, and the ability to control crises and prevent risks, which would play an important role for China and the US to enhance mutual trust, strengthen cooperation, prevent risks and promote the development of Sino-US military relations.

2.2. The US views on the "Belt and Road Initiative"

The "Silk Road Economic Belt" and the "21ˢᵗ Century Maritime Silk Road" proposed by China's leaders in 2013 have sparked widespread concern. The "Belt and Road Initiative" is regarded as China's plan to expand its economic partnership by overriding the land and sea southwards and westwards. The US Jamestown Foundation expert Lauren Dees believes that, as China signs a series of strategic agreements with Central Asian countries and Russia, the ambitions to build the Silk Road on the sea and land are rapidly turning into reality.[5] For China, the economic belt is helpful to promote regional energy cooperation, to ensure energy security, sustainable economic growth and to confront the threats endangering domestic stability. With the continuous expansion of the new Silk Road, Russia and the Central Asian countries will continue to "focus on the east (China)". China's Silk Road Strategy will have global geopolitical influence, and the trade route connecting three continents, once completed, will pose challenge to sustainability of the Eurasian economic circle and the North American trade networks.

Some scholars believe that the Silk Road economic belt and the Maritime Silk Road are the opportunity to expand China's influence and show the gentle side of China. The plan, once turned into reality, will promote the trade between China and the whole Eurasia. In this process, China will take the responsibility to build the essential infrastructures, so this large trading network will make more and more countries see China as a friendly country rather than a threat. This is a win–win situation, in which China could not only create a more moderate image, but also improve its influence in the region around.

---

[5] Lauren Dickey: "China Takes Steps Toward Realizing Silk Road Ambitions", China Brief, June 4, 2014. Retrieved from http://www.jamestown.org/programs/chinabrief/single/?tx_ttnews%5Btt_news%5D=42466&tx_ttnews%5BbackPid%5D=758&no_cache=1#.VHmprtK2e0Q.

The US World Politics Review published on the website the article of Jeffrey Wade of the Australian National University, believing that this is part of China's action to carry out soft power diplomacy and to expand China's economic and political influence to the other side of Asia. Behind this plan, there is a purpose not revealed, i.e. to legalize most of the China's propositions to claim the sovereignty over the South China Sea. He believes that the Maritime Silk Road plan is basically the "friendly version" of China's "string of pearls" strategy, just as the assertion that has long been made by the other countries. The way to achieve this plan is mainly to build the connective chain of infrastructure, energy, financial systems and trade around China. The goal of this plan is to build a new Asia-Pacific trade and economic system with China as the center.

On November 9, 2014, China's Chairman Xi announced that China would invest 40 billion dollars to establish the Silk Road Fund, which will break the bottleneck of the interconnection within Asia by ways of building a financing platform. This Fund will provide investment and financial support for the countries involved in the "Belt and Road Initiative" for infrastructure construction, resource development, industrial cooperation and other related interconnection projects. It is generally believed that the "Silk Road Economic Belt" and the "21st Century Maritime Silk Road" are China's strategic initiatives to contain the US intention to pivot to Asia and to develop the Silk Road by reintegrating Afghanistan.

2.3. The Sino-US game on establishing AIIB

On October 24, 2014, 21 countries including China, India and Southeast Asian countries signed in Beijing the memorandum of understanding on building the Asian Infrastructure Investment Bank (AIIB), to strive to put the AIIB into operation before the end of 2015. According to the plan, the AIIB will be headquartered in Beijing, with a statutory capital of 100 billion dollars and China as the major contributor. The countries participating the official sign-ing of the *Memorandum of Understanding (MOU) on Establishing AIIB* include Bangladesh, Brunei, Cambodia, China, India, Kazakhstan, Kuwait, Laos, Malaysia, Mongolia, Myanmar, Nepal, Oman, Philippines, Qatar, Singapore, Sri Lanka, Thailand, Uzbekistan, and Vietnam. Japan was not invited for the deteriora-tion of Sino-Japan relation. Some countries having been intended to be involved into the AIIB building process, like Republic of Korea, Australia, Indonesia and other countries did not represent at the signing ceremony.[6]

In early April, China's Premier Minister Li Keqiang proposed to build the AIIB at the Boao Forum for Asia and began to promote this idea. Since then, the US not only expressed its opposition, but also obstructed the building of the bank by political means. The Obama Administration opposed for the following three reasons: first, the building of the AIIB is a deliberate intention to compete with the World Bank and the Asian Development Bank deliberate move of the competition; second, AIIB is the geopolitical tool of China to absorb the Southeast Asia, South Asia, and East Asia into its sphere of influence; third, AIIB will not reach the environment, the procurement standards and other safety regulations adopted by World Bank and the Asian Development Bank. According to the report of the Australia's newspaper *Financial Review*, the US Secretary of State Kerry, when attending the inauguration ceremony of the new President of Indonesia, bluntly expressed the intention of not attending the building of AIIB to Australian Prime Minister Abbott. In this regard, although the US denied this, its strong vigilance to the AIIB is unequivocal. The US thinks that China's move is intended to pose challenge to the US-dominated international financial order as well as the Asian financial structure

---

[6]On November 25, 2014, the Indonesian government signed the *MOU on Establishing AIIB* in Jakarta, being the 22nd intended founding members of AIIB. Retrieved from http://finance.chinanews.com/fortune/2014/11-25/6814454. shtml, October 2, 2016.

with Asian Development Bank as the platform, thus having strong vigilance against this conception.

Under the US-dominant strategic framework of "returning to Asia", any move of China intending to build an independent platform will be seen as a potential threat to the US strategy. As for China, the policy to build a China-dominant independent platform is just to respond and fight against the US "returning to Asia" strategy. The construction of AIIB will be the beginning of the new Sino-US game.[7]

3. The Influence of the US Asia-Pacific Rebalance Strategy on China's Implementation of "Belt and Road Initiative"

The "Belt and Road" Initiative is a mid- and long-term strategy of China to maintain the stability of the peripheral areas and achieve connectivity and common prosperity with the neighboring countries. The implementation of any strategy needs to rely on the external environment. Due to the complex security situation in Asia-Pacific area, China is facing some obstacles and difficulties in implementing this strategy. Especially, the US Asia-Pacific Rebalance Strategy, combining with other factors, may make the issue more complicated.

3.1. The US strengthens the "India-Pacific" maritime security deployment, increasing the complexity of the South China Sea disputes and the difficulty in solving the problem

As the maritime competition of the East Asia intensifies, the US put more diplomatic and military resources into the maritime disputes of the East Asia. The US frequently criticized China for its

---

[7] Research Headquarter of Anbound Group (China): "AIIB begins the new Sino-US game cycle", *Financial Times (Chinese Network)*, October 27, 2014.

"confidence" and "dominance" through the defense policy documents and the speeches of the senior government officials. In March 2014, the New American Security Center released a report, which uses "Tailored Coercion" to describe Chinese diplomatic and paramilitary moves on maritime disputes. The report concluded that the moves of China are kind of advocacy of revisionism, posing threat to the regional stability and maritime security.[8]

On February 5, 2014, Russell, the assistant Secretary of State in charge of the East-Asia and Pacific affairs, stated at the congressional meeting that China's action of claiming the maritime rights and interests according to "nine-dotted line" in the South China Sea does not confirm to the international law.[9] He requested China to clearly clarify the legal meaning of "nine-dotted line".

This marks that the US has changed the obscure policy it has long been adopted, and intervenes in the South China Sea dispute from the legal, military, and diplomatic perspectives. Due to the intervention of the US, the difficulty of resolving the South China Sea disputes are increasingly growing and China's efforts to safeguard maritime sovereignty are facing increasing pressure.

The South China Sea disputes have become the major concern of the US to adjust its military deployment in Southeast Asia, in which the Philippines is the core of the deployment. In July 2010, at the ASEAN Regional Forum, Clinton announced in a high profile way that the navigation freedom in the South China Sea, the openness of the Asian high seas and the respect for the international law are the core interests of the US, and that the US will, together with Vietnam, the Philippines and other countries, promote to internationalize the South China Sea. Since then, the US attitude towards the South China Sea issue is becoming more and more proactive and tough. On February 13, 2014, General Jonathan

---

[8] Patrick M. Croin, Ely Ratner, Elbridge Colby, Zachary M. Hosford and Alexander Sulivan: "Tailored Coercion: Competition and Risk in Maritime Asia", Center for a New American Security, Washington, March 2014.

[9] Daniel R. Russel: "Maritime Disputes in East Asia", Testimony before the House Committee on Foreign Affairs Subcommittee on Asia and the Pacific. Retrieved from http://www.state.gov/p/eap/rls/rm/2014/02/221293.htm. March 1, 2014.

Greenert, the Chief of Staff of the US Navy, delivered a speech at the National Defense College of the Philippines, saying that if conflicts occur between the Philippines and China on the South China Sea sovereignty, the US will stand by the Philippines. "The diplomatic encouragement, armament assistance and security commitments from the US changed the basic policy of the Philippines in coping with the South China Sea issue in the past, being the strong pushing hands of influencing and changing the policy of the Philippines on the South China Sea issue".[10]

The US high profile involvement contributed to the fantasy and adventurous moves of the Philippines and Vietnam, exacerbating the tense situation of the South China Sea.

3.2. The risk of Sino-US maritime power competition and conflict is increased

The US Asia-Pacific Rebalance Strategy has exposed an important intention of the US, i.e. to restrict the rise of China by way of the power of allies and partners, so as to avoid the situation that China poses challenges to the US on the sea. The concepts or strategies of "Air–Sea Battle" and "Intervention by Joint Action", etc., are largely in response to China's so-called "Anti-Access" and "Area Denial" strategies.[11]

The US thinks that China's anti-access and area denial capability are challenges for the freedom of action of the US troops. To meet this challenge, apart from adjusting the operational concepts and proposed the "Air–Sea Battle" strategy, the US also strengthens the military deployment and military cooperation with the relevant countries within this area. This is actually a road of "gunboat diplomacy", which will certainly cause the concern and anxiety about China and

---

[10] Ju Hailong: "The Philippines Policy on the South China Sea Issue: The Policy Choice Driven by Interests", *Contemporary Asia-Pacific Studies*, 3, 2012, p. 46.
[11] David W. Kearn Jr: "Air-Sea Battle and China's Anti-Access and Area Denial Challenge", *Orbis*, 58(1), 2014, pp. 130–138.

China will definitely take countermeasures.[12] This may result to the imbalance of the strategic powers of the Asia-Pacific area.

With the implementation of the US Asia-Pacific Rebalance Strategy, the US strategic focus will gradually shift from the land of the West to the sea of the East.[13]

During this period, the Chinese military power is improved greatly and China continues to implement the maritime strategy adapting to the national strength and influence. China confronted with the US more and more frequently during its rise in the maritime field. Maritime power competition and game between China and the US continues to be intensified, and will impact on the future of Sino-US relations to a great extent.

Although there are some difficulties and obstacles, through our efforts, we still can turn the crisis into an opportunity to achieve stability of China's surrounding environment and the common prosperity of the East Asian countries. The Southeast Asia is a key part of China's Maritime Silk Road; whereas, the South China Sea dispute continuing to heat up, as well as the relationships, keeping to be intensified in recent years, might pose a challenge to the implementation of the Maritime Silk Road. At the China–ASEAN Expo in 2014, China's Vice Premier Zhang Gaoli pointed out the necessity to strengthen the maritime security cooperation in the security field and gave suggestions on establishing the exchange and cooperation mechanism among the maritime law enforcement agencies. Given that, many countries exercise their sovereignty claims in the South China Sea through their Coast Guard and other paramilitary organizations, so the interaction and cooperation between these law enforcement agencies can be an important step in easing tensions on the sea. The countries having disputes with China, like the Philippines and Vietnam, have strengthened their

---

[12] Christian Le Miere: "The Return of Gunboat Diplomacy", *Survival*, 53(5), 2011, p. 65.

[13] Christian Le Miere: "Rebalancing the Burden in East Asia", *Survival*, 55(2), 2013, p. 32.

cooperation with the US, Japan and Australia and other countries in recent years, in order to improve their maritime capability to fight against China. If China and ASEAN enhance the cooperation and exchanges on the sea, this can be the first measure taken to establish the mutual confidence, so as to defuse conflicts and crises, thus creating an atmosphere of peaceful cooperation.

The stability of the Central Asia and Afghanistan is essential for building the Silk Road Economic Belt. The Central Asia still faces the threat of three forces. Due to the complex situation in Afghanistan, President Obama recently announced that the US troops would remain in Afghanistan in 2015. If the security situation in Afghanistan cannot be effectively controlled, there will be a huge potential risk for China's Silk Road Economic Belt initiative. Complex security situation requires China to strengthen security cooperation with relevant countries, to provide public goods for the regional security so as to facilitate the economic cooperation and interconnection.

In the US, after the mid-term election, the Republicans not only won control of the Senate, but also managed to keep the status of the majority party in the House of Representatives, for which reason Obama was called a "lame duck president". This political pattern in which the Congress is totally under the domination of the Republicans would make the governance by President Barack Obama fall into the containment of the Republicans. As to the diplomatic policy, the Republicans might be more inclined to grant the president the fast track for trade, which will be favorable for the Obama Administration to advance the currently difficult negotiations on the *Trans-Pacific Strategic Economic Partnership Agreement* and the *Trans-Atlantic Trade and Investment Partnership Agreements*. Whichever party wins the upcoming general election, the US will take a tougher policy toward China. Meanwhile, the US would be more and more deeply involved in the South China Sea issue.

In recent years, the confrontation in the strategy of China, the US and Japan has become more severe. The South China Sea dispute is just the reflection on the surface, the underlying reason is that the rapid development of Chinese economy has brought about changes in the power structure, and thus the regional order of Asia is facing new adjustment. The Abe Cabinet, through the exercise of collective self-defense, attempts to further strengthen the US–Japan security cooperation to safeguard their own security, on one hand, and tries to constrain the maritime rise of China by strengthening cooperation with the Philippines, Vietnam, Australia, India and other countries, on the other. It is gratifying that China and the US reached agreement on crisis evading by signing on November 12 the *Code of Conduct to Maintain Security in the Case of Meeting at Sea or in the Air*, with the aim to prevent ships and aircraft sporadic conflict. In the future, the three countries, including China, US and Japan, need to make greater efforts in controlling differences and avoiding conflicts, so as to avoid collision and confrontation in strategy.

Chapter 4

The New Tendency of Abe's Government and the Strategic Dilemma in Sino-Japanese Relations

Li Chengri

National Institute of International Strategy
Chinese Academy of Social Sciences
licr@cass.org.cn

Shinzo Abe has been actively promoting the policy of "getting over the post-war system" since he returned to power, trying to break the "restricted zone" in exercising the right of self-defense and strongly advocating a constitutional amendment. He hyped the "China Threat Theory", denied the Diaoyu Islands dispute, and tried to win over the United States so as to revise Japan-US Defense Cooperative Guidelines. He has also been pursuing value oriented diplomacy and strategic aid diplomacy in China's surrounding area, intending to restrain China strategically. These movements not only set strategic dilemma for improving Sino-Japan relations, but also created significant external pressures and challenges for China to promote the "Belt and Road Initiative" and to achieve "Asia-Pacific Dream".

1. Shinzo Abe Makes an Utmost Effort to Get Over the Post-War System, Attempting to Achieve Country Normalization

In December 2012, since Shinzo Abe returned to power, in the name of so-called "Protecting Diaoyu Islands", he has been doing his utmost to instigate Japanese domestic nationalism, attempting to break the "restricted zone" in exercising the right of self-defense after the war and achieving "getting over post-war system". "Getting over post-war system" indicates the amendment of Japanese Constitution in order to carry out right of self-defense and finally get rid of American control. Among them the core issue is to carry out right of self-defense for two main reasons: firstly, Japan Self-defense Force has reached world advanced military level. Even if constitutional amendment expressly regards it as armed force, this action is a mere acknowledgment of this "symbolic measure" through legal procedure; secondly, in respect of dispatching soldiers overseas from Self-defense Force, Japan has passed many acts such as *The United Nations International PKO Cooperative Act*, *Special Anti-terrorism Measures Act*, *Peripheral Affairs Act*, *Special Measures Act to Support the Reconstruction of Iraq* and *Acts to Deal with Pirates*, in order to take part in various peace keeping activities, which turns out to be a kind of "Afterwards Measure". Currently, in the opinion of Abe, to "get over the post-war system", Japan must break the "restricted zone" in exercising right of self-defense. As a result, the essence of "withdrawing the restrictions of right of self-defense" is actually Japan's attempt to regain the rights to start war overseas.

According to the Constitution of Japan, Japanese government "gives up the use of force in settling international disputes", "does not retain warfare force of army, navy or air forces", and "does not recognize the capacity to declare war". Therefore, the logical consequence of the 9th article in the Constitution is that Japan shall not exercise force that is beyond minimum national self-defense. Japanese government explains this logic as "Even though Japan owns right of self-defense, we cannot exercise it", which is the core factor to regularize Japan's post-war security strategy.

In February 2013, Shinzo Abe set up a "Talkfest on Reestablishing Fundamentals of Security Law" consisting of 15 experts in prime minister's mansion (called Expert Meeting on Security Law for short) headed by president Shunji Yanai (former ambassador to the US) and committee members including Kitaoka Shinichi and mainly those international political scholars with obvious conservative tendency.[1] The Expert Meeting on Security Law summarized lessons and experience on relevant issues during first Abe Regime and had a further discussion of right of self-defense as well as relevant government's interpretation of the Constitution.

In November 2013, Japanese both houses of Congress passed the amendment of *Self-defense Force Act* in succession. The amendment states that when emergency happens overseas, Self-defense Force is entitled to transport Japanese via vehicles by land. Besides, Japanese and foreigners who "need to be protected", and "their family and people concerned" are also added up to become the group of people to be transported. So Japanese Self-defense Force not only expanded its range of activities overseas, but further promoted to solve the problem in exercising right of self-defense. On December 6, 2013, Abe forced to pass *Special Secrets Protection Act* in Congress, regardless of civil public opinion and disagreement from the opposition such as the Social Democratic Party and the Communist Party. On December 7, Japan passed its first post-war *National Security Strategy*, *New National Defense Program Guidelines* and *Mid-term Defense Force Preparing Plan* (2014–2018) in the Cabinet Council.

In April 2014, Japanese Cabinet Council decided to revise the *Three Principals of Arms Export* drafted since 1967 and to make *Three Principals of Transferring Weaponry*.[2] According to the new

---

[1] Retrieved from the official website of the Kantei (Prime Minister's Official Residence): http://www.kantei.go.jp/jp/singi/anzenhosyou2/dai1/gijiyousi.html. November 10, 2014.

[2] As per newly-made *Three Principals of Transferring Weaponry*, Japan will allow export of weapon equipment and technology mainly under the following circumstances: firstly, if it helps to advance peace and international cooperation; secondly, if it helps Japan's security assurance. Retrieved from the official website of the Ministry of Defense (Japan): http://www.mod.go.jp/j/press/news/2014/04/01a_1.pdf. November 10, 2014.

Three Principals, Japan can not only export weapons and technology to USA under certain circumstances, but also export weaponry at sea to countries like the Philippines, Vietnam, and India. In addition, it can develop and produce weaponry together with the US-led security domain partner countries in order to strengthen security and defense cooperation among allied nations. The birth of new *Three Principals* marks that, decades after the war, the lawful "chains" on Japan's arms export have been removed thoroughly. On May 15, *Expert Meeting on Security Law* submitted a report on this issue to Prime Minister Abe officially at the seventh meeting. This report interprets right of self-defense as "when the country closely concerned for our country is under armed attack that may cause significant impact on the security of our country, even if we are not attacked directly, given explicit invitation or agreement from attacked country, we shall exercise force within lowest limit and take part in excluding attack so as to contribute to sustaining and recovering international peace and security".[3] On July 1, Japanese Prime Minister Abe convened a cabinet meeting, officially passed the resolution concerning "the constitutional interpretation of the exercise of collective self-defense" and clearly put forward new version of "three conditions for exercising military force": firstly, when Japan or the nation that is closely related to Japan is under armed attack, when it poses threat to the survival of Japan, and poses a clear danger to Japanese nationals' fundamental rights of life, liberty and the pursuit of happiness; secondly, when there are no other appropriate means to exclude above attacks in order to protect the country and nationals; thirdly, the exercise of military force is limited to "necessary minimum".[4] In this way, Abe finally broke the "government's interpretation" that states "even if Japan owns but cannot exercise" right of self-defense for decades after war,

---

[3] Retrieved from the official website of the Kantei (Prime Minister's Official Residence), May 15, 2014: http://www.kantei.go.jp/jp/singi/anzenhosyou2/dai7/houkoku.pdf. November 10, 2014.

[4] Retrieved from *Upgrading of the laws aiming to provide continuous protection for the nation's existence and people's daily lives,* Cabinet Decision, Decision of National Security Council, July 1, 2014. The official website of Cabinet Secretariat of Japan, p. 7. http://www.cas.go.jp/jp/gaiyou/jimu/pdf/anpohosei.pdf. November 10, 2014.

and open up access for Japanese Self-defense Force to exercising armed forces overseas, which fundamentally changed Japanese national security strategy of exclusive defense-oriented. Therefore, Abe's attempt at unfreezing the exercise of right of self-defense will radically transform the path of peaceful development based on the Constitution after war.

At present, the so-called Abenomics in Abe regime prompts to devalue Yen and make stock market rise in order to boost domestic consumption. However, given Yen's devaluation, in fact, the price and wage have not been raised much, which on the contrary triggers consumption stagnation. In addition, Abenomics is only in the favor of the large enterprises, still lacking powerful recovering momentum. As a result, Japan needs to increase consumption tax more. Yet Shinzo Abe's decision to postpone the increase of consumption tax has brought vast change to his support strength. According to latest findings[5] from Japanese Asahi Shimbun on November 21, 2014, currently the support rate of Abe's cabinet has fallen to 38% reaching the lowest point since the second time it was founded. What's more, 62% of people are against the dismissing of congress and presidential election. The percentage of people who disagree to take increasing consumption tax as the reason to dismiss congress has reached 65%. Now Prime Minister Abe has announced to dismiss congress and scheduled to hold House of Representatives Election on December 14, trying to change the situation of dejecting support rate and to further consolidate his political status so as to be in power for long term. During the election, the comment on Abe Regime's economic policy "Abenomics" is probably going to be the biggest focus.

2. Strengthen Japan–US Alliance, Actively Woo the Involvement of the US

After the end of Cold War, in order to strengthen the Japan–US alliance, the US has urged Japan many times to allow the exercise

---

[5] Retrieved from *Asahi Shimbun*. November 21, 2014.

of right to collective self-defense that is forbidden in the Constitution. America's strategic attempt is to transform Japan into a reliable helper to support America in global military action as well as intervening international affairs, thus dominating the order in Asian-Pacific region. The *Japan–US Security Guidelines* made in 1997 stipulated joint measures when Japan is under armed attack (so-called when Japan is engaged), or when peripheral affairs happen, however, it did not make clear what if there is dispute with "offshore island". So Japan's purpose of changing its interpretation of exercising self-defense rights while revising *Japan–US Defense Cooperative Guidelines* including the defense of "offshore island" (such as China's Diaoyu islands), is to strengthen the restriction of China. Meanwhile, America actively pushes forward the revision of *Japan–US Defense Cooperative Guidelines* and tries to extend the application range for Japan to exercise self-defense rights from the US-centered area in the past to reach partner countries like Australia and India.

The nature of the US *Asia-Pacific Rebalance Strategy* is to contain or restrain the rise of China by strengthening alliance relationship with Japan, Australia, and Korea. It "restrains China by Japan" instead of "keeping balance between China and Japan". This strategic trend has become a principal axis in the US *Eastern Asia Policy* or irreversible strategic direction. The US believes that China is its main challenging country and Japan is its core allied country. Currently the US is on one hand strengthening the military alliance with Japan, and on the other hand, indulging Japan's exercise of self-defense rights to make Japan serve its strategy continuously. In June 2013 when there was a domestic discussion about the exercise of self-defense rights in Japan, the US former Deputy Secretary of State Armitera and other people that know Japan well held a press conference in Tokyo. They claimed that it shall be Japan that decides whether to allow the exercise of right of self-defense. They also stressed that forbidding its exercise would impair Japan–US alliance relations.

Japan makes use of the US strategic intention and shares more and more security responsibilities from the US in Asian-Pacific region, attempting to enhance Japanese Self-defense Force and expand military influence. In July 2013, at the press meeting after Senate Election Shinzo Abe stated that, "in order to strengthen Japan's security and the alliance with the US, Japan is revising security outlines, setting up a national security meeting and discussing the exercise of collective self-defense".[6] He emphasized that Japan shall solve the problem of exercising right of self-defense, so as to strengthen Japan–US alliance. The core of exercising collective self-defense advocated in Abe regime is to coordinate with the US more proactively in military actions in the international community and to gradually turn Japan into military power. For this purpose Japan must break the "forbidden zone" in exercising right of self-defense and reinforce its military force.

In February 2014, Japanese Foreign Minister Fumio Kishida visited the US and had a meeting with US Secretary of State Curie, former Defense Secretary Hagel, President and National Security Adviser Rice, etc. Japan and the US reached an agreement on revising *Japan–US Defense Cooperative Guidelines* as soon as possible and further strengthening the Japan–US military alliance. Japan and the US decided to officially start the negotiation of revising *Japan–US Defense Cooperative Guidelines*. They are going to discuss in details how Japan would exercise collective self-defense as well as how Japan and the US would cooperate and divide military duties in the Asian-Pacific region. On April 6, the former US Defense Secretary Hagel paid a visit to Japan and talked with Defense Minister Itsunori Onodera. He clearly expressed "welcome" concerning the issue of unfreezing self-defense rights and emphasized that "Japan and the US need unbreakable relations, and the US supports Japan to expand the function of Self-defense Force".[7] On April 25, the US and Japan published a joint declaration after the summit meeting, stating that "the *Japan–US Security Treaty* that

---

[6] Retrieved from Press Conference by the Prime Minister. July 27, 2013. The official website of the Kantei (Prime Minister's Official Residence) http://www.kantei. go.jp/jp/96_abe/statement/2013/0727kaiken.html. November 11, 2014.
[7] Retrieved from *Mainichi Newspapers*. April 6, 2014.

stipulates the US responsibility for Japan including Senkaku Islands (China's Diaoyu Island and its affiliated islands) and are applied to all the regions that are under Japanese regime". The US also expressed clear "welcome and support"[8] towards Japanese efforts on unfreezing right of self-defense. The US support stimulates Japanese government to break "forbidden zone" as soon as possible and gives Abe regime a strong impetus.

In October, during local elections in Okinawa, the relocation issue of Futenma Airport (located in Ginowan, Okinawa Prefecture) became the focus of the election. November 16, independent representative Takeshi Onaga, who was against the relocation in Okinawa Prefecture defeated Hirokazu Nakaima supported by Liberal Democratic Party who advocated the idea of relocation and was elected as governor of Okinawa Prefecture. The failure of Nakaima who supports government policy may bring blow to Abe government. The elected Onaga said, "Through my being elected, it is clear that the popular will in Okinawa is against the construction of new bases in the prefecture a second time, and emphasized that relocation to Honoko would cause a structural difference in Okinawa. The US military base is the biggest obstacle for economic development in Okinawa.[9] Although the Japanese government tended to implement established policy, the public opinion clearly opposed to the relocation in Okinawa Prefecture, which is bound to affect the relocation plan of the US military base.

Mid of October 2014, mid-term report on revision of the *Japan–US Defense Cooperative Guidelines* has to be published. At present, Japanese government takes into consideration the agenda of Lower Houses Election as well as the discussion about unfinished revision of *Japan–US Defense Cooperative Guidelines*, it decided to put off the scheduled revision agenda until spring next year. Even so, Abe will give up "Exclusive Defense-oriented" policy in virtue of exercising self-defense rights and turn into "aggressive" military strategy step

---

[8]Retrieved from The official website of the Ministry of Foreign Affairs of Japan: http://www.mofa.go.jp/mofaj/na/na1/us/page3_000756.html. November 10, 2014.
[9]Retrieved from *Jiji Press*. November 16, 2014.

by step without any change. In addition, Abe's actual intention is to enhance Japan's military intervention capacity and influence in Asian-Pacific region through the exercise of right of self-defense with the help of Japan–US alliance. Therefore, in the future Japanese Force will be able to go abroad after its "rectification of name" and stretch its reach to any corner in the world.

3. Japan Strengthens the Diplomatic Strategy in the Surrounding Areas of China, and Its Trend of Competing with China is Obvious

Since Shinzo Abe returned to power, he visited Southeast Asia for five times in succession, becoming the first person who visited all the ten ASEAN countries among the previous Japanese prime ministers. Abe specially elaborated the "Five Diplomatic Principles" between Japan and ASEAN: firstly, Japan should create together with ASEAN countries and expand freedom, democracy, basic human rights as well as other "universal values"; secondly, the free and open ocean dominated by the law rather than the power is public property, Japan is willing to work with ASEAN countries to safeguard maritime rights and interests as well as freedom of navigation, and to welcome the US to attach great importance to Asian policies; thirdly, to actively boost the economic and trade cooperation between Japan and ASEAN countries, promote investment, propel Japan's economic recovery and the common prosperity with all countries; fourthly, to promote common development with ASEAN and maintain the diversity of Asian culture and tradition; fifthly, to further promote the exchanges among young people of Japan and ASEAN countries.[10]

In recent years, Japan has unfurled the banner of official development assistance (ODA), and increased the investment and aid to Southeast Asia. Since 1992 when Japan recovered the development and assistance to Vietnam, Vietnam has been Japan's biggest

---

[10] Retrieved from the official website of the Kantei (Prime Minister's Official Residence), http://www.kantei.go.jp/jp/96_abe/statement/2013/20130118speech. html. November 11, 2014.

beneficiary country, the total amount of development and assistance Vietnam obtained from Japan in 2012 was worth $1.646 billion.[11]

May 2013 Abe first visited Burma, announcing to discharge all the Yen debts of Burma, increasing 51 billion Yen loans and providing the non-reimbursable assistance worth 40 billion Yen in the fiscal year of 2013. In July of the same year, Abe visited the Philippines, expressing that in order for the Philippines to promote coastal guard ability, Japan would adopt ODA to provide over 10 patrol ships for the Philippine coast guard, and the construction cost each is over $1000. In return, the Philippines put forward to support Japan's claims in the international arena. In the Fifth Session Mekong–Japan Summit held in December, Japan promised to provide the official development assistance worth a total of 600 billion Yen to Cambodia, Laos, Myanmar, Thailand and Vietnam and other countries within three years (as of the fiscal year 2015). Then in the Japan–ASEAN Special Summit held in Tokyo in December 2013, Japan promised to allocate $100 million to "Japan–ASEAN Integration Fund" so as to promote the integration process of speeding up tariffs, investment, transportation and other aspects in internal ASEAN. In addition, Abe also promised, Japan would provide the development assistance and loans of $19.23 billion to ASEAN countries within five years.

April 2013, a Japanese Cabinet Meeting passed the new *Marine Basic Plan* to be the basic principle of Japan's maritime policies over the next five years. According to the new *Marine Basic Plan*, Japan will transform from "a country guarded by the ocean" into "a country guarding the ocean", which means that Japan's maritime policy would turn from "passive" to "active". In September of the same year, Japan called in the Philippines, Vietnam, Indonesia and Malaysia as well as other 13 marine countries located in the maritime strategic routes and held "a seminar supporting the capacity building of emerging marine nations" in Tokyo, and expressed to

---

[11] Retrieved from Ministry of Foreign Affairs of Japan, *Official Development Assistance White Paper 2013 on International Cooperation of Japan*, February 2014, p. 184.

the participants that it would provide the relevant support measures of improving maritime safety ability.

In June 2014, "ODA Outline Modification Expert Forum" made a formal report, according to the *National Security Strategy* that was passed in the Cabinet Meeting in December 2013, emphasizing to use ODA strategically and efficiently, recommending the government to continue to play the main role, and implement the concept of "active pacifism".[12] On November 19, the first Japan–ASEAN Defense Minister Conference was held in Myanmar and both sides reached an agreement to strengthen cooperation in the security field. The Japanese Defense Minister Akinori Eto expressed in the conference that Japan would increase support strength to Southeast Asian countries with maritime safety, disaster relief and personnel training as the center.[13] Japan held the Defense Minister Conference with ASEAN countries and became only second to the US and China that ever held the Defense Minister Conference in ASEAN countries. Therefore, the assistance of Japan in Southeast Asia pays more attention to the strategic assistance investment in system construction and democratization process as well as other deep fields, which will further paves the way for Japan seeking the status of political power. Meanwhile, Japan forced Southeast Asian countries to be "far away from" China with the help of assistance, in an attempt to form the united front of containing China.

The Japanese government is increasing the aid and investment in South and Central Asia, in a further attempt to enhance the influence in the region. In September 2013, Japan and India reached an agreement to expand the currency swap lines between the two countries from $15 billion to $50 billion. In January 2014, Japan's Prime Minister Abe visited India and issued *Joint Statement*

---

[12] Retrieved from *Report of the Employment Conversazione Meeting relating to the Revision of ODA Outline*, June 2014, p. 4. The official website of the Ministry of Foreign Affairs of Japan, http://www.mofa.go.jp/mofaj/gaiko/oda/about/kaikaku/taikou_minaoshi/files/yusikisya_report.pdf. November 11, 2014.

[13] Retrieved from *Sankei News*. November 20, 2014.

concerning strengthening Japanese–Indian Strategic Global Partnership.
In September, Modi, India's new Prime Minister, visited Japan.
Heads of the two countries signed *Tokyo Declaration on Japan and
India's Strategic Global Partnership* and *Defense Cooperation and
Exchange Memo*, the two sides reached an agreement and decided
to strengthen the "2 + 2" cooperation mechanism between the
two countries of Japan and India, promoted the conversation
among the foreign ministers of Japan, the US and India, and further strengthen the defense equipment cooperation between the
two countries and bilateral or multilateral maritime joint training
and so on. Modi catered to Japan's constraining China in order to
draw Japanese investment in India. During his visit to Japan, he
barely disguised to criticize China's "expansionism". In response
to this, Abe showed that in the next five years, Japan's investment
in India's private and public projects including ODA would be a
total of 3.5 trillion Yen, at the same time, it will provide the loans
of 50 billion Yen for India's financial communes, and plan to offer
15.6 billion yen loans in order to improve the drainage facilities
in India's Northeast.[14] At the same time, Japan has carried out
assistance and cooperation in the fields of democracy, peace
building, energy, disaster prevention, children's welfare and
other fields through South Asian Association for Regional
Cooperation (SAARC), which has begun Japanese education to
the teenagers in the region and increased talent cultivation year
by year since 2007, enhancing the influence on the region.

Japanese investment in Central Asia is mainly through the
"Central Asia plus Japan" dialogue mechanism (founded in 2004),
and it holds a foreign ministers meeting every year. By 2012, Japan
had provided Central Asian countries with paid fund 95.1 billion
Yen, free assistance 6.1 billion Yen and technical cooperation fund
12.6 billion Yen.

---

[14] Retrieved from the official website of the Ministry of Foreign Affairs, September
1, 2014, http://www.mofa.go.jp/mofaj/files/000050478.pdf. November 11,
2014.

In recent years, Japan's strategic investment and aid in Mongolia and North Korea has begun to increase, especially expanding its strategic diplomatic move towards Mongolia. In March 2013, the Japanese Prime Minister Abe visited Mongolia, both sides agreed on the development of coal resources and the cooperation of environmental field. Japan agreed to provide the low-interest loans of 4.2 billion Yen for pollution regulation and thermal power plan of Mongolia and promised to provide clean and natural environment technology for Mongolia. In return, Mongolia invited Japanese companies to participate in exploiting the world's largest mining coal mine — the Tavan Tolgoi deposits in Mongolia. In September of the same year, Norovyn Altankhuyag, Prime Minister of Mongolia, visited Japan as the first overseas trip, once again express his support in "permanent Japanese membership". The two sides issued the *Joint Statement* and *Medium-term plan Action Plan*, further consolidating the "strategic partnership" between the two countries. In April 2014, Japan and Mongolia signed the *Agreement on Yen Loans and Free Capital Cooperation* in Ulan Bator. Japan decided to provide the development aid of 8.356 billion Yen for Mongolia. At present, Japan's assistance and foreign demands to Mongolia are mainly shown in the following two goals: one is to ensure Japan's energy supply, the second is to make use of Mongolia to contain rising China. In addition, in July 2014, Japan partially terminated economic sanctions on North Korea, attempted to improve relations with North Korea, and "alienated" the friendship between China and North Korea so as to strengthen diplomatic influence in Northeast Asia.

4. Japan's Strategic Intention of Containing China is Obvious and the Structural Contradictions between China and Japan are increasingly Severe

In December 2013, Shinzo Abe worshiped the Yasukuni war shrine, resulting in the most severe "Ice Age" of Sino-Japan relations since the establishment of diplomatic relations between the two countries.[15] In April 2014, Japan's Education Ministry published the verification result of social studies textbook adopted by primary schools since the spring of 2015, and explicitly expressed the disputed Diaoyu islands and Takeshima between China and Korea as the "inherent territory of Japan". In the annual budget estimate requirements of Japan's foreign ministry in 2014, in order to propaganda to the international society that Diaoyu islands, the four northern islands (Russia call them Southern Kurils), Takeshima (South Korea call it Dokdo) are the inherent territory of Japan, the increased fees of adopting measures for territorial security (external publicity, etc.) reached 1 billion Yen.[16] On September 10, Japan's Defense Minister Itsunori Onodera met with reporters and said, "in view of the fact that the Chinese bombers and fleets travel through Japanese Southwest waters, it is necessary to strengthen the monitoring of Chinese warships and aircraft".[17] Thus it can be seen, since Abe came to power, the trend of constraining and alerting China has been very clear and increasingly severe, which is worth great attention.

In August, Japan's defense ministry released *White Paper on Defense* in 2014, accused China of carrying out marine activities with the "high tension" attitude, thinking that China's delimitation

---

[15] From July 24 to August 10 in 2014, the legal person "Speech NPO" of Japanese non-profit specific activity and China Daily jointly held the 10th "Sino-Japanese joint public opinion survey" and received effective answers from 2,539 men and women above 18 years old. According to the survey, the proportion of Japanese who leave a bad impression on China is 93%, reaching the worst value in the past. The main reasons for the bad impression include China "do not keep the international code of conduct" (55.1%), "compete for resources (52.8%),"or "entangle historical issue" (52.2%), "the issue of Diaoyu Islands" (50.4%), etc. Retrieved from Non Profit Organization of Japan (NPO), The official website of Genron-NPO, http://www.genron-npo.net/pdf/2014forum.pdf. November 11, 2014.

[16] Retrieved from *Ministry of Foreign Affairs FY 2014 Budget Request*. August 2013, p. 9. the official website of the Ministry of Foreign Affairs, http://www.mofa.go.jp/mofaj/annai/yosan_kessan/mofa_yosan_kessan/pdfs/h26_yosan_gaiyo.pdf. November 11, 2014.

[17] Retrieved from *Essentials of the Press Conference by Minister of Defense*, September 10, 2013, the official website of the Ministry of Defense (Japan), http://www.mod.go.jp/j/press/kisha/2013/09/10.html. November 11, 2014.

of East China Sea Air Defense Identification Zone "may lead to an escalation of the situation and cause unpredictable events",[18] declaring that the purpose and goal of China to strengthen the military power were not clear, and the decisions related to "military and security were not enough transparent", "China's activities in East China Sea, the South China Sea and other sea areas and airs pace expanded rapidly and became active day by day", etc. these all show that Japan intentionally deceived and misled the public opinion at home and abroad through the white paper, spread and transmitted "China Threat Theory", and provided an excuse for its military ambitions and actions of Abe regime.[19]

On November 7, Chinese State Councilor Yang Jiechi held talks with the visiting Shotaro Yachi, director of Japan's National Security Bureau, and reached four principled consensuses in terms of dealing with and improving the Sino-Japanese relations.[20] On November 10, President Xi Jinping was invited to meet with Japanese Prime Minister Shinzo Abe, who came to China to attend the Informal Asia-Pacific Economic Cooperation (APEC) Economic Leaders' Meetings. At present, the relations between China and Japan, though still in a controllable state, Abe government's

---

[18] Retrieved from the official website of the Ministry of Defense (Japan), August 5, 2014. pp. 32–45. http://www.mod.go.jp. November 10, 2014.

[19] Retrieved from *Japan's 2014 Edition 'White Paper on Defense' Harbour Evil Intent Designs, People's Daily,* August 6, 2014.

[20] Firstly, the two sides confirmed to abide by the principles and spirits of the four political documents between China and Japan, and continue to develop China–Japan strategic reciprocal relations; secondly, the two sides reach some consensus in terms of overcoming the political obstacles affecting the relations between the two countries in the spirit of "facing up to history and facing the future"; thirdly, the two sides recognize that there exist different opinions regarding the recent tense situation surrounding the Diaoyu Islands and other East China Sea waters, and they agree to prevent the situation from being worse, set up the crisis control mechanism through dialogue and consultation to avoid the unexpected events; fourthly, the two sides agree to use a variety of bilateral and multilateral channels to gradually restart political, diplomatic and security dialogue, and make efforts to build political mutual trust. Retrieved from the Chinese Foreign Ministry website: http://www.fmprc.gov.cn. November 11, 2014.

strategy in China cannot be adjusted fundamentally. In view of this, Sino-Japanese relations will not be fundamentally improved in the near future.

First of all, under the circumstance that the right wing forces denied the aggression history in World War II, Abe regime breaks the "forbidden zone" of collective self-defense right in an attempt to push to send troops overseas. This move causes the concerns of Asian countries which once suffered Japanese invasion. Since Abe returned to power, a series of words and deeds advocating nationalism fully exposes that the right-wing ideology comes down in one continuous line with his grandfather Nobusuke Kishi, constantly "turn back the clock" on historical issues, and this is also the root cause for the continuous deterioration of the Sino-Japanese relations. Currently, the Japanese political right deviation and military power tendency are bound to increase the vigilance and aversion of the international community, especially Asian countries, which could trigger a new round of arms race among Asian countries, thus affecting the peace and development in Asia-Pacific region. At the same time, if Japan's Self-defense Forces can "release the forbidden zone of collective self-defense forces so as to achieve "to send troop overseas", Japan's military power and international military influence will increase along with it, which will form a certain strategic pressure on the safe environment for China's implementation of the *Belt and Road Initiative*.

Secondly, Japan's exercise of right of self-defense will accelerate the Japan–US military integration, thus making Japan cooperate with the US troops to carry out military intervention in the future possible Taiwan Strait conflicts and increasing uncertainty for China to achieve unification. At the same time, Japan could increase its influence on the Taiwan Strait by virtue of Japan–US Alliance, becoming a pro-independence accomplice behind the scenes, and maintain the situation of *No Independence and No Unification* on both sides. Especially, Japan draws the US over to intervene in the Diaoyu islands dispute so as to greatly increase the difficulty of effectively resolving the dispute over the Diaoyu islands in China. Besides, Japan may follow the

US to be involved in the South China Sea dispute, draw over the Philippines, Vietnam and other Southeast Asian countries that declare to claim for territorial sovereignty, thus worsening China's peripheral security situation. Therefore, China must clearly understand that Japan is the main external challenge to China's current maintenance of national security and territorial integrity as well as the "troublemaker" of promoting the strategy of *Belt and Road Initiative*.

In the end, the Japanese academic circles pay close attention to *Belt and Road Initiative*, especially the international relations scholars have embarked on the study of domestic situation in China[21] and complicated relations between China and major neighboring countries.[22]

5. Conclusions

Since the first time China's economy surpassed Japan's and became the world's second largest economy in 2010, especially since September 2012 after the Japanese government illegally "purchased island", there have been friction and confrontation between Japan and China concerning the Diaoyu Islands dispute, the East China Sea Air Defense Identification Zone, Japanese history textbooks,

---

[21] The Financial Comprehensive Policy Institute subordinate to Japanese Ministry of Finance holds China Research Society every year since 1993, and conducts research on China's political, economic, diplomatic, and other areas. Since 2013, the research society has been presided over by the president of Japan's Defense University. Retrieved from China Research Conference, The official website of the Ministry of Finance, Policy Research Institute, http://www.mof.go.jp/pri/research/conference/china_research_conference/index.htm. November 12, 2014.

[22] At present, Japan Institute of International Affairs (JIIA) organizes the domestic well-known Chinese and regional research experts and the research expert on Chinese issues Seiichiro Takagi presides to carry out the systematic research on the relationship between China and the major neighboring countries. Retrieved from Views of Major Countries on China: Policy Analysis. The official website of the Japan Institute of International Affairs, http://www2.jiia.or.jp/pdf/research_pj/h25rpj05-kadozaki.pdf. November 12, 2014.

worshiping at the Yasukuni Shrine and many other issues. What is more, Japan is also skeptical and wary about the establishment of the Asia Infrastructure Investment Bank (AIIB).[23] Structural contradictions between the two countries have become increasingly prominent, and the strategic competition between China and Japan will become increasingly severe too. By 2013, in terms of economic strength reservoirs, China has reached 61.2% of Japan, and is expected to reach 70% by the end of 2014, which may become the critical point for both sides to transit comprehensive national strength. Although China and Japan have reached four principled consensus to continue developing strategic reciprocal relations, they are still in a "strategic game" situation readjusting to each other because of the lack of political trust, which probably will take a long time.

Because Japanese existing laws are all based on the constitutional interpretation by previous cabinet that exercise of right of self-defense is forbidden, the exercise of right of self-defense will surely lead to the revision of relevant laws. The anticipated ones include more than ten laws such as *Self-defense Force Act, Peripheral Affairs Security Guarantee Act, Dealing with Armed Attack Act, The United Nations International PKO Cooperative Act, Ship Inspection Activities Act, Civil Protection Law, The Usage of Specific Public Facility Act, Acts to Deal with Pirates, The Setting of Ministry of Defense Act* and *The Setting of National Security Council Conference Act* etc.[24] Even though the Lower House Election in December 2014 may have an impact on Abe's political prospect, Abe Regime's new measure of attempting to exercise right of self-defense will definitely push forward Japanese domestic rightist political tendency and military

---

[23] Japan's well-known expert on China issues Seiichiro Takagi believes that with the existing international financial institutions World Bank, the Asian Development Bank (ADB) etc., Asian infrastructure development banking will bring great challenges to the snatch of international financial talent and the stability of existing international financial order. Retrieved from Seiichiro TAKAGI. The economic influence of China's "New Security Outlook in Asia", *East Asia*, August 2014, 568, p. 3.

[24] Retrieved from *Yomiuri Shimbun*. July 2, 2014.

power tendency, which will bring vast change to domestic politics, security and defense polity. Japan and the US have reached agreement on Japan's revising *Japan–US Defense Cooperative Guidelines* within 2015, which will explicitly stipulate the application range and approach of Japanese right of self-defense. This move will further complete their military cooperation and division system in Asian-Pacific region. In view of this, Japanese series of measures on politics, diplomacy and security will not only profoundly affect the structure of Asian-Pacific Region, but bring external pressure and challenge for China to promote the *Belt and Road Initiative*.

Chapter 5

Construction of Russia's "Eurasian Union" and "Economic Corridor among China, Mongolia, and Russia"

Fan Lijun

Russia and Mongolia Research Institute,
Inner Mongolia Academy of Social Science
nmgskyfanlijun@163.com

It is extraordinary for both China and Russia in 2014. For Russia, "the west is not bright while the oriental is bright". As its strategic space in the west is constantly crushed and extruded by the US and Europe, Russia shifts its focus of "Eurasian Union" strategy to the east. For China, we achieve great success both domestically and internationally. We have proposed the guideline for our neighborhood diplomacy featuring amity, sincerity, mutual benefit and inclusiveness. The "Belt and Road Initiative" and "Economic Corridor among China, Mongolia, and Russia" also act as liaison between China and the world, and construct economic veins among Asian countries. "Interconnection" infrastructure construction brings new vigor and vitality to the recovery of regional and world economy. In dealing with Middle Asia and Mongolia, China and Russia once again encounter each other to develop their own strategies. Apart from "replacing discourse power with national power", what kind of solution China should use to break bottlenecks in developing regional strategy with Russia. This question needs some provoking thoughts.

Putin puts Russia's "Eurasian Union" in his manifesto of new time. Based on the eastward shift of focus in "Eurasian Union" and the foreign development philosophy featuring Mongolia's "Road on Steppe", China's leader proposed the construction of "Economic Corridor among China, Mongolia, and Russia" coordinating developing philosophies of three countries. Considering regional and international *status quo*, this cooperation pattern comes into birth. Although "Economic Corridor among China, Mongolia, and Russia" is still in the phase of planning and constructing, we can make sure it has major significance to the eastward shift of Russia strategy, Mongolia's geographical role in Northeast Asia and Middle Asia, and China's expanding in the "Belt and Road" strategy.

1. Strategic Vision and Development Process of Russian Eurasian Union

In October 5, 2011, Putin published a signed article titled "New Integration Plan for Europe and Asia — the Future is Born Today" in Izvestia. He pointed out that the concept of "Eurasian Union" in this article, of which one critical step was to "formulate "Customs Union" and single economic space through incrementally integration of existing organizations".[1] Putin hopes that "Eurasian Union" could be a bond connecting Europe and Asia and become the third center of Eurasian Continent besides Northeastern Asia Economic Rim and European Union Economic Rim. This indicates Russia's two-headed diplomacy has shifted its focus to Asia-Pacific region.

Putin's "Eurasian Union" emphasizes its own development both domestically and internationally. Domestically, Russia exploits the development potentials of its eastern part in Asia. On one hand

---

[1] Putin V: New Eurasian integration plan — Future is born today, Izvestia. October 5, 2011.

it narrows the gap between eastern part and western part of Russia, on the other hand it sees Siberia and Far East region as springboards to jump into Asia-Pacific region. Internationally, Russia strengthens its relations with all Asia-Pacific countries, including countries of Commonwealth of Independent States. Old friends such as Mongolia, North Korea, Vietnam, and India have also been included in "Eurasian Union". Its planning pattern or roadmap is as follows:

1. Before December 31, include Ukraine, Armenia, and Tajikistan into "Eurasian Union".
2. Before the end of 2014, include Kyrgyzstan, Mongolia, and Uzbekistan into "Eurasian Union".
3. Before December 30, 2016, cooperate with Serbia and Montenegro to turn Belgrade into the fourth center of "Eurasian Union".
4. Continually include Turkey, Scotland, New Zealand, and Vietnam into "Eurasian Union".

From this roadmap, "Eurasian Union" led by Russia still take its neighbors — CIS countries as breakthrough point, gradually expands its territory to former Soviet Union countries and at last covers the whole Asia-Pacific region.

Based on "Customs Union", "Eurasian Union" proposed by Putin integrates "Common Economic Space" formulated during CIS period in order to construct "Eurasian Economic Union". Through "Eurasian Economic Union", "Eurasian Union" can achieve economic integration, free circulation of capital, technology, labor force, and commodity in this region and ultimately political alliance in Eurasian region.

"Eurasian Economic Union" originated from "Customs Union" among Russia, Belarus and Kazakhstan in 2006. On November 28, 2009, Russia, Belarus, and Kazakhstan signed *Agreement on Eurasian "Customs Union"*. (This agreement came into effect on January 1, 2010.) In Eurasian economic Council Summit of Mosco in December 2010, these three countries discussed and decided to find "Eurasian Union"[2] on the basis of Russia, Belarus, and Kazakhstan single economic space. On November 18, 2011, leaders of Russia, Belarus, and Kazakhstan signed a statement on Foundation of "Eurasian Union", short for Alliance of Russia, Belarus and Kazakhstan, including *Joint Statement on Eurasian economic Integration*, *Eurasian Economic Council Treaties*, and *Eurasian Economic Council Charters* and so on. These involved "Free Trade Zone", "Customs Union", "Single Economic Space", "Economic Alliance", and "Absolute Economic Integration".[3] This remarked the launch of Alliance of Russia, Belarus and Kazakhstan, as well as "Eurasian Economic Union".

As per *Joint Statement on Eurasian economic Integration*, on January 1, 2012, Russia, Belarus, and Kazakhstan changed "Customs Union Committee" into "Eurasian Economic Council" in charge of adjustment of internal and external relations of "Customs Union" and "Single Economic Space", and formulation of standing organizations of "Eurasian Economic Union".

"Eurasian Union" is actually a political concept as "Eurasian Economic Union" is the concrete and important step of realizing this concept. In this article, I will firstly introduce the concept of "Eurasian Union" and use "Eurasian Economic Union" in specific economic cooperation. These two concepts are Russia's vision plan and concrete steps.

2. Russia's Eurasian Union and Eastward Shift of Its Focus from Regional Perspective

Russia realized that in order to develop its "Eurasian Union" strategy, it should emphasize its own development both domestically

---

[2] The Common Currency of Russia, Belarus, and Kazakhstan is Called Adler. Retrieved from http://www.aif.ru/dontknows/file/1162396. October 4, 2014.

[3] (Russia) Lukashenko: The Western World Needs to Know, You Cannot Overthrow Belarus. Retrieved from http://www.aif.ru/dontknows/file/1162396. October 4, 2014.

and internationally by shifting its focus of economic development to Siberia and Far East Region and narrowing economic gap between its European and Asian regions. Consequently, Russian government founded Ministry of Far East Development and its Far East plenipotentiary appointed by the president is especially responsible for economic development of Far East region. "These actions are unprecedented in Russian history".[4] Besides preferential policies, Russian government also invests great amount of money. Although Russia's economy is not that optimistic in the past two years, it has been gradually increasing its investment in Siberia and Far East Region, especially the investments in infrastructure construction. Russia also takes its advantage of energy and resource in the Far East to actively expand its economic cooperation with China, Japan, South Korea, and other northeastern countries in hopes of exchange resource for capital which can stimulate economic development of Siberia and Far East Region. Toward this end, Russia held 2012 Asia-Pacific Economic Cooperation (APEC) Summit in Vladivostok expanding its influence in Asia-Pacific region. In November 2014, Putin also promoted Siberia and Far East Region in Beijing APEC Summit saying "we are establishing plans, making some preferential policies and simplifying administration process to welcome competent enterprises to develop in Far East Region where will provide you a wider platform".[5]

In promoting integration of regional economy, Ukraine is trapped in crisis because of choice difficulty in joining European Union or "Eurasian Union". The escalation of Ukraine Crisis leads Russia to readjust its development strategy of "Eurasian Union" shifting its focus eastward to Asia-Pacific region.

---

[4] Chi Ye: Strengthen Far East policy, Putin Founds Ministry of Far East Development, China Youth Daily. May 26, 2012.
[5] From international partnership to policy of Rubles — Vladimir Putin's statements at APEC summit, http://www.1tv.ru/news/polit/271509. November 10, 2014.

2.1. Ukraine crisis stimulates eastward shift of focus of Eurasian union

The promotion of Eurasian Economic integration in Ukraine is not the root cause of Ukraine Crisis, but it serves as blasting fuse. After collapse of Soviet Union, Ukraine has become Eastern Europe Arena on which NATO, European Union and Russia paid against each other due to Ukraine's significant strategic position. NATO and European Union drew Ukraine to their side for narrowing Russia's strategic space which is the last thing Russia wants to see. As a result, the trial strength between Russia and western countries turns into battles between factions of pro-Russia and pro-west inside Ukraine. From anti-government parade since the end of 2013, independence of Crimea and joining Russian Federation to autonomy and independence movement in Donetsk and Lugansk, Ukraine crisis is constantly escalating and expanding.

Along with expansion of Ukraine crisis is the trial of strength among Russia, America, and Europe. European Union and NATO have imposed several rounds of sanctions on Russia, from economy, energy to finance in hopes of forcing Russia to give in concerning Ukraine issues. In response of sanctions, Russia implemented soft policies as cutting off gas supply and trade embargo in 1996 and 2005. After taking Crimea, Russia quickly changed its strategy by putting extension of "Eurasian Economic Union" in Ukraine on hold and emphasizing development focus in the east. Though this, on one hand Russia can fight against the west with the help of the east, on the other hand Russia may relieve its pressure brought by sanctions from the western world and prevent border crisis between Russia and Ukraine from spreading into Russia.

Russia's strategic shift eastward mainly focuses on developing relations with Asia-Pacific countries in Middle Asia, Middle East, Northeastern Asia, and Southeastern Asia. Fully restoring and reestablishing relations with traditionally friendly countries in Asia-Pacific region is a salient step of Russia's strategy. Here we take five Middle Asian countries, Mongolia and China as the main research subjects and analyze Russia's relations with these countries, its influence on "Eurasian Union", problems and development tendency of "Economic Corridor among China, Mongolia and Russia" proposed by China.

2.1.1. *Speed up construction of Eurasian Union with Middle Asian countries*

According to planned roadmap, led by Russia, the Union has established international treaties compatible with "Customs Union" and the Single Economic Space, cleared all the obstacles on way of operating "Customs Union" and the Single Economic Space and provided legal support for comprehens launching "Eurasian Union" on January 1, 2015. The second step is to promote "Eurasian Union" among CIS countries, especially in five Middle Asian Countries.

On December 24, 2013, Russia, Belarus, and Kazakhstan, the three founding countries, took Armenia into "Customs Union" and the Single Economic Space. On October 10, 2014, Armenia became the member country of "Eurasian Union". So far there have been four member countries in "Eurasian Union", which are three founding countries and Armenia. Uzbekistan, Kyrgyzstan, and Tajikistan, which are Eurasian Economic Community countries inside CIS, have signed entry protocol, but they are still reserved about joining "Eurasian Economic Union". Negotiation with Kyrgyzstan, is still in progress without specific results. Although these countries have not joined "Eurasian Economic Union", they are still great help for Russia to fight against the western world.

Being member countries of "Eurasian Economic Union", Russia, Kazakhstan, and Armenia formulate a single market, among them, in which Russia's leadership in economy is strengthened. Integration of nuclear corporations in Russia and Kazakhstan could effectively control regional development of world economy. Similar to this, integration in industries of national defense, machine manufacturing, non-ferrous metal processing, chemical engineering, oil and gas processing could also exert great influence on regional economy. Under the framework of "Eurasian Economic

Union", Russia's integration with Kazakhstan, its largest neighbor in Middle Asia, not only secures its eastward shift of "Eurasian Union", but also safeguards the stability of its southern part which means a lot in Russia's national defense strategy.

2.1.2. *Strengthen strategic partnership with Mongolia*

After the signature of Joint Statement on Strategic Partnership by Russia and Mongolia, relations between these two countries had great development. Putin put more emphasis on Russia's relation with Mongolia after he came to power in 2012. Russia develops relations with Mongolia with Soviet-Mongolia economic legacy as an entry point, economy as a platform and traditional culture as a bond, so as to deeply strength its relation to Mongolia. On May 12, 2013, the president of Russian Railway Corporation, Vladimir Yakunin visited Mongolia to discuss the reform of electrified railway in Mongolia. Besides, Minister of Foreign Affairs, Minister of Culture, and State Duma Delegation visited Mongolia this year and discussed with Mongolia concerning cooperation in the fields of economy, trade, culture, education, health and military. Putin's whirlwind visit to Mongolia early September 2014 had fruitful results.

On September 4, 2014, Putin paid a visit to Mongolia at invitation, joined the 75th anniversary of victory in Battles of Khalkhin Gol and signed 15 cooperation agreements with regards of politics, economy, culture, education, and military. At this time, Russia and Mongolia did not sign any political paper to improve their relations, nevertheless the weight of these 15 agreements is far more than that of comprehensive strategic partnership. Among these, visa exemption agreement is of great importance in citizens' travelling between two countries and regional cooperation and reflects high trust to each other. According to Putin, "we discuss further about every key question under the structure of strategic partnership, plan our future especially our cooperation on economy and trade... we outline our roadmap about future which leads cooperation between our two countries in every field in future".[6] The roadmap mentioned before includes the route from "Eurasian Economic Union" to "Eurasian Union". The largest achievement of promotion of "Eurasian Economic Union" in Mongolia is the trial operation of Altanbulag Free Trade Zone located in border of Mongolia and Russia on June 22, 2014. So far there have been 28 enterprises settling down here. The operation of this free trade zone reduces more than 1,000 km of importing China's goods and drives economic development in Mongolia.

For Russia, both development strategies of Siberia and Far East Region and conception of "Eurasian Economic Union" are dependent on Mongolia's cooperation. Russia strengthens its relation with Mongolia not only for economic benefits, but also from the perspectives of geopolitics and national security. What Russia values is geographic politics of Mongolia, diplomatic stance of Mongolia and butterfly effects rising from it.

2.1.3. *Deepen and consolidate comprehensive strategic partnership*

Recently, thriving bilateral relations between China and Russia have become the focal point of the whole world. In 2012, both China and Russia went through leadership transition as new leaders emphasized a lot on developing bilateral relations. In 2103, Putin approved new version of Russia Foreign Policy Ideas which mentioned that "Russia will continue strengthening equal, trustful and comprehensive strategic partnership with China and expand cooperation actively in all fields".[7] In April 2013, Xi Jinping chose Russia as the first country to pay visit to after he was elected as president of China, which demonstrated his emphasis on relations between the two countries. In May 2015, two countries signed Joint Statement on New Phase of Establishing Strategic Partnership

---

[6] Putin's Speech on Press Conference in Mongolia Retrieved from http://asiaiussia. ru/news/4142/. September 4, 2014.

[7] Hu Xiaoguang: Russia Will Continue Strengthening Comprehensive Strategic Relations with China. Retrieved from http://news.xinhuanet.com/world/2013-02/17/c_124351244.htm. February 20, 2013.

which improved relations between two countries. Currently, people hold the view that comprehensive strategic partnership between China and Russia has reached the best level in history. "We have high trust of each other, firmly support each other and deepen cooperation in all fields. Profound friendship built by leaders of two countries plays a significant role in relations of two countries".[8] Especially after the outbreak of Ukraine crisis, relations between China and Russia became closer. Concerning international and regional issues, China and Russia keep close cooperation, support each other and rely on each other under the structure of Security Council.

With more western sanctions on Russia, especially in financial areas, Russia will lean more to Asia and continue its Asian diplomacy strategy of resource for fund until its strained relations with America and Europe relive. China, Japan, and South Korea are primary choices for Russia to apply its policy of mineral resource for fund. In May 2014, China and Russia signed a gas supply contract worth 400 billion USD during the period of CICA summit. On November 12, 2014, Russia and Iran signed weapon purchase deals worth 50 billion USD to help Russia's industry transformation and upgrading and increase high end employment opportunity. Russia keeps five Middle Asian countries, Mongolia and North Korea at bay through their traditional bonds and makes sure these countries take a neutral stand in geopolitics. Putin's visit to Mongolia and 15 agreements regrading traditional industries in September 2014 are good examples of this. On November 17, 2014, North Korea sent a special envoy to visit Russia and proposed that they would resume Six-Party Talks unconditionally which had something to do with Russia's mediation and lobby, as well as North Korea's policy adjustment. One step of shift focus of "Eurasian Union" to Asia-Pacific region is to build economic alliance with the above Asian countries.

---

[8] Wang Yi: Currently Relations between China and Russia Have Reached the Best Level in History. Retrieved from http://news.xinhuanet.com/politics/2014-03/08/c_133170394.htm. March 8, 2014.

2.2. Intersection of Eurasian Economic Union and silk road economic belt in Middle Asia

The nucleus of "Eurasian Economic Union" led by Russia is CIS countries after collapse of Soviet Union. As Kazakhstan is one of the main initiators in CIS, five Middle Asian countries become priorities in "Eurasian Union" development. This coincides with Silk Road Economic Belt proposed by China. Although China and Russia have different development ideas and purposes in Middle Asia, Russia still has much concern about this.

Firstly, Russia concerns about national security. Russia always worries that penetration of extreme religion force from Middle Asia may cause instability of southern border in Russia and endanger national security. "Cut off drug trafficking routes and communication channels between Middle Asian terrorists and their ally", "protect our traditional positions in politics and economy of Middle Asia and contain influence from unfriendly power outside this region".[9] Although China does not belong to unfriendly power, Russia is reluctant to welcome another power to enter Middle Asia.

Secondly, Russia concerns that China's economic integration with five Middle Asian countries through Silk Road Economic Belt could undermine Russia's economic relations with Middle Asian countries. Actually, Russia's worry does make sense. In recent 10 years, China's economic and trade links with five Middle Asian countries have become closer and closer with increasing value of trade. Until 2013, China was the largest trading partner of Kazakhstan and Turkmenistan, the second largest trading partner of Uzbekistan and Kyrgyzstan, the third trading partner of Tajikistan.[10] Trade volume among Russia and Middle Asian countries is increasing, but with smaller range compared to the volume between China and Middle Asian countries. In these two years, due to continuous falling of energy price in the world, Russia is

---

[9] (Russia) Mikhail Titarenko: Russia and Its Asian Partners under the Framework of Globalization, translated by Li Yanling, China Social Sciences Press, p. 273.

[10] Zhong Siyuan: China and Middle Asia Make Dreams Come True Together, *People's Daily*, February 7, 2014.

experiencing economic slowdown and losing its trade volume with Middle Asian countries. On the contrary, China is progressing day by day.

Last but not least, Russia worries that China's economic integration with five Middle Asian countries will have impact on Russia's promotion of "Eurasian Economic Union" in Middle Asia. "Eurasian Union" led by Russia includes four of five Middle Asian countries. In accordance with the roadmap, before the end of 2014, Tajikistan, Kyrgyzstan, and Uzbekistan should join this union and "Eurasian Economic Union" should be launched on January 1, 2015. However, *status quo* is that only Russia, Belarus and Kazakhstan, three "Customs Union" countries, have signed and joined this union while other countries are in the process of negotiation without confirmed results. The future of "Eurasian Economic Union" still remains in mist.

Focusing on economic interests, the "Belt and Road Initiative" including Silk Road Economic Belt proposed by China try to formulate economic diplomacy, without political ends, featuring a regional economic cooperation pattern, point to face. "Eurasian Economic Union" launched by Russia mainly aims at promoting economic integration to reach a big union featuring integration of politics, economy and military ultimately. China has taken Russia's interests into consideration when constructing Silk Road Economic Belt, and Russia fully support China's construction of Silk Road Economic Belt. For Russia, the union will not be a favorable economic entity if "Eurasian Union" does not include all five Middle Asian countries. Meanwhile, strategic space of Russia's "Eurasian Union" will be considerably narrowed without participation of five Middle Asian countries, which is the last thing Russia wants to see. Consequently, Russia and China need to find their cohering interests under the framework of The Shanghai Cooperation Organization and Confidence Building Measures in Asia.

At present, China has founded Silk Road Fund to support infrastructure construction of the countries along the Belt and Road. Due to sanctions from America and Europe, Russia is not capable of investing large amount of money into Middle Asian countries.

Large amount of China's capital flow into Middle Asian countries will definitely exerts influence on Russia's relations with these countries. China should consider Russia's conventional influence on these countries and try to avoid interest competing with Eurasians Economic Union when cooperating with five Middle Asian countries. China should subtly use history legacy from Russia and these countries so that Silk Road could be lubricants of the economic engine in Middle Asia.

2.3. The influence of Eurasian Economic Union on China–Mongolia relations

Russia and Mongolia are no longer in the relationship of shackles as they were back in the period of Soviet Union, but develop bilateral relations on basis of equality, mutual benefit and mutual trust. Mongolia's geopolitics are of great significance to Russia while NATO and European Union expand eastward, America goes back to Asia-Pacific region and China has become the second largest economic entity. Mongolia's choice will directly influence Russia's strategic space in Asia-Pacific region and implementation of "Eurasian Economic Union" strategy.

Firstly, Russia and Mongolia share long common borders where transnational people of two countries are located. Any movement in Mongolia will inevitably have some impact on Russia. The bilateral or multilateral communication and cooperation in the fields of politics, economy, culture, military and foreign affairs between Mongolia and third neighbors headed by America will certainly exert influence on national security of Russia. Russia must be cautious that disasters like Ukraine crisis should not happen in its eastern part.

Secondly, Russia would not like to see the spread of China's force in Mongolia. In the future, Russia will deepen its relations with Mongolia using economic legacy from Soviet Union and Mongolia as breakpoint, economy as platform and traditional culture as bond. Actually, taking Mongolia into "Eurasian Union" is a strategy for Russia.

As per roadmap established by Russia, before the end of 2014, Mongolia should join "Eurasian Economic Union". Mongolia has not signed any treaty or agreement on joining "Eurasian Union" with Russia, but we can see that Mongolia is approaching this union step by step from a series of agreements signed when Putin visited Mongolia in September 2014.

Apart from strengthening cooperation in the traditional basic industries of railway, mineral resource and energy development, Russia loosens cooperation conditions in fields of economy, trade, culture and technology and expands cooperation scope. Mutual exemption of visas means that Mongolian citizens can freely enter and leave Russia providing much convenience for economic communication between these two countries. Russia's lowering its entry bar for Mongolian beef and mutton has vital realistic significance to improving export rate of Mongolian livestock. Through this increasing export rate, Mongolia's decrease in foreign currency because of sharp reduce in energy export is offset. Putin promised that oil and gas pipeline designed for entering China would go through Mongolia demonstrating his concession for Mongolia in Russia's strategy in "Eurasian Union".

China signed *Joint Statement of Comprehensive Strategic Partnership* with Mongolia and 26 compatible agreements when president Xi Jinping visited Mongolia in August 2014. Comparing these to agreements signed by Mongolia and Russia, it is not hard to find that cooperative agreements between Russia and Mongolia are more targeted, which is one-on-one cooperation like department on department or unit on unit with designated person to take charge of. We still need to observe what influence cooperation projects between Russia and Mongolia will exert on bilateral cooperation between China and Mongolia. However, we can see that three basic industries leading national economic development of Mongolia, especially railway construction, are included in the cooperation projects between Mongolia and Russia. If China wants to invest, China needs to negotiate with not only Mongolia, but also Russia, the invisible force.

Mongolian railway is a 50–50 joint venture shared by Mongolia and Russia. Russians and Mongolians serve as general managers of this company every two years by turns. All the rail facility in Mongolia, from sleepers, engines to related equipment, is made in Russia. Railway could be the trump card for Russia in dealing with Mongolia. In these two years, Mongolia actively negotiates with Russia trying to extend railway construction in Mongolia. During Putin's visit to Mongolia, he promised that Russia will offer 250 million USD in extending Mongolian railway. Putin intends to expand Russia's influence on Mongolia through exporting equipment, technology and capital, and extending railway cooperation. He wants to exclude third force in Mongolia, among which China is regarded as the potential rival. However, it seems very difficult for Russia to implement this cooperation project.

Mongolia values infrastructure construction of domestic transportation. On November 2, 2014, president of Mongolia was interviewed by national television station, "railway is different from truck transportation, which can extend the route to harbors reaching the third country. This could facilitate international trade of Mongolia. It is necessary to improve traffic efficiency of railway and converge with China's railway. "Will China's capital enter Mongolia smoothly? Will Russia agree to accept the capital from China? This will depend on how China negotiates with Russia and Mongolia.

From October to November 2014, Mongolia went through reelection and reorganization of government administration. Firstly, the parliament passed impeachment of the current premier. There are two candidates running for the office but the final result is yet to know. Secondly, 16 ministries of Mongolia were reduced to 13. Some ministries are split but new ministers have not been elected. The resultant force of new Mongolian government and president decides Mongolia's say in domestic and international affairs, regional cooperation and future development of China, Russia, and Mongolia. We can make sure that new Mongolian government will not change holistic diplomacy strategy. As for certain cooperation projects, we still wait to see their further movement.

Mongolia appears both in "Eurasian Union" led by Russia and the "Belt and Road Initiative" formulated by China. The problems existing in cooperation among Mongolia, Russia, and China also come into existence in their cooperation with Middle Asian countries ranging from traditional bond issues to realistic development problems. As time goes by, we will see how "Economic Corridor among China, Mongolia, and Russia" plays in these problems.

3. Economic Corridor among China, Mongolia and Russia, and China's Reactions

The idea of "Economic Corridor among China, Mongolia, and Russia" is originated from "China, Mongolia, and Russia Dialogue Mechanism" proposed by president of Mongolia. President of Mongolia, Nambaryn Enkhbayar, attaches great importance to relations between Mongolia and China, between Mongolia and Russia as well. One important leverage of this reelected president is to develop traditionally friendship with Russia while formulate comprehensive strategic partnership with China as balance. Mongolian president proposed China, Russia and Mongolia Dialogue Mechanism when president Xi Jinping visited Mongolia on August 22, 2014.

In order to keep up with the "Belt and Road Initiative" proposed by China and the idea of "Eurasian Economic Union" proposed by Russia, the president of Mongolia put forward the idea of Steppe Road intending to reopen Mongolian commercial routes in history. The commercial routes include the road on the steppe connecting two oceans and the road on Mongolian grassland for Chinese tea to enter Europe during Ming and Qing Dynasties. Mongolia wants to restore its role as a bridge in Northeastern Asia and Eurasian Continent.

In September 2014, considering international situations and proposals from Russia and Mongolia, China's leader raised the idea of "Economic Corridor among China, Mongolia, and Russia" at Dushanbe summit of Shanghai Cooperation Organization. This idea is a new regional cooperation pattern in consideration of relations among China, Russia, and Mongolia under the framework of the Belt and Road Initiative. It is of vital significance to China, Russia, and Mongolia for regional safety and stability.

3.1. Strategic importance of Economic Corridor among China, Russia, and Mongolia

"Economic Corridor among China, Mongolia, and Russia" is to "converge with Trans-Eurasian rail projects initiated by Russia, Silk Road Economic Belt and Steppe Road in Mongolia".[11] The Corridor is an essential channel for China's Belt and Road Initiative and Russia's Trans-Eurasian rail projects. Although "Economic Corridor among China, Mongolia, and Russia" is currently under planning and construction, it has enormous realistic importance to connectivity of China, Russia, Mongolia, and regional cooperation in Northeastern Asia.

After the collapse of Soviet Union and Third Neighbor strategy proposed by Mongolia, the strategic position of Mongolia is becoming more and more salient. World powers and some international organizations have entered this country one after another. On one hand Mongolia wants to contain China and Russia with third force, on the other hand so-called third force, including the US, European Union and NATO, with complicated intentions also wants to balance regional force through Mongolia.

If Mongolia becomes the ally or quasi-ally of third neighbors, world pattern will change in a foreseeable way. If Mongolia allows military force of NATO and the US enter Mongolia or democratic thoughts spread and go deep in Mongolia, the balance of interests in Middle Asia, Northeastern Asia and even Asia-Pacific regions will be influenced. As a result, China and Russia's deepening cooperation with Mongolia could effectively control geopolitics and economic pattern of Eurasian continents.

---

[11] Xi Jinping attends meetings among leaders of China, Russia, and Mongolia. Retrieved from http://news.xinhuanet.com/mrdx/2014-09/12/c_133638177.htm. September 12, 2014.

Politically, China and Russia should strengthen communication and cooperation with Mongolia. Through this, both bilateral relation between China and Russia, and multilateral cooperation mechanism led by China and Russia could be strengthened. Presently, China, Russia, and Mongolia are strategic partners to each other. Sino-Russian relations are closer than China–Mongolia relations and Russia–Mongolia relations. Other than Six-Party Talk, there is no multilateral talk mechanism in Northeastern Asia. Meetings among leaders among China, Russia, and Mongolia start new multilateral talks in Northeastern Asian region. Russia's "Eurasian Union", "Eurasian Economic Union" and China's Belt and Road Initiative deepen cooperation among them, Mongolia and Middle Asian countries in all fields, further strengthen China and Russia's influence on countries in this region and their controlling power over regional situation so that influence from the US and Europe on Middle Asia and Northeastern Asia could be effectively contained.

Economically, Mongolia always wants to throw away dependence on China and Russia with the help of third neighbors. However, due to the limitation of geopolitics, third neighbors penetration towards Mongolia is not that effective as expected. China and Russia still act as vital trade partners to Mongolia and engage a lot in Mongolian economy. From the end of August to the beginning of September in 2014, leaders of China and Russia visited Mongolia and provided convenient conditions for economic recovery of Mongolia in the future.

Eastern part of Mongolia is located in Northeastern Asia while the western part is in Middle Asia, keeping very deep ethnic relations with Middle Asian countries. Mongolia wants to participate in not only economic activities of Asia-Pacific region, but also transregional cooperation in Silk Road Economic Belt, consequently Steppe Road was proposed. China opens Tianjin Harbor and Jinzhou Harbor to Mongolia to facilitate Mongolia's joining Maritime Silk Road and regional cooperation in Northeastern Asia, and Eastern Asia.

"Economic Corridor among China, Mongolia, and Russia" is northward extension of Silk Road Economic Belt on land and a new transnational cooperation idea that connects 21ˢᵗ Century Maritime Silk Road in the south and converges with Russia's "Eurasian Union" and China's Belt and Road Initiative. Three parties can set up effective coordination mechanism managing overlapping and intertwined interests, sharing common destiny and seeking common grounds while shelving difference.

China can take advantage of its capital, technology and human resource, make full use of all active factors in cooperation among Russia, Middle Asian countries and Mongolia, follow the guidance of neighborhood diplomacy featuring amity, sincerity, mutual benefit, inclusiveness, and strengthen infrastructure construction under the framework of Asian Infrastructure Investment Bank and Silk Road Fund at the time when China is needed during economic development of Russia, Mongolia, and Middle Asian countries.

3.2. Foster strengths, circumvent weaknesses, and break bottleneck in regional cooperation among China, Russia, and Mongolia

From planning and roadmap of "Eurasian Union" including "Eurasian Economic Union" led by Russia and the "Belt and Road Initiative" including Economic Corridor among China, Russia and Mongolia led by China, five Middle Asian countries and Mongolia are places where interests are overlapped and intertwined. However, these countries are in complicated relationships with China and Russia. We need to clear up all the relations inside, find out common interests, seek common points while reserving difference, and provide small countries with benefits while inputting energy into cooperation between China and Russia.

3.2.1. *Take traditional advantage of five Middle Asian countries, Mongolia, and Russia to promote the Belt and Road Initiative*

From the viewpoint of world politics and economy, national relations among China, Russia, Mongolia and five Middle Asian countries are short while the ethnic relations are quite long-standing and well established. We can put it in this way, national relations among China, Russia, five Middle Asian countries and Mongolia are printed with deep ethnic and religious marks.

Buddhism in five Middle Asian countries was passed over by Mongolian people while Islamism inside Mongolia is passed over by Middle Asian people. Besides, there are frequent interactions between ethnic groups in five Middle Asian countries and Mongolian people. Currently large amount of transnational ethnical people of five Middle Asian countries and Mongolia are living in China and Russia. The relations among China, Russia and those countries mentioned above directly have an impact on ethnic relations while Ethnic and religious relations also exert influence on safety and stability of border areas of these countries, even national relations.

Relations between China and Russia are crucial to those among five Middle Asian countries, Mongolia, China, and Russia. Simultaneously, relations between these countries and Russia also affect those between China and these countries to some degree. Actually, how to deal with relations is a practical problem for putting forward the "Belt and Road Initiative" and Economic Corridor among China, Russia and Mongolia. China should take advantage of existing traditional legacy from relations among Russia, five Middle Asian countries and Mongolia to advocate the "Belt and Road Initiative" on the basis of Five Principles of Peaceful Coexistence and under the guidance of our neighborhood diplomacy featuring amity, sincerity, mutual benefit, and inclusiveness.

Russia and five Middle Asian countries used to be brothers in Soviet Union while Mongolia was part of Russia in the past. So far cooperation among these countries are still affected by previous connections. Five Middle Asian countries all develop holistic diplomacy with multi pillars, diversities and multilayers by taking advantage of their geopolitics and resource. However, they cannot bypass Russia, the invisible force, when speaking of specific cooperation projects. 90% of pillar industries of these countries were born in Soviet Union in which the core parts are controlled and led by Russia. Based on this, Russia proposed "Eurasian Economic Union" and "Eurasian Union". Consequently, China must take Russia's interests in these areas into consideration, avoid risks and seek common grounds while reserving difference when cooperating with Middle Asian countries and Mongolia.

Russia's political and military intentions are to unite Middle Asian countries and Mongolia to fight against strategic encirclement by the US and Europe. Besides, Russia is cautious about Chinese power entering this area. After trade-offs, Russia decides to cooperate with China to contain the contagion from the US and Europe into Middle Asia and Mongolia. As so China, Russia's action helps to sustain safety and stability in northern and western borders, extend outer space of China and guarantee geopolitical interests of China.

Price collapse in fossil energy and a series of issues caused by Ukraine crisis put pressure on Russia's internal affairs and diplomacy. Under such circumstances, China's huge investment in Silk Road Economic belt makes Russia restless. Russia as capital shortage withholds Russia's influence and investment in Middle Asian countries. Nevertheless, historical relations between Middle Asian countries and Russia will not disappear in a short period of time. Therefore, China should resort to and make full use of the "legacy" when implementing cooperative projects, especially "trademark projects", sticking to the cooperation principle of "mutual markets, mutual resources, mutual investment, mutual benefits, and win–win results".

While cooperating with five Middle Asian countries and Mongolia in economy and trade, China should put emphasis on historical and ethnical relations with five Middle Asian countries and Mongolia and insert more cultural significance to connectivity between China and these countries. The Belt and Road Initiatives are brought up to "inherit and enrich the ancient Silk Road and boost exchanges and collaboration in both economy and culture, basing on historical great passage for cultural and commercial exchanges between China and Middle Asia, Southeast Asia, West

Asia, East Africa and Europe".[12] The soft power of China's diplomacy featuring cultural exchanges and cooperation will be the focus of China's diplomacy towards countries along the Belt and Road.

3.2.2. *Improve "soft power" of cultural diplomacy in political and economic diplomacy*

Cultural diplomacy is a vital part of the whole diplomatic strategy of a country. Compared to political, economic and military diplomacy, cultural diplomacy demonstrates a kind of culture that can release its charm in a quiet way. At present, China has good relations with most neighboring countries. 80% of these neighboring countries have strategic relations with China. Meanwhile, China is the largest trade partner and investment funder of 70% of its neighboring countries.

In the context of political and economic communication, cultural communication becomes more and more important. On November 4, 2014, Xi Jinping pointed out at the 8th Conference of the Central Finance and Economy Leading Team Office, "we need to carry forward economic cooperation and cultural exchange at the same time, strength cultural communication with neighboring countries in education, tourism, academics and art to bring to a new level".[13] Cultural communication, especially ethnical cultural communication, should be the vital entry point of facilitating political and economic communication between China and countries along the Belt and Road in the process of constructing the Belt and Road and "Economic Corridor among China, Mongolia, and Russia".

Firstly, ethical cultural communication is the answer to many difficult questions. Ethnic relations among China and countries

---

[12] Xi Jinping: China Will Invest 40 Billion USD in Silk Fund. Retrieved from http://news.xinhuanet.com/world/2014-11/08/c_1113170681.htm. November 8, 2014.

[13] Xi Jinping: Set up Silk Road Fund and Support the "Belt and Road Initiative" with Our Investment. Retrieved from http://funds.hexun.com/2014-11-07/170153382.html. November 7, 2014.

alongside Silk Road Economic Belt, Russia, and Mongolia are way back to history and even longer than national relations among them. Due to historical reasons, a lot of transnational ethnic groups are formulated. Separation from mainstay ethnic groups changed their living habits and lifestyle while recognition of ancestors and traditional culture remained the same. We can nurture characteristic culture of Chinese minority ethnic groups with the help of transnational ethnic groups. On one hand this could be in favor of rejuvenating traditional national culture, on the other hand mutual recognition could be fostered. In this way, ethnic cultural communication could be the answer to resolve conflicts, disagreements and distrust due to misunderstanding.

Secondly, ethnic cultural communication is also the significant guarantee of secure neighborhood of China. As is known to us all, the geopolitics of Middle Asia and Mongolia are very special where all kinds of religions, ethnic groups and powers with different purposes gather together. Major powers also compete against each other in this area. The US, European Union, NATO, Russia, India, Turkey, and Iran all want to exert influence on Middle Asia and Mongolia with different purposes. Whatever power enters here will directly affect security environment around China. It is vital for China to deepen ethnic cultural communication with countries above, eliminate ethnic recognition difference, and strengthen sense of identification in ethnic culture so as to prevent non-traditional culture from spreading inside ethnic groups, fight against the invasion from extreme nationalists and religious extremists effectively and secure the environment around China.

Thirdly, cultural communication is the vital complement to connectivity in politics and economy. Before APEC Beijing Summit, China's leader invited leaders of neighboring countries, leaders of two international and regional organizations to hold a host dialogue concerning strengthening partnership of connectivity. After the meeting, a joint communique titled Dialogue on Strengthening Interconnection and Partnership was issued, and stated "connectivity in 21st Century in Asia consists of three parts, which are hardware interconnection including transportation infrastructure, software interconnection including legislation, standards and policies, and also cultural interconnection encouraging mutual trust among people, and five fields which are policy communication, infrastructure construction, trade, capital, and communication among people. Infrastructure construction is the priority and basis".[14] All political communication, economic interaction and infrastructure construction need people to execute. Interaction between people is also interaction and exchange of culture. Therefore, when planning Silk Road Economic Belt and "Economic Corridor among China, Mongolia, and Russia", based on the fact that transnational ethnic groups of these countries exist in China, China should focus on ethical cultural communication, make fully use of soft power of ethic culture recognition, carry forward top design and development concepts from national leaders and occupy the advantages in the context of intertwined interests.

China's encounter with Russia in regional cooperation with Middle Asia and Mongolia is inevitable. Although China would not like to have a major power leading the "Belt and Road Initiative" and "Economic Corridor among China, Mongolia, and Russia", which are both proposing transnational cooperation patterns of formulating community of interests and destiny. As with the execution of interconnection projects in these above countries, Chinese factors are entering Russia's historical sphere of influence by a large-scale and exert influence on implementation of "Eurasian Economic Union". What will be Russia's reaction? How will Sino-Russian relations affected? We still need further evaluation.

We are approaching the end of 2014. As per the planned roadmap, Russia's "Eurasian Economic Union" will be officially launched on January 1, 2015. However, so far Tajikistan, Kyrgyzstan, and Uzbekistan are still in the process of negotiation without the confirmation of joining. The competition between China and

---

[14] Joint Conference Communique on Strengthening Connectivity Partnership. Retrieved from http://news.xinhuanet.com/2014-11/08/c_127192126.htm. November 8, 2014.

Russia in Middle Asia has begun quietly. Russia and Mongolia's reactions towards the idea of "Economic Corridor among China, Mongolia, and Russia" will be reflected in 2015. The complicated historical relation among China, Russia, five Middle Asian Countries and Mongolia is just like an invisible cloak that you cannot see it but can feel it. I think we can take off this invisible cloak through soft power like culture and let people in those countries benefit from Chinese economy. This is also the basis of China's "Go out" strategy and establishing friendly relationships with neighboring countries.

Chapter 6

The Belt and Road Initiative: India's Strategy and its Effect

Song Haixiao

India Study Center, Guangdong Institute for International Strategies
lazydog@126.com

India believes that China proposed the "Belt and Road Initiative" based on its domestic and international situation. It is a grand strategy focusing on infrastructure and free trade zone, using trade and cultural exchanges as a linkage in order to build China's "Central Kingdom". India is wary of China's presence in the Indian Ocean, worrying that this will gradually weaken its regional control and strengthen the dependence of South Asian countries on China. India responds with a cautious welcome to China's initiative and rejects to take a stand. At the same time, India tests the bottom line of China while maintaining communication, and brings up "India Manufacture", trying to retake the say. This is not conducive to the development of India and its long-term national interests, putting the neighboring countries in South Asia into a dilemma, and is also harmful to the deepening of Sino-Indian strategic partnership relation.

Since September 2013, China's Chairman Xi proposed the strategic initiatives in succession, including the "Silk Road Economic Belt" and the "21ˢᵗ Century Maritime Silk Road". The Belt and Road Initiative, as China's foreign strategy in the new period, gradually became an important issue of China's diplomacy, and got positive responses from the majority of invited countries. Different from the positive response of other countries, India showed a tepid response. This attitude is thought-provoking. In fact, there is no information asymmetry between China and India. Early in February 2014, at the 17th round meeting of the special representatives on the Sino-Indian border issue, China invited India to participate in the construction of the "21st Century Maritime Silk Road". Later, the mainstream English newspapers in India and comprehensive web portals made clear reports.[1] However, until December 2014, except for some responses from scholars and the media, the Indian authority only showed a cautious welcome and rejected to take a stand. Faced with the grand strategy actively promoted by China, what should India's strategy be? What factors make India refuse to show its attitude directly? How will India's position and responding strategy affect China's Belt and Road Initiative? These problems are worth our thinking and research.

1. India's Interpretation of the Belt and Road Initiative

1.1. India's interpretation of China's purpose and motivation of the Belt and Road Initiative

India believes that the foremost strategic goal of China's implementation of the Belt and Road Initiative is to meet the needs of domestic economic development and restructuring. Indian scholars generally believe that China "plans to maintain competitiveness in export and eliminate the negative impact of the rising labor cost by port and maritime infrastructure construction or the establishment of special economic zone in partner countries",[2] so as to realize economic transformation.

---

[1] "China invites India to join its Maritime Silk Road initiative", *Rediff*, February 14, 2014, China http://www.rediff.com/news/report/china-invites-india-to-join-its-maritime-silk-road-initiative/20140214.htm.
[2] Ateetmani Brar: "China and India: Prospects for Maritime Cooperation", October 28, 2014, http://www.maritimeindia.org/Archives/CHINA-AND-INDIA.html.

Secondly, India believes that China's Belt and Road Initiative is against the US strategies in Asia-Pacific and South Asia, one being the "Pivot to the Asia" strategy, and the other the "New Silk Road Plan" (NSRP) that aims at turning Afghanistan into a pivot in economy, trade, and energy.

On November 9, 2014, Chairman Xi attended the Asia-Pacific Economic Cooperation (APEC) CEO Summit and the Dialogue on Strengthening Connectivity Partnership, announced that China invested $40 billion to establish the Silk Road Fund and to provide financial support to the Belt and Road project construction. In this regard, 'The Hindustan Times' interpreted China's motives as: to break America's hope of return to Asia and to upset its plan to build a Silk Road in Afghanistan.[3]

1.2. India's interpretation of the specific plans of the Belt and Road Initiative

After April 2014, Indian media published their own interpretation of China's Belt and Road Initiative. The typical one is that China tries to build a "Central Kingdom". It is a widely held opinion among Indian media that China's Belt and Road Initiative is a strategy focusing on infrastructure and free trade zone, using trade and cultural exchanges as a linkage in order to build China's "Central Kingdom". In this regard, some scholars believe that "China publishes the details of the Maritime Silk Road plan for the first time, announced to center on the Indian Ocean, and took the port construction and improvement of coastal countries such as Bangladesh and Sri Lanka's infrastructure as the key considerations. China is also planning to set up free trade zone in Indian Sea area. The Belt and Road Initiative is a great blueprint — the Silk Road Economic Belt and the Maritime Silk Road link three continents into a ring. China, with trade and cultural exchange as a link, will connect the

---

[3] "Xi adds $40 billion for Silk Road plan", *The Hindu*, November 9, 2014, http://www.thehindu.com/todays-paper/tp-international/xi-adds-40-billion-for-silk-road-plan/article6579367.ece.

world to be a 'Central Kingdom' with China as its center".[4] Similar interpretations can also be found in the article "China's New Silk Road Vision Revealed".[5]

2. India's Strategy to China's Belt and Road Initiative

Since China proposed the Belt and Road Initiative, Indian authority has never stated its stand publicly. Opposite to the authority, Indian media and scholars make a variety of interpretations. Through Indian scholars' analysis and induction, we can understand the policy tendency of the Indian government towards China's Belt and Road Initiative from one perspective. In general, India's policy towards China's Belt and Road Initiative has the following characteristics.

2.1. Cautious welcome, careful observation, no stance

India's responses to China's three initiatives, which are Bangladesh–China–India–Myanmar (BCIM) Economic Corridor, the Silk Road Economic Belt and the 21st Century Maritime Silk Road, are not the same. BCIM Economic Corridor is the first one to be started, and now the four countries have reached a preliminary consensus on cooperation. To BCIM Economic Corridor, India's first reaction is passive, but gradually became more active, and began to respond positively in Sino-Indian relation documents. India's official declaration of stance on Silk Road Economic Belt was lacking, and most were found in indirect report from China. As to the 21st Century Maritime Silk Road, India refuses to air its opinion.

---

[4]Ananth Krishnan: "China's 'Maritime Silk Road' to focus on infrastructure", *The Hindu*, April 20, 2014, http://www.thehindu.com/news/chinas-maritime-silk-road-to-focus-on-infrastructure/article5929297.ece.

[5]Shannon Tiezzi: "China's 'New Silk Road' Vision Revealed: A new series in Xinhua offers the clearest vision yet of China's ambitious 'New Silk Road'", *The Diplomat*, May 9, 2014, http://thediplomat.com/2014/05/chinas-new-silk-road-vision-revealed/.

About India's initial attitude, Chinese media once reported: on February 2, 2014, the then Prime Minister of India Singh said, India would actively participate in the construction of the BCIM Economic Corridor and the Silk Road Economic Belt.[6] Later on June 30, the Economic and Commercial Counselors' Office of Chinese Embassy to India quoted the Indian Economic Times, "India recently declared its support to the Chinese proposal on the construction of BCIM Economic Corridor, but hoped to know more details about the Maritime Silk Road before it decided to participate. It is reported that the Indian vice president Ansari, during his visit to the Academy of Social Sciences Scholars, said that BCIM Economic Corridor is a good proposal and the Indian side would support the plan".[7] But some India media believed that this was "India's refusal to declare their position".[8]

Xi Jinping made a state visit to India in September 2014. During the visit, the two countries published the *Joint Statement between the People's Republic of China and the Republic of India on the Construction of Closer Development Partnership* in New Delhi. The joint statement had a total of 28 items and about 3,600 words, covering the new Sino-Indian cooperation progress in energy, infrastructure and so on, also involving the BCIM Economic Corridor, but making no mention of the Belt and Road Initiative. That is to say, as to the BCIM Economic Corridor, the consensus between the two sides manifests as "the two sides noted the progress made in promoting the BCIM Economic Corridor. Recalling the Joint Working Group's first meeting on the BCIM Economic Corridor, the two sides agreed to continue to work hard,

---

[6] "Chinese ambassador to India: the Belt and Road construction will become a new growth engine for Sino-Indian cooperation", international online, May 22, 2014, http://gb.cri.cn/42071/2014/05/22/7551s4551466.htm.

[7] "India expressed support for the development of Bangladesh–China–India–Myanmar Economic Corridor", July 1, 2014, http://in.mofcom.gov.cn/article/express/jmxw/201407/20140700647278.shtml.

[8] "Saibal Dasgupta, TNN, India silent on China's ambitious sea route plan", http://timesofindia.indiatimes.com/india/India-silent-on-Chinas-ambitious-sea-route-plan/articleshow/42884936.cms.

implement the consensus reached at the meeting".[9] It is proper to believe that India's stance on the BCIM Economic Corridor is also very cautious, as to the Belt and Road Initiative, India refused to respond, and its dubious and defensive attitude is blindingly obvious.

2.2. Continuous communication, close contacts and bottom line probing

Although India has doubts about China's Belt and Road Initiative and stays alert, the friendly exchanges between the two countries still remain the mainstream, especially when the new Modi government pursues a realistic foreign policy. Therefore, the political interactions, economic and trade cooperation between the two countries are still relatively frequent. Since China put forward the Belt and Road Initiative, India pays close attention to the new trend and new development in China's diplomacy, watched over the implementation details of the Belt and Road Initiative, tried to test the bottom line of the Belt and Road Initiative. In the meantime, the academic exchanges themed on "Maritime Silk Road" in the Indian academic community are fairly frequent, and business and civil exchanges are mostly about the issue of "Maritime Silk Road".

On September 9, 2014, during the "Invest in India" promotion within the 18th China International Investment and Trade Fair held in Xiamen, Indian Consul General in Guangzhou, K. Nagaraj Naidu, said in his speech, "the two sides (China and India) have achieved fruitful results in the field of energy, communications and other infrastructure projects, laying a solid foundation for Maritime Silk Road". Another participant, project manager from India's Gujarat Municipal Industrial Organization Development Bureau, Rupas Prohit said that "the proposal of Maritime Silk Road would

---

[9] "Joint Statement between the People's Republic of China and the Republic of India on the Construction of Closer Development Partnership (full text)", *Xinhua Website*, September 19, 2014, http://news.xinhuanet.com/world/2014-09/19/c_1112555977.htm.

provide new opportunities for developing the Gujarat into India's national automobile, medical bases and defense production center".[10] It is proper to say that the Indian business community is full of expectation towards the "21st Century Maritime Silk Road" at large, values the potential opportunity it brings to the Indian business community.

Indian academic community made many kinds of interpretation on China's Belt and Road Initiative, although some believe that, from the geographical politics perspective, China's strategy will strengthen China's influence across Indian Ocean, therefore challenging India's regional influence. However, quite a few Indian strategy analysts believe that India should play an active role in the Belt and Road Initiative by taking three big moves in action, diplomacy and ecological politics.[11] Indian strategic analyst Raja Mohan believes that, India really needs interconnectivity, in order to realize the upgrading of the infrastructure in India border area, India can cooperate and compete with China. If Modi neglected the cooperation and competition with China, India will be marginalized in the geo-economics of Asian and Indo-Pacific region which is in continuous transformation.[12]

2.3. Put forward "'Made in India' initiative", dilute the Belt and Road Initiative, and take back the say

Faced with China's endeavor to advocate Belt and Road Initiative on international stage, the entreprenant new Indian leader launched the initiative of the 'Made in India', and peddled it around the

---

[10] "Maritime Silk Road to Set up a New Platform for the Sino-India Investment Cooperation", *Xinhua Web*, September 10, 2014, http://news.xinhuanet.com/world/2014-09/10/c_1112424942.htm.
[11] "India is an important partner in co-building One Belt One Road", *Yunnan Daily*, September 18, 2014, http://www.yndaily.com/html/2014/qiaotoubao_0918/6248.html.
[12] C. Raja Mohan: "Chinese Takeaway: One Belt, One Road", *the Indian Express*, August 13, 2014, http://indianexpress.com/article/opinion/columns/chinese-takeaway-one-belt-one-road/.

globe, tried to dilute the effect of China's Belt and Road Initiative, in order to take back the say in economics in Asia-Pacific, even the Indo-Pacific region.

On September 25, 2014 when Modi unveiled "Made in India" campaign, he proposed the initiative of "Made in India" and emphasized that the initiative advocated not the manufacture of India-featured goods, but establishment of foreign-funded factories by making full use of three advantages of India, i.e. democracy, population and needs. In fact, PM Modi first proposed "Made in India" on August 15, Indian Independence Day. "Come and make everything in India. Your products can be sold anywhere, but please produce them in India".[13] Modi government takes service industry as a key point for national development. Therefore, India government founded the 'Invest in India' web portal (www.investindia.gov.in) as a one-stop service platform for foreign businesses investing in India. As is promised, all inquiries will be responded in 72 hours, otherwise they will be handed over to relevant government departments to be dealt with.[14]

Indian government lavishes its efforts in propagating the "Made in India" initiative. On September 26, 2014, the day before Modi visited the US, Indian government invited CEOs from Airbus, Mercedes-Benz and Samsung Electronics to present in the "Made in India" campaign, and the government also started to market its idea to the US.[15] During his visit to the US, Modi met 17 leaders from the US business community, including officers from Boeing, Goldman Sachs. As to this matter, foreign media hold that PM Modi is pragmatist, who would soon lead Indian

[13] "Five Big Industrial Corridor taking shape, Time for Indian manufacture Development", *Oriental Fortune Web*, September 28, 2014, http://finance.eastmoney.com/news/1351,20140928429175574.html.
[14] "Made in India Starts", *Wenhui Newspaper*, September 27, 2014, http://whb.news365.com.cn/gj/201409/t20140927_1323623.html.
[15] "Modi visits US today to sell 'Made in India' initiative", *Phoenix*, September 26, 2014, http://news.ifeng.com/a/20140926/42094749_0.shtml.

economy to prosperity as the initiative was raised to build India into an international manufacturing hub.[16]

On November 14, 2014, Indian Embassy to China organized a seminar themed as "Invest in India", which, as Indian government said, would be part of the "Made in India" serial activities that Indian Prime Minister Narendra Modi launched in New Delhi on September 25, 2014".[17]

3. Factors Affecting India's Attitude towards the Belt and Road Initiative

3.1. Concerns about China's military presence in Indian Ocean worsen tense situation

Despite demands for cooperation in maritime security, the presence of China in the Indian Ocean, for whatever reason, will immediately arouse strong concerns from India. A Chinese submarine and warship docked at Colombo harbor on October 31, 2014. Though they had docked there for five days for crew refreshment and refueling, India was seriously concerned and complaining. "The frequency of Chinese visits has become a concern for New Delhi," Indian officials told Reuters.[18] As to this point, R. Hariharan, an associate at the Chennai Centre for China Studies, said India was concerned about the latest docking of a Chinese submarine at a Sri Lankan port for many reasons. He stated that "Chinese submarines has been added for the first time to

---

[16] "Modi eyed Made in India to build Global Manufacture Center", Xinhua Web, September 28, 2014, http://news.xinhuanet.com/world/2014-09/28/c_127044529.htm.

[17] "November 14th, Invest in India Seminar in Chongqing", *Indian Embassy to China*, November 14, 2014, http://www.indianembassy.org.cn/Chinese/newsDetails.aspx?NewsId=553&BId=1.

[18] "Indian Officials: the frequency of Chinese submarine docks in Sri Lanka raises Indian concerns.", November 4, 2014, http://mil.huanqiu.com/observation/2014-11/5189891.html.

the People's Liberation Army Navy (PLAN) for piracy fight matters in the Gulf of Aden, which is not a common practice".[19]

Besides, the US has established a military dominant position in the Indian Ocean, which has aroused serious concerns from India. Up till now, Indian maritime power and the US military presence in the Indian Ocean Region are seriously asymmetric. Although India has established homeland-based Andaman–Nicobar–Lakshadweep Islands maritime defense system in the Indian Ocean Region, using the bio-aircraft carriers as the core, its entire power is no match for the US Fifth Fleet. At present, the Indian Navy enjoys domain only from coastal lines to the Bay of Bengal, while the US centers on Diego Garcia and monitors nearly half of the Indian Ocean. As more and more superpowers get involved in the Indian Ocean Region, together with the deterioration of non-traditional security situation in the region, India is worried that the superpower competitions will bring more complexities to the situation, and more chaos to orders of the region.

3.2. Concerns about losing regional dominance with China's involvement in the Indian Ocean

Five years ago, Robert S. Kaplan, an American Scholar predicted that China and India would end up in rivalry in the Indian Ocean given situations of energy security and geopolitics. Objectively speaking, though Kaplan's prediction about the superpower confrontation between China and India has proved to be subjective, the Belt and Road Initiative raised by China, especially the "21st Century Maritime Silk Road" initiative makes India keep concerns about the future superpower games in the Indian Ocean Region. The Indian Media comments that so far, China has become the third player in the Indian Ocean Region following the US and India. In the long-term, China aims at becoming the largest player in the region. Therefore, India is worried that "New Delhi's years of dominance over the Indian Ocean is being chipped away by

---

[19] *Ibid.*

billions of dollars of aid from Beijing and gargantuan Chinese construction projects".[20]

The former Chief of Indian Navy Sureesh Mehta has pointed out that China's capacity of exerting pressure on India in Indian Ocean Region would become one of the key driving forces for Asian security.[21] From India's standpoint, the country craves for benefits from the economic rise of China, while it tries to hold down China's prominence in the region.

3.3. Concerns about India's northeastern area and other South Asian countries' increasing dependence on China

Srinath Raghavan, a Senior Fellow at the Centre for Policy Research in New Delhi, argues that "although India has finally agreed to consider the BCIM Economic Corridor, it is unlikely to move with alacrity. India's own backward linkages from the Northeast leave much to be desired. In such a situation, going ahead with a corridor — connecting the Northeast with these countries — will be seen as working mainly to China's advantage".[22]

In addition, it is widely held that China's prosperity has drawn great attraction to other South Asian countries. India believes that the Belt and Road Initiative will reinforce China's presence and influence in the Indian Ocean region while weaken its own influence and even worse. As a major power in South Asia, India worried that neighboring countries will "walk away" from India. Therefore, during Chairman Xi Jinping's visit to India, India didn't

---

[20] "India, China quietly struggle in Indian Ocean", *The Times of India*, September 20, 2014, http://timesofindia.indiatimes.com/india/India-China-quietly-struggle-in-Indian-Ocean/articleshow/42980396.cms.

[21] Sureesh Mehta: "Geopolitics of the Indo-Pacific in the Next Two Decades", http://www.maritimcindia.org/article/chairman-address-adm-retd-sureesh-mehta-chairman-nmf.

[22] Srinath Raghavan: "Talking trade and peace with China", *The Hindu*, September 20, 2014, http://www.thehindu.com/opinion/lead/talking-trade-and-peace-with-china/article6427459.ece.

talk much about Maritime Silk Road Strategy out of fear of "giving away" its traditional partners to China.[23]

4. Comments on India's Strategy to Belt and Road Initiative

4.1. No good for India's development and long-term state interests

China's Belt and Road Initiative will connect the market chain between China and economic sector, including Central Asia, Southeast Asia, South Asia, West Asia, North Africa, Europe, develop a strategic cooperative economic belt for the Pacific and Indian Ocean, and it is in accordance with the common interests and common demands of all parties. The Belt and Road Initiative is a both bilateral and multilateral strategy on international connectivity, win–win and multi-win. China has been actively and effectively promoted the cooperation with South Asian countries through other channels. However, the strategy is not only for India. It is a linkage across the Eurasian continent, and an international vessel that connects the Pacific and Indian Ocean, connects Asia, Africa, and Europe. India acts as a "fulcrum" in this strategy. If India refused to participate in the initiative, the Maritime Silk Road might circumvent it.

Some Indian scholars admit that cold treatment to the Belt and Road Initiative not a good idea. It is worth noticing that India's absence, to some extent, does not affect the implementation of the "Maritime Silk Road" planning. There are alternatives other than India for China to cooperate in South Asia. Besides, most countries along the route have a high expectation on large-scale infrastructure development and Chinese financial support. Sri Lanka and the Maldives, for example, have accepted the Road Initiative. India could gain huge benefits from these investments. However,

---

[23] *Ibid.*

India worries too much about China's presence in the Indian Ocean.[24] In fact, most scholars have a clear judgment on the opportunities and challenges of Belt and Road Initiative to India. "When China invested more than 40 billions of dollars in a land route construction to Europe via central Asia, Russia, and sea route to the Middle East and Africa via Southeast Asia, South Asia. There is a vital region that may miss the opportunities to join the new economic and infrastructure network and this region is South Asia. In many ways, choices have been put in front of India. For India, there are only two choices. One is to be part of this order, and the other be out of it. It is too late for India to build up its own Asian order".[25]

4.2. Put South Asian countries into a dilemma

To China's Belt and Road Initiative, India expresses seemingly disinterest, but objection indeed. It makes other South Asian countries trapped in a dilemma. On one hand, they want to keep the traditional friendly relations with India, make closer cooperation in the region, maintain peace and promote development. On the other hand, they want to strengthen the contact with countries outside, speed up the development of their economies, and improve the national overall strength. The contradiction between national interests and geopolitical political struggles make them feel hard to choose. To some extent, even those who have showed clear support to the Belt and Road Initiative, for example Sri Lanka, have to consider India's position on this issue.

---

[24] Srinath Raghavan: "Talking trade and peace with China", *The Hindu*, September 20, 2014, http://www.thehindu.com/opinion/lead/talking-trade-and-peace-with-china/article6427459.ece.

[25] Akhilesh Pillalamarri: "India Needs to Join Asia's Emerging 'Chinese Order'", *The Diplomat*, November 20, 2014, http://thediplomat.com/2014/11/india-needs-to-join-asias-emerging-chinese-order/.

4.3. Impede enhancement of Sino-Indian strategic partnership

Economically speaking as the two largest developing countries and emerging economies, China and India's development goals are concordant. The Vice president of India's Planning Commission, Ahluwalia held that India and China, as emerging developing countries, share common grounds regarding social development, for which reason the competition between China and India should be cooperative, not hostile.[26] Therefore, the two countries should support each other to achieve each other's goals of development and regard "developing partnership" as key content of bilateral strategic and cooperative relationship.

From geographical perspective, the Belt and the Road run across Eurasia, connecting Asia-Pacific economic circle in the East and the Europe economic circle in the west. India is located in the intersection of the Belt and the Road which is of strategic significance: north of India connects the Belt in Central Asia and South of India the Road in the Indian Ocean.

However, the lukewarm response of India is not conducive to the development of Sino-Indian strategic partnership. As to Modi's government, its foreign policies focus on South Asian region and establishing partnerships with the US, Japan, Australia and ASEAN countries, and its domestic policies prioritize social and economic development and look forward to regional and trans-regional connectivity of infrastructure. Actually, the inclusive Belt and Road Initiative is in accordance with India's economic and social development strategy and it can even complement India's policies to facilitate its development. The Belt Initiative, in particular, advocates establishing a new marine order based on free navigation, maritime security and joint deployment of marine resources, and eventually forming a coastal economic belt. The goals agree with India's maritime interests. At a foreign affairs conference in Beijing,

---

[26] "The Indian economic planner: cooperative competition between China and India", *Nanfang Daily*, September 8, 2013. Retrieved from http://www.nandu.com/html/201309/08/220010.html.

Chairman Xi Jinping stressed that the implementation of the Belt and Road Initiative should be done and boosted via common interests of parties involved and by doing this can we harvest win–win results and pragmatic cooperation. It is believed that after a period of time, India's indifference to the Initiative will change.

In short, as China's largest neighbor in Asia, India is a crucial point in the Indian Ocean region for the Belt and Road Initiative. Thus, dealing well with the relations with India, strengthening mutually beneficial cooperation with India and advertising China's neighborhood diplomacy of "amity, sincerity, mutual benefit and inclusiveness" are of symbolic meaning to enhance recognition of and support to the Belt and Road Initiative in countries involved.

The Belt and Road Initiative and Regions

Chapter 7

Situations in Northeast Asia and the Belt and Road Initiative

Piao Jianyi

National Institute of International Strategy
Chinese Academy of Social Sciences
piaojy@cass.org.cn

The eminent shifts in economic strength of Northeast Asian countries in 2014 indicate the trend of big power relations within this region, along with which subtle changes occur to the central issues that beset the region. As to the Belt and Road Initiative, governments in Northeast Asia give a response in different but clear ways.

By Northeast Asian region, it refers to the region covered by bulk of eastern part of the Chinese mainland, Taiwan of China, North Korea, South Korea, Japan, Transbaikalia and the Far East of Russia, and the eastern part of Mongolia.[1] The economic and political patterns internationally of this region keep altering in a subtle fashion. For instance, the US, who takes a "return to Asia" move, China, Japan, and Russia are continuously adjusting themselves to

---

[1] As to the definition of the scope of Northeast Asia, see Piao, J. *China's Regional Safety Environment and the Issue of Korean Peninsula* (First Edition), Minzu University of China Press. 2013, pp. 51, 99.

a new type of big power relation by virtue of handling with bilateral and multilateral problems. Focuses like situations across the Taiwan Straits, of the Korean Peninsula, and of Mongolia present delicate variations and a tendency of interaction. Besides, the situations of Northeast Asia become more and more impressionable to that of adjacent Central Asia and Southeast Asia and even of the world. Compared to other regions, Northeast Asia demonstrates a stronger response to China's ideas of the Road and Belt in their own ways.

1. A Turning-Point Alteration to Economic Strength

In 2014, Northeast Asian countries start to implement their new domestic and foreign policies which were brought forth in 2012 when they successively had their heads changed and governments shuffled and were tested, adjusted and enriched in 2013. The year 2014 is also a year that witnesses the sensational and significant turns in the pattern of their economic strength since the end of Cold War.

Generally speaking, we can compare the economic power of two nations by their Gross Domestic Product (GDP). However, the GDP of one specific year cannot show the whole picture of a country's economic strength but merely the wealth created within its jurisdiction in that year. Only by aggregating the GDP of all years in a quite long period can the economic power of a country or region be properly depicted. In other words, a country's economic strength should be described by the GDP sum of a period in an "integral" way, instead of by the GDP per year in a "differential" manner. The longer the period, the closer the result will be to the fact. For this reason, the author explains how economic powers of the Northeast Asia and the USA have changed after the Cold War through aggregating their GDP from 1992 to 2014.

In reference to the predictions made by the World Bank in November 2014, the GDPs of Northeast Asian countries and the USA in 2014 are expected to lift by 0.4–15% compared to 2013.

Specifically, the GDP of Chinese mainland will rise by 7.4%, Hong Kong of China by 2.2%, Macau of China by 10%, Taiwan of China by 3.44%, South Korea by 4%, Japan by 0.4%, Russia by 0.5%, Mongolia by 15%, and the US by 2.2%.[2] Accordingly, the predicted GDP values of these countries in 2014 can be calculated based on the statistics of 2013 and added to the following Table 1.

Table 1: GDPs of Northeast Asian countries (Regions) and the USA in post cold war period

Year	China	Taiwan, China	North Korea	South Korea	Japan	Russia	Mongolia	USA
1991	4720	1843	—	3082	35368	5094	24	59307
1992	5968	2187	—	3299	37818	4602	13	63377
1993	7385	2309	—	3621	43409	4351	8	66574
1994	7006	2522	—	4234	47790	3951	9	70722
1995	8788	2738	—	5171	52644	3955	14	73977
1996	10217	2893	—	5576	46425	3917	13	78169
1997	11357	3000	—	5163	42618	4049	12	83043
1998	11926	2761	—	3454	38570	2710	11	87470
1999	12525	2988	—	4454	43687	1959	11	92680
2000	13737	3212	—	5334	46675	2597	11	98170
2001	14979	2917	—	5046	40955	3066	13	101280
2002	16246	2977	—	5760	39183	3451	14	104700
2003	18075	3056	—	6438	42291	4303	16	109610
2004	21077	3310	—	7220	46059	5910	20	116860
2005	24471	3559	—	8449	45522	7640	25	124220
2006	29179	3663	—	9518	43626	9899	34	133989
2007	37208	3848	—	10492	43780	12997	42	140618
2008	47579	3942	—	9314	48870	16608	56	143691
2009	52211	3790	—	8341	50690	12220	46	141191
2010	61316	4270	—	10145	54742	10145	62	146578

(Continued)

---

[2] See http://www.worldbank.org.cn.

Table 1:   (*Continued*)

Year	China	Taiwan, China	North Korea	South Korea	Japan	Russia	Mongolia	USA
2011	75779	4668	—	11162	58694	18504	85	150940
2012	85733	4670	—	11171	59080	18496	99	156848
2013	92403	4693	—	13046	49015	20968	115	168000
2014	102608	4854	—	13568	49211	21073	132	171696
Σ/Σ 92–14	768091	78827	—	169966	1071464	207371	861	2624403
Σ/Σ Japan 92–14	71.7%	7.4%	—	15.9%	100%	19.4%	0.08%	244.9%
Σ/Σ USA 92–14	29.3%	3.0%	—	6.5%	40.8%	7.9%	0.03%	100%

Note that firstly China includes Hong Kong and Macau and North Korea has not right to release the statistics, and secondly, as statistics in 2014 are predicted values, Σ 92–14, Σ/Σ Japan 92–14, Σ/Σ USA 92–14 are all estimated.

Source of statistics: http://www.worldbank.org.cn.

The upper part of the table shows GDPs of Northeast Asian countries and the US from 1991 to 2014. The data of 1991 is the base year data serving for comparison with years after the collapse of the Soviet Union and the Cold War. The Σ 92–14 in the bottom part of the table is the aggregation of GDPs of each country from 1992 to 2014. The Σ/Σ Japan 92–14, described in the form of percentage, is the ratio of Σ 92–14 to the sum of Japan's GDPs within the same time frame. Likewise, Σ/Σ US 92–14 represents the ratio of Σ 92–14 to America's GDPs of the US in total from 1992 to 2014.

By analyzing the table, the following conclusions are reached which are of significance to observe the situations in Northeast Asia.

To begin with, in the 1991 when the Cold War came to a close, the Northeast countries are ranked in the high to low order of Japan, Russia, China, South Korea, Taiwan of China, North Korea, and Mongolia as far as GDP is concerned. The GDP of Japan was preponderant, being approximately 240% of the total of all other Northeast Asian countries.

Secondly, there has been four times of changes in the GDP rank from 1992 to 2014. In 1992, China superseded Russia to be the second right next to Japan while Russia became the third. In 1994, Russia was exceeded by South Korea, falling off to the forth. In 2006, Russia retook its third place by out-competing South Korea. In 2009, China rose to the top, followed by Japan.

Thirdly, the order by GDP has remained the same for six years since 2009, which is China, Japan, Russia, South Korea, Taiwan of China, North Korea, and Mongolia. In 2014, China gains a GDP that is 116% of the aggregation of all other nations in the region, but still far from the 240% that Japan achieved in the last year of the Cold War. Nevertheless, China's GDP is 2.1 times of Japan's, 4.9 times of Russia's, 7.6 times of South Korea's, 21.3 times of Taiwan's, and 59.8% of America's. Thereinto, China's GDP reaching more than twice as much as Japan's and approaching 60% of America's are remarkable changes of transformational meaning.

Nonetheless, the order by cumulative GDP values from 1992 to 2014, which is more accurately reflect the economic strength of each nation, is Japan, China, Russia, South Korea, Taiwan of China, North Korea, and Mongolia. The cumulative GDP of Japan is 1.4 times of China's, 5.2 times of Russia's, 6.3 times of South Korea's, and 13.6 times of Taiwan's. In view of this, Japan is still considered as the most economically powerful country in Northeast Asia. As for China, its cumulative GDP reached 3.7 times of Russia's, 4.5 times of South Korea, and 9.7 times of Taiwan. Moreover, the cumulative GDP achieved 71.7% of Japan's and 29.3% of America's, being another stunning advancement.

Fifthly, the ratio of America's cumulative GDP to those of Northeast Asian countries other than Japan has been decreasing year by year since 1992. Compared to that by 2013, the ratio of America's cumulative GDP to Japan remains to be 2.4 in 2014; however it reduces from 3.7 to 3.4 to China, from 13.2 to 12.7 to Russia, from 15.7 to 15.4 to South Korea, and from 117% to 114% to the aggregation of the cumulative GDP of the whole Northeast Asia. This suggests that it seems unrealistic for any Northeast Asian country to create a sudden change to the regional order elaborately established by the US after the Second World War in the foreseeable future, although there is a tendency that the aggregation of cumulative GDP of nations in the region and the cumulative GDP of the US become equivalent one year after another, which is also a significant change.

Besides, South Korea believes that its comparative edge in economy, compared to North Korea, has been greatly lifted since 1992.[3] However, the rank of South Korea as far as the GDP each year is concerned has retrogressed to that before 1994 since 2006. And in light of the cumulative GDP from 1992 to 2014, South Korea is lagged further behind by China and Russia despite that its gap between Japan is bridged.

Lastly, North Korea and Mongolia have not seen their positions changed in terms of their GDP and cumulative GDP values from 1992 to 2014. However, the 21st Century witnessed remarkably increasing economy for both countries. As to North Korea, its economy, after a rally in 1998, returned onto a stable path of revival and development in 2002. Mongolia walked out of its first post-Cold War decade of wandering and entered into a fast development stage in the 21st Century.

2. The Evolvement of Big Power Relations and Regional Hot Issues

As what is described above, the most striking and significant changes in 2014 are China's GDP in 2014 exceeding Japan's twice and approaching 60% of the USA's, China's cumulative GDP from 1992 to 2014 surpassing Japan's 70% and reaching 30% of the USA's, and the sum of the cumulative GDP of Northeast Asian countries and regions from 1992 to 2014 being equal to the America's cumulative GDP. These changes are helpful for comprehending the evolvement

---

[3] In recent years, some research and media institutions in South Korea, motivated by the government policies towards North Korea, carry out comparative studies of the economic strength of the two nations. They conclude that the GDP of South Korea is 30–33 times of that of North Korea at present. But as North Korea has never acknowledged the concept of GDP, nor published any GDP statistics, the conclusion cannot be used as a basis for serious academic study.

of relationship between major Northeast Asian countries and hot regional topics in 2014 for the reason that economic power has become fundamental elements in measuring total strength and competitiveness of countries after the Cold War and ensuring comprehensive safety interests of a nation.

Although it is not an exact reflection of economic comparison of China with Japan and the USA, China's GDP reaching more than twice of Japan's and almost 60% of the USA's is of pressing affect and of symbolic significance to the three nations. Nevertheless, it is of practical implementation for China's cumulative GDP to surpass 70% of Japan's and to get close to 30% of the USA's. It means that, with the present economic growth rates in China, Japan and the USA, China will catch up with Japan by 2019 and with the USA by 2047. The total amount of cumulative GDP of Northeast Asian countries and regions from 1992 to 2014 is getting closer to the cumulative GDP of the USA, casting more light on key issues where the USA is involved in Northeast Asia.

In a nutshell, objectively speaking, these three changes are playing important although different roles in the evolvement of major power relations and hot issues in Northeast Asia in 2014 no matter whether they are acknowledged subjectively by all nations in that region, especially by major countries and the USA.

2.1. Trends in major power relations

These three changes directly exert influence on Japan, who is still the second largest economic power around the world but with the most unpleasant conditions among Northeast Asian countries. On the one hand, the ratio of China's GDP to Japan's climbed up from 188.5% in 2013 to 208.5% in 2014. Although it doesn't demonstrate that China has its economic power surpass Japan's, it do gives a great shock to the psychological limit of the latter for it has been making light of China and other Asian countries. The ratio of China's cumulative GDP to Japan's rose from 65.1% in 2013 to 71.7% in 2014. In this case, Japan, like the USA who had to take steps when the Soviet Union's GNP reached beyond its 70%, was repelled to think how to deal with China. On the other hand, the ratio of China's GDP to the USA's climbed up from 55% in 2013 to 59.8% in 2014 and the ratio of its cumulative GDP to the USA's increased from 27.1% in 2013 to 29.3% in 2014. Those give a hint to Japan that China is rising up while the USA is suffering a decline of its power. Therefore, it is necessary for Japan to think over its strategies in dealing with its relations with China and the USA against the background of not only Northeast Asia, but beyond in Asia and Pacific region and even the whole world.

Therefore, it seems that Japan, who has a record of military aggression into China and Asian countries and difficulty in becoming a political and military superpower under the constraint of the United States, has set its strategic focuses on China nearby, the USA afar, and Russia with tactics. With regard to China, the long latent dispute over the sovereignty of Diaoyu Islands and the delineation of the territorial sea of the East China Sea were used by Japanese government to stir up peace with China and even aggravate contradictions. By doing this, Japan tries to divert China's manpower and material and financial resources from its economic construction to fighting against Japan. Moreover, taking as an excuse that China might respond militarily to Japan with its rising military power and opaque amount and use of military expenditure, Japan is speeding up the pace of upgrading to a military power.

In the case of the US, since Japan knows well that the US is growingly worried about and eager to hold back China's process of rising up, it strengthens its alliance with the US by co-developing military technologies and improving joint military command system. Moreover, taking lifting the ban on collective self-defense as a breakthrough, Japan modifies the pacifist constitution in a fundamental manner in order to become familiar with and master the operation of military technology and military command system of the US as soon as possible and thus eventually get free from the manacle set by the US. At the same time, Japan denies and beautifies its history of being once an invader in Asian countries including China by paying homage to the Yasukuni Shrine and negating its atrocities in the Nanjing Massacre and the recruitment of "comfort women" so that it can make preparation to completely get rid of the postwar system in aspects of morality and international justice.

Japan cast as bait the mass economic cooperative proposals for Russia's strategic development in its outer Baikal and Far East, winning over Russia. Japan solves the protracted dispute over territory and delimitation of the maritime boundaries between Japan and Russia in the Four Northern Islands (South Kuril Islands), thereby strengthening the strategic partnership between the two countries and undermining China–Russia strategic and cooperative partnership to drift them apart and to offset their growing mutual trust. At the same time, the increasingly close relations with Russia embolden Japan to force the United States to compromise and to gradually lift bans and restrictions on Japan.

However, the major power relations in Northeast Asia in 2014 did not go as Japan wished. China, growing more and more confident in its future, continued to cast high pressure over perverse actions of Abe's government. As to safeguarding its sovereignty over Diaoyu Islands and the East China Sea, China had its military force patrol in the sea areas of and air areas over the two regions on a regular basis in a moderate manner instead of making escalation regarding the issues. As regard to Abe and Japanese cabinet members and political figures visiting the Yasukuni Shrine, Japan's denial of its aggression into China and other Asian countries, its wrong doings in the Nanking Massacre and recruiting comfort women during the war, and its attempts to revise the pacifist constitution in order to become a military big power, China responded firmly by condemning both in speech and writing and freezing its contacts and dialogues with Japanese officials of all levels including the senior ones to urge Japan to acknowledge and repent its aggressive records true-heartedly and to resume a way of peaceful development.

At the same time, in order to unite Asian countries who have suffered Japanese aggression and international forces for good in deterring the reactionary behaviors of Abe's government, China is applying a series of unprecedentedly positive measures through bilateral channels and on international arenas like the US Despite that China and Japan reached four point consensuses accompanied by a summit meeting between both countries at the APEC Summit held in Beijing, China still keeps highly alert to any attempting perverse moves by Abe's government by watching how Japan do its promises.

The USA, as the superpower, attaches great importance to the situations in Northeast Asia for that region is the home to many political, economic or military powers. However it regards as more crucial the maintenance of a perpetual and sound international economic and political order where it dominates. So it needs to be extremely vigilant to keep its sanctimonious image as the "international police", as well as to resort to other nations' help in protecting existing world order. Given this plus its holding a safe lead over any Northeast Asian countries in terms of comprehensive national strength, it is unnecessary for the USA to make substantial responses as it is fully aware of the intention of Abe's government.

Besides, the USA speaks highly of Japan's actions such as provoking conflicts in the issues of Diaoyu Islands and of East China Sea, irritating China and trapping China into an arms race against Japan, and lifting the ban on Japan's right of collective self-defense and revising the Ninth item in the pacifist constitution. Nevertheless, it gives unshaken objection to Japan's other behaviors like paying frequent homage visits to the Yasukuni Shrine by Abe and Japanese key officials, the release of the announcement to deny the history of Japanese invasion into China and other Asian countries, of its guilt in Nanking Massacre, and of its call on military comfort women, and the attempt to fundamentally overthrow the pacifist constitution. It is because that the USA is worried about being involved in potential military conflicts between Japan and China if Abe's government, with the US at its back, fearlessly and overly irritates China and losing China's helping hands in dealing with complicated regional hot issues and global problems. Nonetheless, the USA is waiting and seeing even though it knows that Japan is trying to get rid of its constraint.

Japan "makes eyes at" Russia by starting with solving the sovereignty issue of the Four Northern Islands (known as South Kuril in Russia), which is risky and likely to invite the enemy inside. The United States appears to be unable to do anything about this. But in fact it is making a feint to the west but attack in the east. Specifically, by poking into the contradictions between Ukraine and Russia over the Crimean peninsula, it joins hands with NATO, the EU countries, and Japan to impose sanctions against Russia. Russia, in this case, resists vehemently, making Japan hesitate in leaning towards Russia.

As to Russia, another big power in Northeast Asia, its GDP is 20.5% of China's and 42.8% of Japan's in 2014, its cumulative GDP being 19.4% of Japan's and 27% of China's in the same year. We can see that Russia's economic growth and strength are far behind China and Japan. But the three amazing changes that are mentioned above demonstrate a reduction in the gap between Russia and Japan the top one in economy in Northeast Asia, and meanwhile an enlargement in the gap with China. At the same time, like other countries or regions in Northeast Asia, Russia is faced with challenges of America's skillful intervention into major power relations and regional hot issues in Northeast Asia.

According to the general principle in international relations theory, Russia seems to seek for balance in power among big nations in the region. But specifically speaking, its economic strength is far behind Japan and China and it sets its economic, political and cultural focuses on Europe, so it is hard for Russia to mobilize power as much as China and Japan do. Therefore, at present what Russia cares most is how to fasten to create a sound regional environment for its economic and social development. In order to continuously push ahead with its development strategy in outer Baikal and the Far East, Russia actively carry out economic cooperation with all Northeast Asian countries including China and Japan, while it will hold same or similar position as China, who is also on its way of rising up, does whenever big power relations and orders are to be concerned.

Russia is wary of the United States to squeeze Russia's development space by setting up military bases in Japan as the frontier and posing military threats. Russia is also vigilant against the United States being in Japan's way of improving relations with Russia and therefore causing damage to its interests. Therefore, Russia mobilizes its strategic nuclear submarines and bombers from time to time, cruising in the waters and airspace surrounding Japan to remind the Japanese to be independent and do not take others' orders and also to warn the United States not to be arbitrary. Besides, it tries to pull Japan to its own side by inviting Japan for joint naval exercises.

What's more, as a nation that has smashed Japanese armed invasion in the eve of the World War II,[4] Russia is on guard for Japan's move in denial to and beautification of its invasion history into Asian countries to challenge post-war regional and international systems in a fundamental manner and to speed up the pace of becoming a political and military power. For that reason, Russia continues to hold joint military exercises on land and in sea with China on a regular base and decides to commemorate the 70th anniversary of the end of World War II and of anti-fascist war victory in 2015, same as what China will do.

However, Russia is fully aware that, compared to the continuously developing China–Russia strategic and cooperative partnership, it is hard for relations with Japan to achieve any breakthroughs neither at present nor in the foreseeable future no matter what measures Russia takes, be it severe or mild, given the military alliance between Japan and the US. Under such circumstances, Russia pays much more attention to regional hot issues in Northeast

---

[4] Here it refers to the Chang Kufeng Incident (from July to August in 1938) and the Nomonhan Incident (also known as the Battle of Khalkhin Golfrom May to September in 1939), where the Soviet Union crushed the intrusive attempt of the Japanese Kwantung Army along the borders between China and the Soviet Union, and China and Mongolia respectively.

Asia than any other powerful nation while China, Japan, and the US are mediating with one another with both skill and dash.

2.2. Subtle changes in the regional focus

Apart from the above results in bilateral relations directly got from the three remarkable changes in economic power contrast among Northeast Asian countries and regions in 2014, Northeast Asian countries and the US are indirectly affected in aspects of situations across Taiwan Strait, in Korean Peninsula, and in Mongolia and are experiencing subtle changes occur to those regional focuses.

2.2.1. *The situation across Taiwan Strait*

After the Kuomintang (KMT) came to power in Taiwan in 2007, the mainland China set up a policy of further strategic foresight towards Taiwan. Taking the 2008 Beijing Olympic Games as an opportunity, tensions in Taiwan Strait came to ease. Striking while the iron is hot, both sides of the Taiwan Strait brought the relationship to settlement and cooperation. In 2010, the mainland and Taiwan reached Economic Cooperation Framework Agreement (ECFA),[5] offering institutional guarantee for bilateral economic collaboration on a new platform of peaceful development and at the same time facilitating the establishment of Free Trade Area (FTA) among China, Japan, and South Korea. The signing of the ECFA was the maiden substantive embodiment of peaceful and stable development across the straits and its positive effect upon the whole Northeast Asia, and an agreeable suggestion to the Korean Peninsula who is also suffering problems in relation to ethical and national unity.

However, it is still remain unclear where cross-straits relations will lead to, because issues of unification which are of essential significance haven't been reached consensuses yet by both sides.

---

[5] "Cross-Strait Economic Cooperation Framework Agreement", *People's Daily*, June 30, 2010.

Upon the singing of the ECFA, in particular, the Taiwan authorities failed to grasp the sound development in cross-straits relations and convert it into benefits to the welfare of the Taiwanese, thus encouraging "Taiwan independence" forces who had been holed up for a while staged a comeback. These forces, backed up and egged on by some big powers, viciously propagated that some items in the ECFA are to threaten economic safety of Taiwan due to the large economic gap between mainland China and Taiwan. The pity was that the ruling KMT authority did nothing about this but to miss the opportunity, distrust towards the authorities among Taiwanese growing day by day. Consequently, discontent against KMT finally broke out at the nine-in-one election in late November 2004, where the Democratic Progressive Party (DPP) who advocates Taiwan independence trounced the ruling KMT.

The sheer victory of DPP in the election led to bleak prospects of KMT in the 2016 election and new uncertainties for the future of cross-straits relations. Nevertheless, the pragmatic negotiation on FTA between mainland China and South Korea acted as insurance to the ECFA, creating delicate environment for the evolvement of cross-straits relations. In fact, since that Taiwan and South Korea have similar industrial structures, their competitive industries are also the fields where they compete fiercely with each other. That requires the ruling "Taiwan independence" force take people's interests and their increasingly strong appeal for a peaceful cross-strait development into consideration instead of blindly challenging the ECFA.

On the other hand, South Korea felt pressure from the stable situations in Taiwan Straits and the signing of ECFA being put on table after 2008 Beijing Olympics. It dropped hesitating and wait-and-see attitude, and accelerated FTA talks with China to yield eventual substantive results by the end of 2014. Now, the completed China–South Korea FTA talks in return become the escort of ECFA. And interactions between ECFA and China–South Korea FTA have built a fine stage where situation in Taiwan Strait interacts with that in Korean Peninsula within Northeast Asia.

2.2.2. *Situations on the Korean Peninsula*

The substantive FTA talks between China and South Korea are accomplished through several important diplomatic activities in 2014 like President Xi paid official visit to South Korea and President Park Geun-hye was invited to the APEC leaders' meeting in Beijing. The FTA has become the most significant event for both relations between neighboring countries and Korean Peninsula, and those between neighboring countries in relation to Korean Peninsula.

As is known to all, only China and Russia of the four big nations including Japan and the US have been keeping normal diplomatic contacts with both North and South Korea after the end of the Cold War. Japan and the US still refuse to carry out normal diplomatic activities with North Korea. This asymmetric feature in relations of neighboring big powers with the northern and southern parts of Korean Peninsula is the prevailing international environment for the ups and downs and periodic and chain evolvement in Korean Peninsula after Cold War.[6] It also accounts for the retarded process of economic integration in Northeast Asia and of multilateral security cooperation. The signing of China–South Korea FTA and boosting bilateral economic integration will help ease the adverse situations and bring about external conditions that are favorable for realizing independent development, peace and unification for both southern and northern sides on Korean Peninsula.

The USA was the first among the four neighboring countries to make the FTA with South Korea. In negotiation, South Korea requested that commodities coproduced by the South and North Korea Peninsula in Kaesong are listed in the FTA list but the request was refused by the USA. Upon the signing of FTA between

---

[6] For more information about the periodic and chain nature of evolvement of the situations in Korean Peninsula after Cold War, please see Piao, Jianyi, 2011. Root causes and prospects of current crisis in Korean Peninsula. *China's Regional Security Environment Review: 2011.* Hong Kong Social Sciences Press Group, pp. 30–46. Piao, Jianyi. 2013. China's Regional Security Environment and the Issue of Korean Peninsula. *Minzu University of China Press*, pp. 279–304.

South Korea and the USA, the latter urged South Korea to sign FTA as soon as possible. During negotiation between South Korea and Japan, South Korea took its FTA with the USA as the blueprint and requested that Japan should reach comprehensively high-level FTA. However, the request was rejected by Japan. South Korea suspended indefinitely its negotiation with Japan but signed FTA with the EU. Same to the case with Japan, South Korea asked for a high-level comprehensive FTA with China based on US–South Korea FTA. But it finally compromised and accepted the reasonable suggestions of China as it had no way to go in face of the ECFA and the Free Trade Zone (FTZ). These facts demonstrate that the US is making use of its FTA with South Korea to directly pin down the reconciliation and cooperation between North and South Korea, and moreover to exert influence on the FTA process between Northeastern big countries and South Korea indirectly through South Korea.

At the same time, China accepted South Korea's request of putting products from Kaesong into their FTA list with pleasure, offering strong support to the reconciliation of the North and South Korea. Moreover, the process where China talked about the FTA plan seriously and honestly and eventually got its suggestions accepted offered experience to South Korea about reaching an FTA with Russia later on.

In contract with China–South Korea, China–North Korea relations kept a low profile in 2014. The theory of "abnormal China–North Korea relations" was hyped up by some overseas forces with ulterior motives upon President Xi Jinping's visiting South Korea first and separately. Even some Chinese blindly agree to that. Nevertheless, the visit arrangement was more a strategic consideration than a reflection of relations with the two countries as far as then and following situations in Korean Peninsula, especially the evolvement of international relations in Northeast Asia are concerned. Presumably both North and South Korea were aware of the intentions of Xi's visit. In fact, China–North Korea relation is going forward on a normal level. Both central and local governments and the folk in the two countries are carrying on with established and new economic cooperation projects. North Koreans coming to China for economic cooperation are still over 120 thousand.

At the same time, the relations of other big Northeast Asian countries with North Korea are remarkable as well. Japan continues to challenge South Korea in the sovereignty issue of Takeshima (South Korea call it Dokdo) and the issue of "military comfort women". An increasing number of Japanese political figures are to worship at Yasukuni Shrine. All these lead to the two countries being on a bad term with each other. Even though Japan almost begged for leader's meetings with South Korea, the latter requested Japan rectify its wrong doings as the precondition for improving their relations. In contrast, Japan and North Korea are progressing a lot in the issue of the "kidnapped Japanese" through more than a year of negotiation. North Korea agreed to re-check on the case in an all-round way and included all Japanese held up in North Korea after the Second World War as the objectives of investigation. In return, Japan removed its sanctions against North Korea.

As to relations of Russia with the Korean Peninsula, what Chinese media and the public don't know is that Russia notices that the continuous favorable turns in the economy of North Korea are constrained by outdated infrastructure, the two parties on the Peninsula wish to conciliate although they appear to be in antagonism with each other, and the US intends to pin down the peaceful cooperation in Northeast Asia by taking advantage of the nuclear issue on the Peninsula. Thus Russia, in hope of promoting its relations with the Peninsula, lays stress on the three-party economic cooperation with both North and South Korea involved. Under financial support of South Korea, Russia completed the modernization of No. 3 pier at Rajin Port and transported 400 thousand coal of good quality to South Korea by railway and sea in 2014, followed by the reconstruction of the 54 km railway route from Hasan to Rajin Port of North Korea in 2013. Based on these achievements, Russia continues its collaboration with North and South Korea with the first phase project of modernization of inland railway in North Korea.

Moreover, the relation of intergovernmental international organizations like the UN and of NGOs with the Korean Peninsula is one of the key influencing factors for the situations on the Peninsula, as well as is closely related to the relations of nations mentioned above with the Peninsula and the evolvement of the relations among those nations centered on the Peninsula. For the past decade or more, the US and other western countries have posed as human rights defenders. They have proposed condemnation of human rights practice in North Korea by taking the words of the North Koreans who fled to South Korea or lived in western countries as the evidence in the UN Conference on human rights.

Since Lee Myung-bak administration came to power in 2009, South Korea joined the sponsor group for the proposal willingly, upgrading the so-called "human rights issue in North Korea" to be a crucial point for the evolvement of situations of the Korean Peninsula. In 2014, the United Nations Human Rights Commission (UNHRC) passed bill of prosecuting Kim Jong-un, the highest leader of North Korea, in the International Crime Court (ICC) and the bill was approved by a majority at the Third Committee of the UN General Assembly.

Although the prosecution takes effect only upon the approval of the UN Security Council but it will not as China and Russia will reject, the action under the incitation of the US, Japan and the EU severely undermined the relation of North Korea and the UN and damaged the authoritative image of UN in international society. The UN manipulated by the US then announced that it only acknowledge the separate election of the southern part of the Korean Peninsula and the government of South Korea that came into being by that election while it refused to acknowledge the legitimacy of Democratic People's Republic of Korea by the election across the whole Peninsula later on. The announcement rooted the Korean War. Nowadays, the US, Japan, and EU instigated this so-called human rights problem regardless of the facts is little more than a proof of North Korea's being ineligible to represent its citizens with its anti-people policies and of South Korea's being the only legal government and representative of the whole peninsula. In this case, the issue of Korean Peninsula is faced with the danger of going back down to the initial state 70 years ago and no one could assure that the destructive Korean War will not break out one more time if the situations go on like this.

Nevertheless, apart from relations between big neighbors and Korean Peninsula, relations among big neighbors centered on the Peninsula, and relations of intergovernmental international organizations and NGO with the Peninsula, the critical element that influence the evolvement of situations on the Peninsula in 2014 goes to the trend of south–north relations decided by interior governance and diplomacy of each nation. In 2014, Park Geun-hye administration commenced to put its ideas into action after almost one year of policy tests and adjustments since Park's assume the position in February 2013. Based on its own understanding of the interior politics and diplomacy, Park's government built and officially put forward with the North Korea-oriented policy system by combining the "Korean Peninsula Trust Process", "Northeast Asia peace initiative", and "Eurasian Initiative" that were proposed long before with "Dresden speech" and "Manulife unification theory" that were published afterwards.

But in the point of view of North Korea, what Park's administration does is of little difference to the Lee Myung-bak's. South Korea neither stops its large-scale war exercises with the US targeted at North Korea in spring and autumn each year nor eases its separate military manoeuvres in non-military zones. The South Korean armies take the highest leader of North Korea as the shooting target in manoeuvres and the government let them have their way. Besides, it still actively takes part in the bill charging North Korea of the latter's human rights conditions at the UN Assembly on human rights each year, sets strict bars on communications of folk organizations with those in North Korea, and acquiesces in throwing down demagogic leaflets into North Korea with balloons by North Korean group who defected to South Korea. Given all those, North Korea has to suspect that what Park's government does aims at disturbing normal citizen life and economic construction of North Korea and thus forcing Kim Jong-un to give up his route of equal attention to economic and nuclear force construction.

Therefore, given that South Korea repeatedly asked for inter governmental dialogues, North Korea, taking the opportunity of entering for the Asian Games in Inchon, sent a delegation made up by high-rank military and government officials to South Korea when both sides reached a consensus about holding high-level inter-governmental dialogues. However, during the preparation for the meeting and at the meeting which turned out not as high as it was originally conceived, North Korea realized through observing behaviors and actions of South Korea that the latter was not a sincere communicator or a doer in hope of easing the explosive and tense military stand-off. As a result, the intergovernmental dialogue ended up in unpleasant abortion. The precious chance for the two to conciliate fleeted away. Shortly after, South Korea and the US held a new-round large-scale joint military exercises, pushing south–north relations on the Peninsula to freezing point.

After the end of Cold War, the interior politics and diplomacy of South Korea and North Korea, their bilateral relations and relationship with neighboring countries, relations of neighbors in regard to the two countries, and relationship of the two countries with intergovernmental international organizations and NGOs are all reflected in the issue of nuclear on the Korean Peninsula that has a history of over 20 years. In September 2015, the Six-Party Talks among China, North Korea, South Korea, Japan, Russia and the US reached a consensus, namely the September 19 Joint Statement. The statement proposed an all-round, fair, and reasonable solution to the Korean Peninsula in a phased manner. Unfortunately, situations on the Korean Peninsula went worse and backwards upon the Lee Myung-bak assuming the reign in 2008 and Six-Party Talks was suspended afterwards. In 2014, the DPRK reaffirmed in many occasions that it was willing to accept what China and Russia suggested and go back to the Six-Party Talks unconditionally. However, the US, the ROK and Japan kept making preconditions for resuming the Six-Party Talks, requesting that the DPRK demonstrate its good faith in a nuclear-free country with concrete moves. Consequently, the Six-Party Talks remained idling.

2.2.3. *Situations in Mongolia*

In 2014, Mongolia has a firsthand experience of the three stunning and important changes mentioned above, in economic power balance of Northeast Asian countries from both advantageous and disadvantageous aspects. During carrying out international cooperation, Mongolia learnt a lesson from former bitter experiences and adopted new measures like overthrowing the irrational bans on foreign-owned enterprises dealing in mine exploitation, thereby lifting the country's openness up to a new phrase. At the same time, Mongolia stressed on its geological attribute to the whole region, made endeavor to heighten its engagement in and influential power on regional economic and political issues, and upgraded its relations with both China and Russia to a comprehensive strategic partnership.

Mongolia's economy has slided all the way with ups and downs for the first 10 years after the end of Cold War. The social, economic, and political systems have gone through a critical transformation period from Russian socialism to total westernization. The transformation of economic structure has been basically accomplished, which is from traditional animal husbandry to the combination of modern mining industry and modern animal husbandry, by introducing large-scale foreign fund mining enterprises. The GDP of Mongolia began to rocket at double-digit rates upon entering the 21st Century and its economy started to recover and develop rapidly due to favorable conditions like the mining industry dominated by foreign enterprises, vigorous Chinese markets in need of minerals, and high prices of minerals globally.

In the meantime, Mongolia grows to realize its favorable and unfavorable conditions in international geopolitics and geo-economy. On the one hand, the country owns a vast territory, abundant natural resources, and ethnic history and culture that are of great influence to the whole world. On the other hand, as the country is located in between China and Russia and far from the sea, transportation to the outside world is inconvenient; the small population gives few spaces for domestic market. Both economy and technology in Mongolia, in particular, are outdated and under the danger of being marginalized by the region and even the world. Thus, in order to extend its exterior relations economically and politically, Mongolia commenced "the third neighbors" policy that advocated independent, multi-pivot and flexible diplomacy with the US, Japan, India, EU (mainly Germany), and Turkey, while developing traditional friendship and cooperation with China and Russia.

The first decade of 21st Century witnessed the rapid and continuous increase in the economy of Mongolia, unceasingly stronger economy and remarkable changes in diplomatic relations. Both its two neighbors, China and Russia, and all "third neighbors" have intensified their relations with Mongolia. NGOs in the US and Japan organized activities that popularizing environmental protection and participation in public politics, playing an important role in promoting the process of social democratization in Mongolia. More countries including South Korea invested in the country, which fastened the pace of its economic transformation, facilitated the formation of the production-processing-market network in both Mongolia and Northeastern countries and regions, and assisted its economy to resume the path of fast and stable development. Besides, China, Russia and its "third neighbors" launched training and education programs for Mongolia so as to optimize its human resources and structure. Thanks to the policy of "third neighbors", Mongolia has won larger and more prominent place on international arena, which initiated a platform for balancing the influence of big powers.

However, a series of severe problems have come along with rapid economic increase for the reason that modern social, economic, and political systems have not been completed yet. A part of economic dominance of Mongolia is in the hands of foreign enterprises. Some government officials who accepted bribes sell out important economic interests of their motherland. National information system grows more and more dependent on technologies of other countries. Characteristics of ethnic and traditional culture are replaced by foreign cultures. The order of social life goes worse and the environment is struggling against increasingly severe damages. All those and many more have aroused great concerns from the government. Fierce argues and discussions are likely to take these as problems that threaten national economy, technology, culture, society and ecological conditions and to put the blame on foreign mining enterprises. Consequently, the Mongolia Ulsyn Ikh Khural amended the law in relation to foreign investment on mining industry so as to set legal standards on exploitations of foreign enterprises in the country.

But the prices of mineral products in international market come down gradually; mineral products transported to China are beset with the highlighted problem of excessive costs due to low transportation conditions; the profit space of foreign mining enterprises is almost squeezed to none with its spheres of activities being strictly delimited and many are force to stop production and withdraw their capital from Mongolia. For those reasons, the increase rate of GDP in 2013 turned out to be apparently lower than that in 2012, and results in 2014 was also negative. Under such grave circumstances, Mongolia came to realize that if things went on like that, what the country would lose is never as simple as specific interests in some fields of national security but the whole interests of national safety. Therefore, the Mongolia Ulsyn Ikh Khural passed a new law to reopen the access of foreign mining industries to exploitation activities.

Nonetheless, those foreign enterprises which had once in competition with Chinese ones and already left then had little intention of coming back. Fortunately, President Xi Jinping visited Mongolia shortly after when the two countries reached consensuses on strengthening cooperation on three key fields as infrastructure, mining, and finance, creating rather favorable conditions for Mongolia. Before long, Russian President Vladimir Putin paid a visit to Mongolia. The three countries held their first meeting together, proposed by Mongolia, showing that Mongolia felt for real the changes in economic power balance in Northeast Asia and marking the shuffle of its foreign relations by Mongolia in 2014.

3. Responses to the Belt and Road Initiative

During the evolvement of big power relations and regional hot issues in Northeast Asia, Chinese government, taking advantage of leaders' meetings with Russia, the ROK, and Mongolia, and the ripple effect of the meetings, raised Belt and Road Initiative to which Northeast Asian countries responded quickly.

As is known to all, the Belt and Road is the shorter form of the Silk Road Economic Belt and the 21st Century Maritime Silk Road brought forth by President Xi on behalf of Chinese government during his visits in Kazakhstan in September 2013 and in Indonesia in November of the same year respectively. Shortly before the Chinese academia started to make any deepened and extensive research on the initiative, Mongolia, which was the weakest in economic strength and eager to boost its economy and improve the wellbeing of its people by extending overseas economic collaboration, took the lead showing great interests towards them.

Russia, according to the prevalent viewpoint of Chinese academia, was expected to be the one which responded most negatively and even rejected the proposal. However, President Putin, after listening to the explanation of Chinese government, expressed Russia's support to President Xi during his visit in Beijing. Later on when President Xi paid a visit to the ROK, President Park Geun-hye affirmed that the ROK was willing to link its Eurasian Initiative with China's Belt and Road strategy. Moreover, the Democratic People's Republic of Korea (DPRK), although has not made any comments on the initiative, has been committed to the construction of the powerful socialist nation since the end of 20th Century and been offering active support and coordination with the construction of connectivity, demonstrating that the DPRK is willing to cooperate with China in building the Belt and Road. Besides, Japan, without any responses to China's proposal, is actually carrying out researches on relations between China and main neighbors of China in the academia presided over by the think tank of the Ministry of Foreign Affairs.

These facts show that all Northeast Asian countries except Japan which competed fiercely with China have responded to China's initiative based on their geopolitical relations with China, the degree of connectivity, situations of economic and political relations. And the fast speed of response is unique among all regions in relation to the Belt and the Road.

As far as geopolitical relations in Northeastern Asia, China is the only country that borders on all other members by land or sea. Mongolia and China share the longest border line and Russia the second. Although the land border line of the DPRK is short, it takes up the majority of the country's whole border line. And China and DPRK are next to each other across sea. As to the degree of connectivity, there are more than ten transit ports and channels of various kinds between China and the three countries. In terms of economic and political relations, China has already become the largest trade partner to all other Northeast Asian countries. Besides, it keeps a traditional friendly and cooperative relation with the DPRK, develops strategic collaborative partnership with Russia, and establishes all-round strategic and cooperative partnership with the ROK and all-round strategic partnership with Mongolia, and remains in a strategic reciprocal relations with Japan.

Thus, all other Northeast Asian countries would like to strengthen connectivity in terms of infrastructure with China or each other even if the Belt and Road Initiative had not been brought up. What is worth noticing is that these countries not only conceive the interconnection of infrastructure with other Northeast Asian neighbors, but as well put the idea into action to varying degrees. That can be traced back to the early 1970s when China–US relations began to enter an ice-thawing stage. At that time, the DPRK and the POK came into contact with each other for the first time and reached the "Three Principles on Unification", namely independence, peace, and ethnic unity. Both parties planned to reconstruct the main railway going through the whole Korean Peninsula and connect it with railway networks of Russia and China. The DPRK was even considering charging fees to transit international freights.

In the mid 1980s, Japan and the ROK intended to open up an undersea tunnel that passed through Korea Strait so as to connect Kyushu with the southeast cost of the ROK upon the accomplishment of the Aomori Undersea Tunnel of tens of kilometers long that linked up Honshu and Hokkaido Island in Japan. But they had to drop the idea considering the high costs and little returns of investment due to the south–north stand-off on the Korean Peninsula till the end of the Cold War when they reverted to it as south–north relations on the Peninsula stepped into a new phase of reconciliation and cooperation. In 2000, the ROK and the DPRK held the first summit meeting of historic significance. The summit meeting was held once more in 2008, since when the idea of building a subsea tunnel under the Korea Strait has become the common concern and key issue that the ROK and Japan have been working on till present. They also get a lot of help regarding engineering design from the folk.

Besides, Russia made major adjustments to its policy to the Korean Peninsula after the first summit meeting between the ROK and the DPRK in 2000. Russia and the ROK restored traditional friendly and cooperative relations. Apart from mutual summit visits between President Putin and Kim Jong-il, the highest leader of the ROK, the two countries also agreed to connect the railway passing through the Korean Peninsula from south to north with the one cutting across the Far East and Siberia of Russia. The railway connection plan was taken by both sides as the main field of economic cooperation. The first phase project was to reconstruct the 54 km railway from the Russian cost of state of Hasan to Rajin Port of the North Korean special economic zone of Razon.

This project is of more significance compared to the reconstruction of Gyeongui Railway that was cut off during the Korean War in 2002. However, the nuclear issue on the Korean Peninsula became outstanding once more and kept worsening, retarding the rate of process of the project. In 2008 when Lee Myung-bak administration came to power, inter Korean relations regressed to suspend the Six-Party Talks. Russia then restarted the reconstruction project of Hasan to Rajin Port railway. At the same time, Russia reminded Mr. Lee to take into consideration the positive suggestions of co-constructing a long-distance natural gas transit pipe between the two countries that was proposed by Mr. Li several years earlier when he visited Russia as the executive manager of modern construction. The pipe was expected to transport natural gas produced on Sakhalin to South Korea through North Korea to maintain the stability of the Korean Peninsula situations and to promote common prosperity of the three parties. However, Lee's administration gradually lost the interests towards the proposal as inter Korean relations continued to worsen.

In 2006, at the time when both South Korean government and public were concentrating on the presidential election to be held next year, Park Geun-hye, the ruling party candidate who was confident in winning the election, inwardly made a proposal to China of picking up one proper place respectively on west coast of South Korea and east coast of China and opening up a subsea tunnel connecting the two points together through the Huanghai Sea in order to promote logistics collaboration. But this idea failed to receive positive response from China probably for the reasons that inter Korean relations was getting better or the maritime transportation between China and South Korea had not been used to the full.

In the meantime, Mongolia ambitiously made up a "new millennium railway construction plan" at the turn of the century, gradually arousing interests of some Chinese companies. The kernel of the project was to build a railway route that traversed the country from east to west and extended to link up the road network in the Northeast and Northwest China and further in Central Asian countries. Apparently, the project meant a lot to China for it would facilitate the transit transportation in the northeast and northwest zones, or to be specific transporting goods in Northwest China to Northeast Asian countries (regions) and delivering goods in Northeast China to Central Asian countries, as well as ease the already saturated east–west railway transportation. For those reasons, some Chinese enterprises offered to give financial support to construct a standard gage railway as same as those in China, the Korean Peninsula, and Japan. But after a long-term study and discussion, and asking for advices of Russia which jointly managed the railway system in Mongolia, Mongolian government decided to build broad-gage railway the same as those in Russia and the Soviet Central Asian countries for the sake of national security.

During that period, connectivity construction between China and North Korea has made new progresses. Under the framework of two economic zones in Granville Island and Rason of joint development and joint management, the New Yalu River Bridge project officially commenced; the reinforcement project of the highway bridge over the area between Quanhe River of China in the lower reaches of Tumen River and Yuanting of North Korea completed; and the secondary road from Yuanting to Rason co-constructed by China and North Korea was put into use. Moreover, the first combined transport test turned out to be a success, where one hundred thousand of coal was loaded on heavy trucks in batches in Huichun of China, delivered to the China-rented Pier 2 of Rajin Port through the transborder highway bridge, and then reloaded on freighters to finally reach Shanghai of China.

At the same time, the reconstruction of Hason-Rajin railway completed as well. Russia, in reference to the continuous observation on situations on the Korean Peninsula since Lee Myung-bak administration rose to power in 2008, decided to extend its cooperation with North Korea to the whole Korean Peninsula. President Putin paid a one day visit to Seoul at the end of 2013 where he talked President Park Geun-hye into participating in the cooperation between Russia and the Korean Peninsula. The cooperation among Russia, the DPRK, and the ROK has been coined as "Hason-Rajin project" in press reports of Russia and the ROK ever since. Years earlier Russia accomplished the modernization and reconstruction of Pier 3 of Rajin Port that rented by Russia under the financial support of South Korea. Shortly after that, the combined transport test succeeded where forty thousand of coal was delivered by a train in Russia to Pier 3 of Rajin Port through Russia–North Korea Transborder Railway Bridge and then was reloaded on freighters heading for South Korea.

The completion of Hason-Rajin port railway reconstruction and the ROK-funded rebuilding of Pier 3 in Rajin Port has deepened the mutual understanding and boosted mutual trust between Russia and the DPRK. The two countries continued to initiate a larger project, which was to renovate the railway of 240 plus km from Namp'o, the largest port city of the DPRK, to Northeast Pyongyang. The project was determined by both as the first phase project of the reconstruction of the whole railroad network in the DPRK.

While the connectivity of infrastructure between Russia and the Korean Peninsula stepping steadily forward, the interconnection between China and Mongolia, between China and Russia, and among the three nations was fruitful, too. As China and Mongolia raised their relations to a comprehensive strategic partnership, Mongolia decided to build two new railways of standard gage as the same in China from its mining areas into China. China and Russia agreed to transform the Port of Zarubino, a small international port near Hason of Russia into a large-scale one with admits hundred-thousand-ton cargo ships so as to activate the transborder railway from Huichun of China to Posyet of Russia that was built years earlier. Moreover, China, Mongolia, and Russia reached an agreement on laying down pipelines to transport natural gas produced in Russia to China through Mongolia.

In summary, there are some points worth paying attention in regard to connectivity construction of infrastructure in Northeast Asia.

Firstly, geopolitically speaking, all countries sharing land borders are promoting connectivity between one another. The construction projects of transit passages are in full bloom not only along the border lines of over ten thousand miles between China and Mongolia, China and Russia, China and the DPRK, Russia and Mongolia, Russia and the DPRK, and the DPRK and the ROK, but also on crossover points of China–Mongolia–Russia borderline and China–Russia–North Korea borderline. The original passages have been broadened and dredged to largely lift the transit efficiency; the newly built future-oriented passages are bearing more and more volume of trans-border goods that is possibly going to exceed that of the old ones.

Secondly, the objectives of construction are dominated by interconnection of transportation infrastructure, such as railways, highways, and pipelines, reaching out to the exchanges of logistics and mobility of people, and further to the aerial and sea lanes. In particular, what are interconnected in Northeast Asia are not only land routes, but also maritime ones, making this region a priority zone for China to co-construct the Belt and the Road. As far as the path of construction is concerned, the connectivity in Northeast Asia starts from the east and ends in the west, extending to the west coast of Japanese Archipelago through the Sea of Japan (Korea East Sea) to the east, to Southeast Asian countries through Taiwan island to the south, and to South Asia, West Asia, Central Asia, and the European part of Russia via west China, west Mongolia and West Siberia of Russia.

Thirdly, there are two protruding hub regions on the map of connectivity in Northeast Asia. One is the lower reaches of Tumen River located along the borders of China, North Korea and Russia. The other one is Mongolia in between China and Russia. The former, in particular, will be the combined zone of the Belt and the Road beyond doubt, therefore bearing special significance to the construction of the Belt and Road.

Lastly, China is endowed with the most favorable geopolitical conditions for realizing connectivity of infrastructure with all other Northeast Asian countries because it is the only one in the region that is adjacent either by land or sea to all other neighbors. But this advantage has not been made the best of yet, while what Russia has done is astonishing. Russia is accelerating its interconnection with other nations in order to rather create a favorable exterior environment for the strategic development of Transbaikalia and the Far East than expand its influence over the Northeast Asia. Therefore, Russia should be the first partner taken into consideration for China to build the Belt and Road in not only Central Asia, but also the whole region.

Chapter 8

Situations in Southeast Asia and Constructing Maritime Silk Road

Yang Danzhi

National Institute of International Strategy
Chinese Academy of Social Sciences
yangdz@cass.org.cn

Southeast Asia is definitely in an extremely important region to China's 21st Century Maritime Silk Road initiative. For China, it is a region where challenges and opportunities coexist during implementing the strategy. Nevertheless, this strategy corresponds current and long-term interests of both China and ASEAN countries, therefore China should have enough patience and perseverance to forge ahead with the strategy.

On October 3, 2013, Chinese President Xi Jinping delivered a speech in parliament, formally expressing the will to construct 21st Century Maritime Silk Road with ASEAN countries. Southeast Asia, with geographical advantages, profound historical origin and common interests with China, is no doubt of significant meaning for the Road initiative.

157

1. Changes in Political, Economic, and Safety Situations in Southeast Asia and Response of Southeast Asia to China's Maritime Silk Road Initiative

1.1. Changes in political, economic, and safety situations in Southeast Asia

In 2014, there have been some new changes of the political, economic and security situation in Southeast Asia, mainly reflecting in the following respects.

First, though domestic political situation of the Association of Southeast Asian Nations (ASEAN) is basically stable, there still exists domestic instability in some countries, which may trigger new instability in the future. In the morning of May 20th, Thailand's army suddenly imposed martial law and take control of the country. This move formally ended months of confrontation between pro-government and anti-government camps but could not fundamentally solve the structural contradiction in Thai society; Joko Widodo won former general Prabowo Subianto in Indonesia's presidential election and may promote reform and anti-corruption during his tenure. Burma's democratization is continuing, but without constitution revision related to Aung San Suu Kyi's qualification for the 2015 presidential election. Besides, conflicts between Buddhists and Muslims are still going on, because of which the relationships of Burma with the west and the Islamic world as well as international organizations are likely to become nervous. The communist party of Vietnam will remain in power in the next five years. Nonetheless, reformist and conservative co-exist in Vietnam, the former emphasizing the rapid increase of Gross Domestic Product (GDP), the latter maintenance of macroeconomic stability.[1] In 2014, Vietnamese Prime Minister Nguyen Tan Dung strengthened his power through the establishment of a National Steering

---

[1] Country Report Vietnam, July 2014, The Economist Intelligence Unit Limited, 2014.

Committee for International Integration. Therefore, Vietnam's original power structure may subtly change.

Second, the ASEAN integration is continuing. In 2013–2014, ASEAN has been dedicated to its Roadmap for an ASEAN Community (2009–2015). Accelerating the construction of ASEAN political and security community, economic community and socio-cultural community. ASEAN has completed 28 items of the original 32 of political and security community building plan in July 2014. To cope with the complex regional security situation, including the South China Sea issue, and to establish mutual benefit relationship with dialogue partners, ASEAN has set up a powerful work platform and promoted regional peace and security by conducting dialogue and cooperation.[2] At the 8th ASEAN Defense Minister's Meeting in August 2014, the defense ministers of all nations present exchange points on strengthening cooperation to eliminate recent tensions in the South China Sea. In the field of non-traditional security cooperation, the defense ministers focused on humanitarian assistance and disaster relief, network security, border security and search and rescue operations. They not only signed the protocol of "Moving forward in Unity to a Peaceful and Prosperous Community", but also passed the documents of "ADMM Work Plan for 2014–2016" and "setting up Direct Communication Mechanisms of Defense Ministers". The "work plan" will determine the priorities of their defense cooperation. The direct communication mechanism for ASEAN defense ministers will provide fast, reliable and trustworthy path for the ministers to communicate with each other in crisis and urgent situations. The ASEAN economic community construction is also accelerating. ASEAN has made progress in trade facilitation, financial services, policy and regulations implementations, infrastructure construction, development of small and medium-sized enterprises, and integration

---

[2] Foreword, Moving Forward in Unity: To a Peaceful and Prosperous Community, *ASEAN Annual Report 2013–2014*, written by ASEAN Secretary-General Li Liangming, p. 1.

into the global economy. ASEAN not only emphasized connectivity, but also pay close attention to cooperation with dialogue partners. Up to July 2014, ASEAN has completed 81.7% of the scheduled tasks in the construction of ASEAN economic community; 90% of the social and cultural community construction blueprint, mainly related to science and technology cooperation, disease treatment, smoke control in the subregion, protection of ASEAN cultural heritage, protection and promotion of the rights and interests of women workers and disaster management, etc. In this process, ASEAN will effectively eliminate the development gap among member states.[3]

Third, the relationship between ASEAN with big powers has entered into a period of adjustment. ASEAN continues to carry out the "balance of power diplomacy". ASEAN member states have enhanced their domestic and international politics.

From 2013–2014, Vietnam, Thailand, Singapore, Myanmar, Cambodia, Malaysia, the Philippines, Indonesia, and other ASEAN member states carried out frequent interaction with the United States, China, Japan, India and other countries, especially Vietnam, the Philippines, Malaysia with the United States and Japan. Given the complicated regional security situation, ASEAN will continue to carry out the "balance of power diplomacy" to avoid difficulty in choosing side from big powers.

In 2014, the change of the regional security situation has exerted a complex effect on domestic politics, foreign relations and foreign policy of ASEAN members. For example, with the warmer situation in the South China Sea, Vietnam, the Philippines and other countries have strengthened the relationship with America and Japan to balance China's "aggression" in the region. China's deployment of "981" drilling platform in the south of Zhongjian Island caused serious anti-China riots in Vietnam; In addition, the change of domestic politics and foreign policy making of ASEAN member states will affect the regional situation. For example, since

---

[3] Foreword, Moving Forward in Unity: To a Peaceful and Prosperous Community, *ASEAN Annual Report 2013–2014*, p. 1.

Joko Widodo became Indonesian President, he has publicly declared to build Indonesia into a maritime power and to mediate South China Sea dispute between relevant ASEAN members and China. At the same time, Indonesia will continue to deploy the most advanced weapon systems on Natuna Islands, which may further complicate the situation in the South China Sea.

1.2. Response of Southeast Asia to China's Maritime Silk Road initiative

At present, Southeast Asia has made preliminary and prudent response to China's "Maritime Silk Road" initiative. Danny Lee, director of the ASEAN Community Affairs Development Apartment, points out that "the creation of the new Maritime Silk Road is a very good concept and will bring new opportunities for China and ASEAN to cooperate in many sectors, such as trade, infrastructure and cultural exchange; ASEAN member states welcome China's initiative of building the new Maritime Silk Road".[4] It is thought that China's new leadership attempts to shape China as a global power in a direct and creative way, the core content of which is to establish economic system through export-oriented cooperation. To revive the maritime silk road is a proof of this idea, which is not only significant for regional stability and world peace, but also a reflection of China's increasingly prominent position in economy, politics, and strategy in the world. By promoting cooperation in building ports and other infrastructure, China trys to ease tension and enhance mutual trust.

Economically, "Marine Silk Road" initiative will not only greatly promote the cooperation on maritime connectivity, harbor, and trade, but also provides a new channel for Chinese companies and capital to invest overseas.

---

[4] "ASEAN welcomes China's new Maritime Silk Road initiatives", China Daily, 15 August 2014, retrieved from http://news.xinhuanet.com/english/china/2014-08/15/c_133559198.htm.

Cooperation will shrink the big gulf in infrastructure among ASEAN members. For China, export-oriented infrastructure investment is significant to promote the development of the manufacturing sector, deal with domestic overcapacity and boost domestic economic growth.

Trade between China and ASEAN members are mostly by sea. "Marine Silk Road" can promote economic growth of ASEAN, enhance communication of people, and increase mutual understanding between China and ASEAN and among ASEAN members.[5]

Singapore is the most active one of ASEAN members to response to "Marine Silk Road" initiative. On September 16, 2014, Singapore Prime Minister Lee Hsien Loong said in Nanning, Guangxi Province of China that Singapore appreciates and welcomes China's initiative of promoting China–ASEAN economic cooperation, including constructing China–ASEAN Free Trade Zone, setting up Asian Infrastructure Investment Bank and jointly build 21st Century Maritime Silk Road. Besides, Singapore is looking forward to cooperating closely with China and discussing further details.[6]

Earlier, Stanley Loh Ka Leung, Singapore's Ambassador to China said in an interview with Xinhua News Agency that Singapore attaches great importance to the relationship with China, and that China and ASEAN try to transform from traditional way of cooperation to new ones in connectivity, finance, electron, and so on by drawing support from the 21st Century Maritime Silk Road.

There are three main reasons for Singapore's positive response. One is the increasingly close economic and trade exchanges and communication between China and Singapore. In 2013, China

---

[5] Goh Sui Noi: "China can try walking in ASEAN states shoes", *The Strait Times*, 8 September 2014, available at http://www.straitstimes.com/opinion/china-can-try-walking-in-asean-states-shoes.

[6] "Lee Hsien Loong: Singapore appreciates and supports to build 21st Century Maritime Silk Road together", Retrieved from http://news.xinhuanet.com/world/2014-09/16/c_1112501403.htm.

became the largest trading partner of Singapore, while Singapore is China's second largest trading partner in ASEAN. China–Singapore bilateral trade has increased from $42 million in 1990 to $92 billion in 2003. Ambassador Mr. Stanley Loh Ka Leung pointed out that Singapore's investment in China were mainly park-based economy, including completed Suzhou Industrial Zone and Tianjin Eco-City, as well as Guangzhou Knowledge City which is under construction and now bilateral cooperation is trying to divert to other fields like finance, food safety, and services. Both sides look forward to more cooperation that meets their development strategies by making full use of their advantages.

Second, Singapore have confidence in the prospects for China's economic development. Lee Hsien Loong predicts that China will continue to maintain strong growth momentum in the next decade or even longer. Third, Singapore expects and believes that China can pull up regional economic growth.

For example, after analysis of many existing problems of global economy, Lee Hsien Loong indicated that "Asia's growth owes much to China's economic growth and China — ASEAN Regional Integration". He also believes that China's economic growth "has a positive impact on regional development," and it will create more win–win cooperation "opportunity" and "bring greater prosperity".

Ambassador Mr. Stanely Loh also noted that "building new Maritime Silk Road is a good opportunity" for ASEAN and to deepen and upgrade their cooperation, from traditional trade to areas such as finance, IT. Singapore will actively collaborate with China and give support in deepening the China–ASEAN relationship.[7]

In addition, many current and former high officials in foreign states who attended the 11th China–ASEAN Expo on September 16, 2014 in Nanning expressed their welcome to China's 21st Century Maritime Silk Road Initiative, including Lao Deputy

---

[7] Singapore ambassador to China said, "China and ASEAN should implement cooperative transformation through 'Marine Silk Road in the 21st century' construction."

Prime Minister Boungnang Vorachith, Thai Deputy Prime Minister and Minister of Foreign Affairs, Indonesia's Deputy Trade Minister Bayu Krisnamurthi and the chairman of IBDC Malaysia, former Malaysia Ambassador Dato Abdul Majid Bin Ahmad Khan.[8] Of course, most of the ASEAN member states just give their response to the Maritime initiative out of courtesy. ASEAN's prudent attitude has two reasons. On the one hand, they want to know China's strategic intentions behind this initiative. On the other hand, China–ASEAN Free Trade Zone is a well-prepared cooperative framework with huge development possibilities, due to which some ASEAN members may have less enthusiasm towards the new initiative.

2. Main Opportunities and Challenges to Maritime Silk Road Construction in Southeast Asia

At present, China faces opportunities as well as challenges in promoting the construction of "Maritime Silk Road" in Southeast Asia.

2.1. Opportunities

First, with the development of the political and economic situation in the Asia-Pacific region, China and ASEAN who experienced a golden decade of bilateral relations are now adjusting and planning a guiding strategy for further cooperation. They are negotiating to make the *Plan of Action (2016–2020)* to implement the *Joint Delaration of the ASEAN-China Strategic Partnership for Peace and Prosperity* and actively discussing to sign a Treaty on Good-Neighorliness, Friendship and Cooperation, which indicate furture directions for China–ASEAN relations.

Second, both sides committed to upgrade China–ASEAN free trade zone to closer China–ASEAN economical relationship, which

---

[8] http://news.xinhuanet.com/world/2014-09/10/c_1112425482.htm.

undoubtedly creates good conditions for Maritime Silk Road construction.

Third, China–ASEAN have finished setting up institutions in the field of connectivity. ASEAN-China Committee on Connectivity Cooperation (ACCC) and Chinese group of ACCC are committed to promoting the construction of China–ASEAN connectivity. Multiple cooperation projects have been launched. In November 2014, at the 17th "10 + 1" China–ASEAN leaders meeting held in Burmese capital Naypyidaw, China's Prime Minister, Li Keqiang, put forward to speed up building basic network for connectivity. He stressed on connectivity planning and construction in fields of communication, electric power, network, financial support and improve soft environment like convenient customs clearance, market regulation and standard specification.[9]

Fourth, China–ASEAN cooperation in finance deepens gradually. ASEAN's ten member states have now become the members of the Asian Infrastructure Investment Bank (AIIB) firstly launched by China. In the original plan, AIIB the investment bank is an intergovernmental Asian regional multilateral development agency, providing key support to infrastructure construction and operating according to the pattern and principle of the multilateral development banks.

According to the Memorandum on the Preparation of Investment Banks, the authorized capital of AIIB is $100 billion and the initial subscribed capital target is around $50 billion with 50% paid in China. It is reported that the registered capital of AIIB is paid in installments by members and the contributed capital in first phase is 10% of initial subscribed target, that is $5 billion, and China invests $2.5 billion.

Previously, according to the Asian Development Bank, 32 Asia Development Bank (ADB) members need $8.22 trillion of infrastructure investment from 2010 to 2020 with $800 billion per year

---

[9] Li's speech in the 17ᵗʰ, China–ASEAN "10 + 1 summit" speech, "(article), http://news.xinhuanet.com/world/2014-11/14/c_1113240171.htm.

on average. ADB thinks that Asian city infrastructure construction funding gap is more than $60 billion every year, while ADB only has about $13 billion in new loans, the new project. At present, it is difficult for the World Bank and ADB to meet the gap in the Asia-Pacific region where the infrastructure financing has reached to trillions of dollars, therefore, new regional financial institutions are urgently needed to fill up the gap soon.[10] ASEAN infrastructure investment fund, annotated in ADB, can only provide billions of dollars, while Indonesia asks for $160 billion for financing. Therefore, AIIB is necessary to be formed. It is predictable that once AIIB begins to operate, China's investment in Southeast Asia will greatly increase and the constructions in Southeast Asian like ports, bridges, roads and other infrastructure will greatly speed up.

In addition, China and ASEAN have strengthened cooperation in the field of traditional and non-traditional security. Given the warming up dispute in South China Sea in recent years, China and ASEAN have had constructive negotiations. At the Declaration on the Code of Conduct on the South China Sea (DOC) 10th China–ASEAN Joint Working Group Meeting, held in Singapore On March 17th and 18th, 2014, and the seventh ASEAN–China senior officials meeting held in Parthia, Thailand on April 21, 2014, China and ASEAN have negotiated related questions of implementing the DOC and designing the Code of Conduct in South China Sea (COC). Besides, on the 17th China–ASEAN (10 + 1) Leaders' Meeting, China's prime minister advocated 2015 as "China–ASEAN Cooperation in Ocean", further deepening maritime cooperation, strengthening dialogue and cooperation between maritime law enforcement agencies and establishing marine cooperation center. Moreover, both sides should implement the Pan-beibu Gulf Economic Cooperation Roadmap well and jointly carry out China–ASEAN maritime cooperation fund projects. In 2015, China and ASEAN will hold China–ASEAN

---

[10] "The Banks will open soon", http://news.xinhuanet.com/fortune/2014-11/24/c_127245680.htm.

informal meeting of defense secretaries to discuss the possibility of establishing a China–ASEAN defense hotline and arrange joint exercises. The enforcement of the Mekong river basin security cooperation will be further deepened. Also, cooperation in new fields such as humanities, science and technology, and environmental protection are also expected to be intensified.[11]

2.2. Challenges

Maritime Silk Road construction in Southeast Asia confronts complex challenges. First of all, because of the influence of the historical and realistic factors, some ASEAN countries have doubts and worries on China's foreign policy of good neighborliness. China has to make efforts to eliminate trust deficit of the Southeast Asian countries on China. In recent years, China's active performance in the South China Sea, especially the stationing of HD-981 oil rig in the south of the Zhongjian Island and the later consolidation and expansion of islands in the South China Sea, widely considered as threats to regional security by ASEAN countries. Chaturvedy holds that, "Given China's acts of assertiveness, it is difficult for the region's smaller states to not feel suspicious of any goodwill gesture from Beijing. It will be difficult for China to build a friendly neighborhood if Beijing's every move is met with distrust and fear. China forgets that because of its sheer size, any move it makes that it views as insignificant could have large implications for its smaller neighbors."[12]

For policymakers of some ASEAN members, China in fact seeks to rebuild dominance in Southeast Asia, and whether ASEAN can unite to response to China on the South China Sea issue has

---

[11] "Li in the 17ᵗʰ" 10 + 1 "China–ASEAN leaders meeting speech" (article), http://news.xinhuanet.com/world/2014-11/14/c_1113240171.htm.
[12] Rajeev Ranjan Chaturvedy: "Decoding China's Silk Diplomacy at Sea", December 11, 2014. Retrieved from http://www.eurasiareview.com/11122014-decoding-chinas-silk-diplomacy-sea-analysis/.

been the touchstone for the possibility of ASEAN security community. In 2014, though ASEAN hasn't passed any agreement against China on the South China Sea issue, it still shows high attention on the South China Sea situation several times in the form of collective declaration. In addition, some claimant countries continue to change the South China Sea situation unilaterally. For example, not only Vietnam, the Philippines show tough attitude on the South China Sea issue, even Indonesia who has kept a low profile has deployed latest procurements including the apache helicopter in Natuna Islands, 200 kms away from the Nansha islands, and publicly announced that Indonesia is determined to take "responsibility as a regional power" to mediate the South China Sea sovereignty dispute between China and Southeast Asian countries and urge China and ten ASEAN member countries to achieve "the South China Sea the COC" as soon as possible. Claimant countries for South China Sea among ASEAN members has showed tough attitude or made actions in the South China Sea disputes, which most likely leads to contradictions and conflicts with China's increasingly growing actions for rights on the South China Sea. In a medium or longer term in the future, if the South China Sea issue is not effectively resolved, there will be negative impacts on the relationship between China and ASEAN as well as the construction of the Maritime Silk Road.

Second, the intervention of the external powers, such as the United States, Japan and India in the recent years may bring interference and impact to "Marine Silk Road construction".

In 2014, the US and Japan continue to increase investment in Southeast Asia by reason of strengthening small countries the ability of safeguard legal rights on ocean. In 2014, the Philippines will receive $50 million in foreign military aid from the US, which is the highest amount of fund during over 10 years, and will get $40 million from the US global security accident spending. Del Rosario, Philippine's defense secretary, says the money will be used strictly to strengthening the navy and the Philippines may obtain its third grade Hamilton high endurance patrol boat. In the past three years, two Hamilton patrol boat that the Philippines received from the United States have been the largest and most advanced warship in the Philippine navy. After eight rounds of negotiations, the US and the Philippines also signed a defense cooperation agreement, which will enhance the sharing of the Philippines bases, to increase US ships, aircraft and abnormal buildup of troops in the Philippines, as well as to make USA allies believe the support capability of the US in limiting the rise of China.[13]

America will use the armed forces of the military installations under the premise of being invited by the Philippine and fully complying with the Philippine constitution and law.[14]

The American government also announced to lose the restrictions of arms exports to Vietnam and lift its ban on arms sales related to maritime police on October 2. According to media reports, loosening the restriction on arms exports may give China a chance to force in Vietnam who is in dispute with China in the South China Sea sovereignty. It is likely because of the high alert to fast closer relationship of China and Russia, who has provided more than 90% of weapons, though has not clearly showed the will to import from USA, Vietnamese state media, close to the Vietnamese army, cited P-3 anti-submarine patrol aircraft and audio equipment that can use sound waves to intimidate enemies from a distance.[15]

The United States and Japan strengthen the intervention of Indo-China Peninsula by intervening the Mekong issues. In 2014, the American secretary of state Kerry and Japanese Foreign Minister Yoshihiko Noda all attended Ministerial Meeting of the Lower Mekong Basin held in Naypyidaw, Burma in September. Enhancing connectivity, narrowing the development gap and realizing

---

[13] http://gb.cri.cn/42071/2014/04/28/6071s4521467.htm.
[14] http://cn.nhandan.org.vn/international/international_news/Item/1904401-the Philippines and USA reached consensus in USA's military in the Philippines. html.
[15] "Japanese economic news" reported on October 4, quoted in reference news network (http://mil.cankaoxiaoxi.com/2014/1005/518109.shtml).

sustainable development in the Mekong region become a hot topic.[16] In 2014, Japan continued to maintain a momentum of investing in Burma, Vietnam, Thailand, Cambodia, and Laos.

In the financial field, the US and Japan keep negative attitude for China's initiative to establish the AIIB. Although Chinese officials have said the AIIB is to improve the existing international mechanism such as the ADB and the World Bank, rather than to compete with others. The US has privately lobbied regional allies including South Korea, Japan, not to join the AIIB, while Japan strongly doubts whether the AIIB can "establish the fair management system" (foreign affairs minister Fumio Kishida said) and whether it has loan review (financial minister Taro Aso said). Therefore, America and Japan feel fear that the AIIB, established by China and other 21 countries including members of the ASEAN may cause negative impacts on the international monetary fund and the ADB respectively dominated by America and Japan. In order to prevent China from influencing and changing the international financial order through the establishment of the AIIB, USA and Japan are likely to intensify the relationship with ASEAN to make member countries not to unite for the AIIB.

India, who put "being a colorful power" as the target earlier, has strengthened participation on Indo-China Peninsula and South China Sea affairs in recent years. Not only has India strengthened cooperation with Vietnam and Burma in the political, economic and defense fields, but also made strong voice on the South China Sea issue frequently. India's Foreign Ministry spokesman Akbaruddin said publicly on October 24th, that "Vietnam has provided some oil fields in the South China Sea and we (India) are examining. As long as there is business interests, we will further consider. The relationship between India and Vietnam does not depend on other countries". Such a high profile involvement in the

---

[16] Ministerial Joint Statement, Four Friends of the Lower Mekong Ministerial Meeting, http://www. mofa.go.jp/files/000049412.pdf.

affairs of the South China Sea is to maintain its strategic interests in the South China Sea and balance on China's power.

Overall, there has been a complex competition among big powers in Indo-China Peninsula and South China Sea. If it eventually evolves into the fierce strategic competition of the big countries, the construction of Maritime Silk Road will definitely be negatively impacted.

At last, the political unrest of some ASEAN countries effects formulation and implementation of its foreign policy, which may lead to fluctuations in the government's policy toward China and affect the implementation of the Maritime Silk Road initiative in the future to a certain extent. For example, change of government led to difficulty in implementing "rice in high speed rail" agreement signed by Yingluck Shinawatra government and China. The contradiction between the Burmese government and the local armed forces not only led to the suspension of Myitsone construction but also the interruption of China–Burma railway construction. Among ASEAN member states, the change of domestic public opinion in Burma and Vietnam who are in political, economic transformation has most obvious effects on the construction of the Maritime Silk Road.

Despite of many realistic obstacles and challenges, the Maritime Silk Road initiative is in the realistic and long-term interests of China and ASEAN countries. Especially for some ASEAN member countries with backward infrastructure and economy, they prefer to promote domestic economy through the Maritime Silk Road construction, at the same time better share dividend of regional cooperation. Even the Philippines who has maritime dispute with China also pays high attention to whether it can be classified into the scope of Maritime Silk Road. Nine in ten ASEAN country members actively participate in the establishment of AIIB, though once missed signing relevant agreements of the AIIB and triggered speculation, Indonesia finally choose to join, which fully reflects the attraction of Maritime Silk Road construction for the ASEAN countries. Therefore, China should have enough patience and strategic concentration in the promotion of the construction of Maritime Silk Road.

3. Strategies of China

The year 2014 has seen the overall steady development of relations between China and ASEAN. How to further consolidate the basis of the relationship between China and ASEAN, find new paths for both sides to deepen cooperation and establish the new model will be the task for China and ASEAN to face and tackle urgently in the next decade. China's "Maritime Silk Road" initiative undoubtedly provides a new opportunity for the development of China–ASEAN relations.

Geopolitically, most ASEAN member countries are island or maritime nations and in the paths of Maritime Silk Road. Therefore, relations between China and ASEAN members will undoubtedly have a significant impact on the smooth transformation of Maritime Silk Road initiative into cooperative practice. Due to the unstable situation in the South China Sea, especially China–Vietnam and China–Philippines disputes in the South China Sea continued to escalate in 2014, ASEAN countries have doubts and anxiety in different degree on China's regional strategy, therefore, getting recognition and support of all the ASEAN member countries on Maritime Silk Road initiative in the short term is not realistic. In addition, the differences among countries involved in Maritime Silk Road are more obvious than that among countries involved in the "Silk Road Economic Belt" in political system, social ideology, religion, culture, economic development level and so on, which forces China to make different strategies in the construction of Maritime Silk Road.

First, to maintain strategy of paying equal attention to land, sea and air, maintaining three-dimensional connectivity and line-point pattern and targeted to carry out diplomacy towards Indo-China Peninsula. Needless to say, Maritime Silk Road is mainly about the ocean, especially involving maritime safety and maritime trade channels. However, given the evolution of the security situation in Southeast Asia in recent years, and political situation of the Indo-China Peninsula countries between the western Pacific and Indian Ocean, foreign strategy adjustment and the support of foreign big powers in this region have become important factors that affect maritime security cooperation. In addition, solid and reliable of "protection" of land is also very important for maintaining the sea lanes safe and sustainable maritime trade. Due to many factors, the strategic position of Indo-China Peninsula is rapidly rising. Therefore, to put Maritime Silk Road initiative into practice, China needs to be more targeted to conduct diplomacy with Southeast Asian nations in Indo-China Peninsula, to strive for the trust of these countries and to strengthen the construction of "protection" in Indo-China Peninsula. More transportation hub combining land, sea, and sky should be created in the process of promoting the construction of connectivity in the Indo-China Peninsula.

Second, designing Maritime Silk Road from the overall situation is the integrity for strategy integrity and the embodiment of the principle, but it is possible to initially start the strategy in some sections involved in the "Maritime Silk Road" in particular period. Especially, most Southeast Asian countries have not made a clear response or kept doubts to China's Maritime Silk Road initiative, China is able to deepen cooperation with countries who response actively such as Sri Lanka, Bangladesh and other South Asian countries surrounding the Indian Ocean. In infrastructure construction, personnel training and resources, information sharing, etc., China and the South Asian countries has a huge potential for cooperation. Besides, the further development of relations between China and several South Asian countries will be also helpful for China to revitalize diplomacy with surrounding countries as well as produce linkage effect in Indo-China Peninsula and the whole Southeast Asia.

Moreover, to seek strategic harmony and Consensus with ASEAN. The Belt and Road is regarded as China's great regional strategy, and Maritime Silk Road is an important part of this strategy. While the great regional strategy of ASEAN is to built political security, economic and social–cultural community as soon as possible. ASEAN has common interests with China in achieving strategic goals, namely, maintain peace and stability in the Asia-Pacific region and promote the prosperity and development of the Asia-Pacific region. There is no conflict between the construction of Maritime Silk Road and "ASEAN Community" in the ultimate goal. To construct the "Maritime Silk Road" and the "upgraded" China–ASEAN Free Trade Zone can be compatible. Both sides need to give more room to each other for development and take care of each other's core interests. Direct confrontation between China and ASEAN or ASEAN's participation with other side to confront with China not only endanger the regional stability, but also go against the interests of China and ASEAN in the long run. Therefore, win–win cooperation is the best choice for China and ASEAN now or in the long run.

At last, effectively utilizing regional cooperation platform and mechanism is necessary for promoting the construction of Maritime Silk Road. The existence and development of these platforms and mechanisms are important safeguards of the smooth construction of "Maritime Silk Road". As the advocator of Maritime Silk Road, China should not only focus on promoting the innovation of the existing cooperation mechanisms, but also make great efforts to promote the effective interaction and mutual cooperation between different mechanisms. Maritime Silk Road construction is not to make a fresh start thoroughly, but to explore new development paths and ways based on the existing mechanism. At present, there have been many forums in the Asia-Pacific region are formally dominated by ASEAN, such as the ASEAN Region Forum (ARF), the Asia-Pacific Security Cooperation Council (CSCAP) and 10 + 3 (APT), which belong to several "tracks" like "first track" and "second track" and cover multilateral mechanisms in security and economy. This kind of domination is historic and reasonable. China needs to keep close cooperation with ASEAN to ensure the existing mechanism to operate well. In addition, as the first advocator of Shanghai

Cooperation Organization and current presidency of the CICA meeting, China is expected to further promote the effective interaction of the existing mechanisms of the SCO, the CICA and the Asia-Pacific region, which undoubtedly has positive and far-reaching significance for the formation of new regional architecture in Asia in the future.

Chapter 9

South Asia and the Belt and Road Initiative: Opportunities, Challenges, and Prospect

Wu Zhaoli

National Institute of International Strategy
Chinese Academy of Social Sciences
wuzhl@cass.org.cn

As a close neighbor to China, South Asia is one of the main targets of China to practice its peripheral diplomatic idea — amity, sincerity, mutual benefit and inclusiveness, as well as a key point to rebuild the 21st Century Maritime Silk Road and economic corridor. Apart from the strategic significance of South Asia to China, the Belt and Road Initiative agrees with strategies of South Asian countries for their social and economic development and offer treacherous opportunities for their growth. Thus, the initiative is received big welcome in most South Asian countries. Nevertheless, security situations in South Asia, international relations within and India's influence on the region, and China–India political mutual trust constitute challenges to the promotion of the initiative in South Asia.

South Asia, being one of the main directions of China's peripheral strategy, means a lot to China's Belt and Road initiative. On the one hand, the 21st Century Maritime Silk Road, Bangladesh-China-India-Myanmar (BCIM) Economic Corridor, and China–Pakistan Economic Corridor (CPEC) dominated by China are of close relations with South Asian countries. On the other hand, proposals or policies brought up by South Asian countries, such as the CCAP, the INSTC, and developing Northeastern India to connect with neighboring countries that are put forth by India, and Pakistan's National Trade Corridor Programme (NTCP) and National Trade Corridor Improvement Programme (NTCIP), are interwoven with China's connection proposal. Moreover, out region countries like the US with its New Silk Road Project (NSRP) show various degrees of influence over other connection proposals or programs. In a word, given current situations, South Asia and its relevant countries have become a critical point for several connection proposals. This paper is to explore China's strategic positioning and appeals in South Asia, the relevance between the Belt and Road Initiative and economic and social development strategies in South Asia, standing and responses of South Asian nations to the 21st Century Maritime Silk Road, and opportunities and challenges China is faced with when forging ahead with its initiatives in South Asia.

1. Role of South Asia in China's Diplomacy for Neighboring Countries

China has been attaching great importance to keep and develop its traditional friendship and cooperation with South Asian countries. Since China commenced its 21st Century Maritime Silk Road initiative, China deems South Asia, being a key point in the Road, as a major region to which China will opens larger in the new era and gives top priority as far as its peripheral diplomatic strategy is concerned. Geologically, South Asia is a relatively independent geographical unit, i.e. the South Asian Subcontinent. Geopolitically, South Asia is very special to China and nations within the region are of different positions under the framework of the Belt and Road. In this region, there are the Kingdom of

Bhutan which has established diplomatic relation with China although limited in space of territory, India that is in deficiency of political and strategic mutual trust with China, and Pakistan, a "four good country"[1] that has high strategic mutual trust with China.

The traditional positions in genealogy of South Asian countries are divided into four sections. Two ends of the genealogy are all-weather strategic partner, and strategic partner to be formed. In the middle, there are strategic partner and full partner. Pakistan is the most special one in the genealogy. As an all-weather strategic partner to China, it is deemed as a "four good country" under the support of China–Pakistan treaty of good neighborliness, friendship, and cooperation. China prioritizes diplomatically its relations with Pakistan all the time and Pakistan in return affirms in many occasions that the friendship with China is a footstone for Pakistan's foreign policy and a country-wide recognition. Both parties consider maintaining their long-lasting friendship as the top priority.[2] Meanwhile, India is on the opposite end of the genealogy to the end where Pakistan is. According to the Chinese government, China in the year of 2014 is committed to developing a closer partnership of development. China's understanding towards its relation with India has grown to be practical and clear since 2005 when it believed that the two countries were building a strategic partnership for peace and prosperity.

Countries in the middle sections of the genealogy are positioned differently to those at the ends. Sri Lanka is strategic cooperative partner who promotes sincere mutual support and everlasting friendship. And the two countries established comprehensive and cooperative partnership with the will of sincere mutual support and everlasting friendship in 2005. They decided

---

[1] A "four good country" means "good neighbor, good friend, good comrade, and good partner".

[2] The Ministry of Foreign Affairs of the People's Republic of China. China and Pakistan Released "Common Vision for Deepening China–Pakistan Strategic Cooperative Partnership in the New Era", http://news.xinhuanet.com/2013-07/05/c_116426628.htm.

to upgrade their relationship into strategic cooperative partnership featuring sincere mutual support and ever lasting friendship in 2013, followed by China's suggesting the two countries become partners in pursuit of common dreams by coordinating development strategies and braving the wind and waves along the way in 2014.[3] China takes Bangladesh, Nepal and Maldives as its full partners. Specifically speaking, China regarded Bangladesh as its important partner in South Asia and Indian Ocean region (2014), decided to establish and enhance the comprehensive and cooperative partnership and everlasting friendship with Nepal on the basis of the Five Principles of Peaceful Coexistence (2009), and resolved to build China–Maldives future-oriented all-round friendly and cooperative partnership (2014).

From the evolvement of the strategic positioning of South Asian countries in China's point of view for the last decade, last year especially, it is not difficult to discern that Pakistan and India remained to be two ends of the genealogy, the former being the pillar of China's strategy in South Asia and the latter the partner of development which China has been pursuing. As to the middle sections, substantial advancement has occurred to the positioning of Sri Lanka and Maldives. China–Sri Lanka relationship was upgraded from comprehensive and cooperative partnership in 2005 to strategic cooperative partnership in 2013 and Maldives became future-oriented all-round partner to China. The promotion of strategic positions of the two countries is in relation with the 21st Century Maritime Silk Road and their importance as hubs of the Road.

Generally speaking, South Asia acquires an affirmative position in China's overall foreign strategic pattern and an increasingly definite role in China's Belt and Road Initiative as China's neighborhood diplomacy evolves. Given its significance, China focuses on developing relationship with South Asian countries.

---

[3] Xi Jinping: "Let us become partners in pursuit of our dreams", *People's Daily*, September 17, 2014. http://politics.people.com.cn/n/2014/0917/c1024-25674241.html.

Pakistan, as a traditional partner, is the backbone country for China's policy towards South Asia; India is placed in a more prominent strategic position as China is seeking partnership of development with India. At the same time, China lays more emphasis on small countries like Sri Lanka and Maldives by exalting their roles in its strategies. In a word, China is looking forward to deepen traditional friendship with South Asian countries, promoting bilateral and multilateral cooperation, and enhancing interregional connection through the Road and two corridors to build a China–South Asia community of common interests.

2. Relations between Belt and Road Initiative and Social and Economic Strategies of South Asian Countries

The blueprint of building the Road and two corridors in South Asia and the community of common interests highly coincides with strategies for economic and social development of South Asian countries. This is not only a golden opportunity for South Asian countries to realize their development goals, but also favorable for China to carry out "the Road and two Corridors" diplomacy in South Asia.

The continent of South Asia has long been suffering turbulence caused by ethnic and religious conflicts, enmity between countries, and terrorist threats. Since the last wave of democratization was gone, most countries in that region have enlisted economic and social development and poverty reduction as one of the principal policy objectives in their medium- to long-term projects and taken infrastructure construction as the key to realize their development goals and therefore invested more on it.

The Twelfth Five Year Plan (from 2012/2013 financial year to 2016/2017 financial year) edited by the Planning Commission of India set up the target of 9% of average economic growth rate so as to realize a faster, continuous and more inclusive growth. In order to reach that goal, India will invest 1 trillion USD, 10% of total GDP, on infrastructure construction. And India has been working on the construction of five industrial corridors as an important part of infrastructure construction since 2006, which are the Delhi Mumbai Industrial Corridor (DMIC), the Bangalore–Mumbai Industrial Corridor (BEMC), the Amritsar–Kolkata Industrial Corridor (AKIC), the Chennai–Bangalore Industrial Corridor (CBIC) and the East Coast Industrial Corridor (ECEC). Pakistan approved the "Pakistan Vision 2025" Plan, outlining seven pillars for economic growth of which achieving sustained, indigenous and inclusive growth and the modernization of transportation infrastructure and greater regional connectivity are more important than the other five. Bangladesh made the Perspective Plan of Bangladesh 2010–2021: Making Vision 2021 a Reality in order to improve comprehensive transportation ability of infrastructure like railways, highways, marine traffic in inland rivers and those connecting to neighboring countries. Sri Lanka drew up a medium to long-term plan called "Sri Lanka: The Emerging Wonder of Asia: Mahinda Chintana Vision for the Future"[4] in hope of making the country a pearl on the Silk Road that is interconnected by modern transportation network across the country. Maldives published the Maldives Economic Diversification Strategy (MEDS), targeting at improving the country into a high-income, energetic and elastic and inclusive economy by 2025, setting up three goals and nine tasks, and taking transportation industry as one of the key industries in the coming decade.

Most of South Asian countries regard economic development as the top priority of government work and infrastructure construction and regional interconnection as pillars to drive economic development. Nevertheless, the long-existing shortages in transportation infrastructure and energy in the region constrain the realization of the goals.

The newest South Asia Economic report released by the World Bank[5] indicates that South Asia, whose economic growth has been

---

[4] Department of National Planning Ministry of Finance and Planning, Government of Sri Lanka, "Sri Lanka: The Emerging Wonder of Asia: Mahinda Chintana Vision for the Future", http://203.94.72.22/publications/npd/mahindaChintanaVision-2010full-eng.pdf.

[5] WB: "South Asia Economic Focus: The Export Opportunity", Fall 2014.

only next to East Asia-Pacific region since global economic crisis, had a poor economic performance for the past few years, and the key to resume fast economic growth for the region is the get through the structure bottleneck by supplying necessary infrastructure.

The substantive investment on infrastructure in South Asia from 2011 to 2020 is necessary to reach the goal of poverty reduction. The report on infrastructure development in South Asia released by World Bank in April 2014 predicted that investment on infrastructure in the whole region will be up to 1.7–2.5 trillion USD by 2020. Demands for transportation would reach 411–691 billion USD, occupying as much as 1.97–3.31% of the GDP of South Asia. Of the total investment demands on infrastructure construction, 340–595 billion USD (and even much more if taking into account the five industrial corridors) are needed in India, 36–45 billion USD in Bangladesh, 17.2–21.5 billion USD in Pakistan, and 10.8–18 billion USD in Sri Lanka.[6] To fulfill these demands, South Asia needs to attain a reliable, stable, and sufficient provision source. But the huge investment gap and limited fiscal and financial resources beset countries in the region.

In this case, three initiatives, namely the Maritime Silk Road, BCIM Economic Corridor and CPEC, envisaged by China fit for the common needs of South Asian countries and offer them with a historic chance to realize their economic and social development objectives.

China promotes the three initiatives in this region to deepen its mutually beneficial cooperation with the region in aspects of infrastructure interconnection, energy, finance, and people's well being by innovative cooperative patterns, and to dock its vision for development with development strategies of South Asian countries in a profound manner, China is also willing to provide necessary support and assistance for them. As President Xi expressed when he visited Maldives, Sri Lanka and India, China would like

---

[6] Luis Andrés, Dan Biller, and Matías Herrera Dappe: "Reducing Poverty by Closing South Asia's Infrastructure Gap", December 2013, Retrieved from http://documents.worldbank.org/curated/en/881321468170977482/Reducing-poverty-by-closing-South-Asias-infrastructure-gap.

to take the wings of the Belt and the Road together with South Asian countries to realize national rise and in the next five years, bilateral trade will be up to 150 billion USD and the investment of China on South Asia will be lifted to 30 billion USD and China's preferential loans to South Asia will be 20 billion USD.[7]

3. Responses and Standing of South Asian Countries to Belt and Road Initiatives

Since President Xi first officially proposed the 21st Century Maritime Silk Road initiative in October 2013, China has been taking diplomatic efforts centered on the Belt and Road Initiative and the outline of the Road has been growing to be clear day after day. South Asian countries who were invited to participate into the construction of the Road have all responded positively except India which is cautious about the idea.

3.1. Pakistan actively support the Belt and Road Initiative and the CPEC

Pakistan has been lavishing full support the CPEC initiative at levels of policy coordination, budgeting, and project planning all the way through from May 2013 when the initiative was put forth for the first time to August 2014 when the third conference of the Joint Cooperation Committee (JCC) on CPEC kicked off. Pakistan thinks that the initiative coincides with its own long-term objective of becoming pivot for regional economy and trade.[8] At present, China and Pakistan have reached a consensus on the planning of

---

[7] Chinese President Xi Jinping delivers speech at Indian Council of World Affairs. Retrieved from http://english.cntv.cn/2014/09/19/VIDE1411095370882449. shtml. December 1, 2015.

[8] To cater for the needs of foreign trade and national economy, Pakistan put forward with the National Trade Corridor Programme in 2007, and National Trade Corridor Improvement Programme in 2011. In 2013, Pakistan issued Pakistan Vision 2025 based on the CPEC. The Vision highlights the development of transportation infrastructure and regional interconnection.

their economic corridor, including path selection, cooperative fields, phase-completion deadlines, and arrangement of Early Harvest Programs. The CPEC Early Harvest Program list was determined in July 2014, on which there are infrastructure construction, energy and port programs and supporting programs. The list is expected to be accomplished by 2017 and long-term programs by 2030.

3.2. Sri Lanka welcomes and supports the belt initiative, willing to participate

Foreign Minister Wang Yi suggested a joint construction of the 21st Century Maritime Silk Road when he met in Beijing with the President's convoy, Sri Lanka Foreign Minister Gamini Lakshman Peiris in February 2014. Mr. Peiris expressed on behalf of the country the support for this initiative. Sri Lanka is one of the countries which respond with the utmost enthusiasm. The country thinks that the initiative agree naturally with its goal of building shipping center on the Indian Ocean and considers China's invitation as a precious chance to make up for the backwardness of the country for the past 30 years. Recently the two countries were upgraded to be a strategic cooperative partner to each other. Both agreed on further boosting maritime cooperation by increasing investment on the Hambantota port project, pushing ahead with the construction of Colombo as a port city and establishing a Joint Committee on Coastal Zone and Maritime Cooperation where maritime issues are to be addressed.

3.3. Bangladesh holds a positive attitude on the BCIM Economic Corridor but is not ready yet for the 21st Century Maritime Silk Road initiative

President Xi indicated when he met in Beijing with Bangladeshi Premier Minister Sheikh Hasina in June 2014 that China welcomes Bangladesh to be a part of the Silk Road Economic Belt and the 21st Century Maritime Silk Road and invites Bangladesh to join the construction of the BCIM Economic Corridor to build a community of common interests. Seen from that, it is obvious that the attitude Bangladesh holds towards China's Belt and Road Initiative and the BCIM Economic Corridor is positive. However, the China-Bangladesh joint statement released in the same month only demonstrated the consensuses on the BCIM Economic Corridor and other interconnection initiatives in the region without definite expression of Bangladesh's standpoint in the Road initiative. That means that Bangladesh had not been studied on or identified its position in the Maritime Silk Road. Nonetheless, to be objective, it is possible that Bangladesh becomes the trade transfer center on the Road by virtue of its geological advantages. And given its uncertain relations with India, Bangladesh, China and Myanmar economic corridor without India being involved can also be another good option for the country.

3.4. Both Maldives and Nepal welcome the 21st Century Maritime Silk Road

Maldives is willing to participate into the construction of the Road and to enhance cooperation with China in fields like maritime affairs, maritime economy, and maritime safety. Nepal hopes to seize the opportunities that BCIM Economic Corridor and the Road initiative bring along so as to improve the well-being of the Nepalese.

3.5. India agrees to study on the BCIM Economic Corridor but keeps prudent towards the road initiative

India has expressed twice that it is willing to carry out preliminary study on the BCIM Economic Corridor when Chinese Premier Li Keqiang visits India in May 2013 and Indian Prime Minister Singh paid a visit to China in October the same year. China sent India its invitation to join the 21st Century Maritime Silk Road construction at the 17th Meeting of the Special Representatives for the China–India Boundary Question in February 2014. However, although both parties reached consensuses on promoting the linking of two markets in China and India, steadily pushing forward cooperation on railway and industrial parks and the BCIM Economic Corridor, and working together to build the Silk Road Economic Belt, India showed blurry attitude towards the Road initiative. Besides, the China–India joint statement released during Chinese President Xi's visit to India in September of the same year mentioned cooperation regarding the BCIM Economic Corridor but none about the Belt and Road Initiative, which shows that India will not drop its deep hesitations until it gets detailed and definite background of the Initiative.

In a word, Pakistan among South Asian countries clearly holds positive and supportive standpoint towards the Belt and Road Initiative and CPEC and has been actively working on the CPEC planning. The response is attributed to the high-level political mutual trust in-between the two nations and perfect consistency of their development strategies. Both Maldives and Sri Lanka, seeing the Road as a great opportunity for their development, responded actively and took part in the construction of the Road. Bangladesh shows positive attitude towards BCIM Economic Corridor and a "wait-and-see" standpoint as to the Belt and Road Initiative. India only supports researches and cooperation in BCIM Economic Corridor and remains cautious and even contradictory to the Belt and Road Initiative, the Road in particular.

4. Major Challenges to Belt and Road Initiatives from South Asia

The longitudinal corridors, the CPEC and the BCIM Economic Corridor, stride over Himalayas and extend to connect the Belt to the north, and to join the Road to the south. It is a strategic arrangement for constructing a transhimalaya economic and development zone. China's initiative is in accordance with economic and social development strategies envisioned by South Asian countries; the latter can accelerate their development by working with China on the initiative. Therefore, the initiative has obtained support and responses from most of South Asian countries, which facilitates the promotion of the two corridors and the Maritime Silk Road in

South Asia. In spite of this, China is still facing with a series of challenges from the perspective of geopolitical situations in that region.

4.1. India has concerns over the Belt and Road Initiative and holds uncertain attitude towards cooperation, which more or less impacts the depth and scope of regional cooperation

The depending boundary problems between China and India are posing substantive influence on the deepening of China–India relations. Apart from this, unbalanced trades, the issue of water resources, and relations of China with other South Asian countries are also reality-oriented problems needs to be addressed by both parties. Being affected by China–India mutual trust, India has grave misgivings about the Belt and Road Initiative, in particular the Road initiative. Sorting out the analyses made in the strategic circle of India, we conclude that there are several misgivings as follows. The First is that as for India, Chinese neighboring diplomacy centering on the Silk Road is a long-term challenge of more significance.[9] Second is that the initiative is in contradictory to the security-oriented cooperative partnership India established with the US, Japan, and Australia under the Indian Ocean-Pacific Ocean framework.[10] Third is that China is adopting "string of pearls" strategy against India economically under the cover of the Belt and Road Initiative.[11] Currently, inviting India into the Maritime Silk

---

[9] Jayadeva Ranade: "New govt will have to formulate policies to protect national interest", *Hindustan Times*, May 11, 2014. Retrieved from http://www.hindustan-times.com/ht-view/new-govt-will-have-to-formulate-policies-to-protect-national-interest/story-WIOzwtitiApMMqFEipwSsI.html

[10] C. Raja Mohan: "Will India Join China's Maritime Silk Road?", *The Indian Express*, February 15, 2014, http://indianexpress.com/article/opinion/columns/will-india-join-chinas-maritime-silk-road/.

[11] David Scott: "China's 'Maritime Silk Road' Proposal — An Uncertain Chalice for India?",http://lkyspp.nus.edu.sg/cag/publication/china-india-brief/china-india-brief-29.

Road project is advisable as to China but is also likely to bewilder India as the latter has to choose one from two adverse opinions, to be specific, carrying out maritime cooperation with China and preventing Beijing in realizing its long-term goals of impacting the Indian Ocean.

India is now in a dilemma. If India does not join the Maritime Silk Road, the Road will round India economically, which will abate its influence over the Indian Ocean region; while India's entering into the Road project will deepen and legitimize China's interference into the affairs in Indian Ocean region and possibly to some degrees devalue the Mekong–India Economic Corridor (MIEC).[12] Generally speaking, the Belt and Road Initiative and the BCIM Economic Corridor are in need of support and coordination of India, so is promoting the CPEC with Pakistan. However, the level of mutual political trust between China and India leads to India's concerns and hesitations and further prevents China from expending its cooperation with South Asia in depth and in scope.

4.2. Relations among countries in South Asia restrict the deepening of regional cooperation, offsetting diplomatic efforts China has made on the region to some degrees

The bilateral relationship between India and Pakistan is decisive element for regional stability. The detente for the two states accords with their practical and long-run benefits and both leaders share the same attitude toward this. In April 2010, the leaders of the two countries reached a consensus on solving all problems through dialogue at the 16th South Asia Association of Regional Cooperation (SAARC) summit in Thimbu of Bhutan. The foreign secretaries from both sides held a meeting in February 2011 where they decided to restore comprehensive dialogue process and made dialogues on eight topics, gaining however limited results. What is

---

[12] *Ibid.*

worse, almost all diplomatic efforts and progresses such as newly signed visa application agreement in September 2012 to facilitate staff mobility, the progresses in expending trade and staff exchanges after Prime Minister Nawaz Sharif assuming power in May 2013, and the new type economy-focused relations emphasized by Prime Minister Narendra Modi in May 2014 have evaporated due to the unceasing firefights over Kashmir disputes.

From the perspective of long-term historical trends, India–Pakistan relations have been lingering at a low level for a long period of time. The comprehensive dialogue process since 2008 made slow progresses and repeatedly fell into the wired circle of "easing up, going worse, and then suspending". American scholars even hold that the two governments are not ready yet for detente in the real sense in the case of domestic political conditions, for the reasons that hardliners are still in firm positions[13] and more importantly the political power of Pakistan is not strong enough.[14]

To some extent, China needs the understanding from India as to promoting the CPEC with Pakistan in western district of South Asia. At the same time, China is in need of the understanding and support from Pakistan to build the BCIM Economic Corridor in eastern region of South Asia. However, given current relations between India and Pakistan, India suspects political, military and strategic intentions of China to advocate the CPEC, while Pakistan has misgivings towards China's diplomatic practices that prefer India by promoting the BCIM Economic Corridor. Therefore, as China is emphasizing on develop relations with South Asian countries as a whole and in a balanced manner, the tensions between

---

[13] Declan Walsh: "U.S. Troop Pullout Affects India-Pakistan Rivalry", NYTIMES, August 16, 2013. Retrieved from http://siasitv.com/u-s-troop-pullout-affects-india-pakistan-rivalry/ and http://sunraynews.com/us-troop-pullout-affects-india-pakistan-rivalry-new-york-times/.

[14] Alison Burke and Delaney Parrish: "Welcoming Indian Prime Minister Modi to the Global Stage: Brookings Experts Weigh in", May 19, 2014, retrieved from http://www.brookings.edu/blogs/brookings-now/posts/2014/05/welcoming-indian-prime-minister-modi-to-the-global-stage.

India and Pakistan will definitely offset China's diplomatic progresses in that region.

There are many problems in bilateral relations between India and Bangladesh. Bangladesh has been supporting the BCIM initiative, although it has divergences on plenty of issues with India. The two countries have carried out frequent high-level mutual visits and resolved the delimitation of shared border and the Bay of Bengal through signing agreements or international arbitration since Bangladeshi Premier Minister Sheikh Hasina paid a visit to India. Nevertheless, conflicts over water resources, illegal immigration, transborder crimes, and transregional terrorism that influence bilateral relations have not been solved effectively. However, a positive progress has been made at the third ministerial level Joint Consultative Committee (JCC) conference in September 2014, where both India and Bangladesh responded positively to the proposal of holding BCIM Economic Corridor in Bangladesh and promoting cooperation among the four countries.[15]

4.3. Terrorism, religious extremism and separatism still exist in the region, posing severe threats to regional and national security

South Asia is the region under the most severe terrorist threat in the world. Regional terrorism, religious extremist forces and separatist forces have always been the major threats. The Bilateral Security Agreement signed between the US and Afghanistan in September 2014 has laid a legal foundation for combating terrorist forces in South Asia, Afghanistan in particular, afterwards. On the other hand, NATO and the American armies remained in Afghanistan after 2014, generating profound influence on the evolvement of situations in that country and regional patterns. The

---

[15] High Commission of India, Dhaka, Bangladesh, "Joint Statement on the Third Meeting of the India–Bangladesh Joint Consultative Commission", New Delhi, September 20, 2014, http://hcidhaka.gov.in/pages.php?id=1582.

agreement lessens the possibility of military force's returning back to Kabul in next several years. At the meantime, the agreement has been used as an excuse for Taliban hardliners to upgrade violent activities; countries in South Asia started to question the intention of the remaining American armies and military bases in Afghanistan, the core region of Eurasian Continent.

Pakistan, where China promotes its CPEC initiative, is one of the South Asian countries under severest terrorist threats. For a long period of time, terrorist forces dominated by Tehrik-i-Taliban Pakistan (TTP) in Khyber Pakhtunkhwa (KP), ethnic separatist forces in Balochistan, religious extremist forces scattered across the country, and underworld forces in Karachi and north Sindh have brought serious challenges to various levels in society and the country. Terrorist attacks have increased dramatically since 2013. The Pakistan Institute for Peace released the 2013 Pakistan Security Report, indicating the there were 1717 cases of terrorist attacks in 2013 killing 2451 and injuring 5438 and both numbers of attacks and casualties raised compared to those in 2012.[16] Besides, according to the statistics by the South Asia Terrorism Portal (SATP), around 54.6 thousand people were killed in terrorist attacks from 2003 to October 2014, of which 19.5 thousand were common people, 5938 were from security armies, and 29.1 thousand were terrorists. Frequent terrorist attacks severely affect the economic development, social stability, and infrastructure construction in Pakistan. Prime Minister Nawaz Sharif set up an anti-terrorist strategy of "negotiation coming first and combining negotiation with combat" and under such framework he expressed in many occasions that the government would like to negotiate with terrorist forces (TTP). This proposal won the support of most citizens. However, it was grounded and finally shattered as interior groups of the forces can reach an agreement on their demands. The terrorists have launched several attacks in Pakistan since 2014. The "Strike of the Sword" aiming at eliminating terrorists received little effects.

---

[16]PIPS, "Pakistan Security Report 2013", Retrieved from http://pakpips.com/securityreport.php.

The BCIM Economic Corridor, according to the plan, passes Bangladesh and Northeastern India, the latter being the harder hit area of turbulences since India obtained its ethnic independence. In that region, terrorist movements, armed violence, bloody conflicts, and terrorist events are prevalent. From 2005 to October 2014, around 18.9 thousand people were killed in terrorist attacks and turbulences across India, of which 5761 people lost their lives in the rebellions and turbulences in northeastern area of India, and 6588 people were dead from anti-government movements by Naxalites, a left-wing extremist organization that controls over 17 provinces and 92,000 km^2. During the same period, 1206 people were killed in terrorist attacks in Bangladesh.[17] And as many as 111.9 thousand people were killed in terrorist activities from 2003 to October 26, 2014 across South Asia.[18]

There are also elements causing uncertainty in Myanmar during the construction of BCIM Economic Corridor. As an ASEAN member that is adjacent to China, Myanmar is a key country for building BCIM Economic Corridor. The uncertainties of Myanmar mainly come from two aspects. One is the trend of China–Myanmar relations. Myanmar has been seeking for big power balance in its foreign policies since the democratic reform and getting closer to western countries both politically and economically. It is enthusiastic in developing friendly relations with the US, Japan, and India. In the meantime, China-Myanmar relations have to overcome many problems and challenges. The other is that the security situations in Myanmar are not optimistic. Myanmar holds positive attitudes towards the BCIM initiative. For example, President Thein Sein when met with Chinese Prime Minister Wang Yi, expressed that Myanmar would like to actively participate in building the BCIM Economic Corridor.[19] However, the BCIM Economic Corridor has to pass the turbulent northern areas of

---

[17] See SATP, http://www.satp.org/satporgtp/southasia/datasheets/Fatalities. html.

[18] *Ibid*.

[19] Myanmar President Thein Sein met with Wang Yi, August 11, 2014. Retrieved from http://news.xinhuanet.com/world/2014-08/11/c_1112029512.htm.

Myanmar that have long been controlled under anti-government armed forces. President Thein Sein has been working on political conciliation and cease-fire with a dozen of armed forces made up of ethnic minorities including Karen National Union since he came to power. But how to deal with armed ethnic minorities and realize national cease-fire and ethnic conciliation remain to be the main challenge to Myanmar government in the future.

4.4. Other connection projects exist in South Asia

The first project is the New Silk Road Plan (NSRP) that was proposed by the US. The NSRP can be traced back to the 1990s. In the very beginning, the US supported the Central Asia Regional Economic Cooperation (CAREC) put forth with by the ADB in 1997. Latter, US government has initiated the Silk Road Strategy Act for two times in 1999 and 2006 respectively but the act wasn't passed by the Congress. In July 2011, the US put forward with the New Silk Road plan once again, hoping to integrate the future of Afghanistan with Pakistan, India, South Asia and even Southeast Asian countries. The purposes of NSRP are to develop a function of "self blooding making" so as to boot its economy and social development, to promote cooperation among nations in the region to improve regional security, to assure dominance of the US in regional development, to maintain and fortify the American influence over the region so as to weaken that of Russia's and China's. NSRP is a comprehensive plan that covers South Asia, Central Asia and even Southeast Asia and West Asia and focuses on clear the way for economic cooperation and energy transportation between Afghanistan with South Asia and even Southeast Asia. However, given domestic economic situations of the US, the shift of global strategic focus, regional safety situations and relations among countries within the region, the US had a tough time promoting the NSRP. By October 2013, the US has offered a financial support of 2 billion USD to Afghanistan for the use of electricity generation and transportation, and energy reforms, built more than 3,000 kms of road, help the country with the establishment of National Railway Bureau and the planning of national railway development, and provided technical support for putting the fiber-optical of 4,000 kms across Afghanistan.[20] But the two key projects of NSPR, namely "CASA-1000" project[21] and TAPI project,[22] made slow progresses.

Second is the CCAP initiative by India. The Connecting Central Asia Policy was originally put forward with at the first India–Central Asia Dialogue in June 2012. The policy appeals to establish colleges, hospitals, information technical centers, long-distance medical network connection, and joint-venture enterprises, to improve aerial connection to boost trade and tourism, and to carry out joint scientific research in fields of defense and security issues and form strategic partners. Prime Minister S. M. Krishna identified CCAP as "commerce, connection, consulate, and community".[23] In

---

[20] Stephen Kaufman: "'New Silk Road' Vision Offers Afghanistan a Brighter Future", 28 October 2013, https://geneva.usmission.gov/2013/10/29/new-silk-road-vision-offers-afghanistan-a-brighter-future/.

[21] "CASA-1000" project refers to the electric system that go through Central Asia and South Asia to connect Kyrgyzstan, Tajikistan, Pakistan and Afghanistan, Transporting surplus electricity in Kyrgyzstan and Tajikistan in summer to Afghanistan and Pakistan which are lack of electricity. The project was put forward with as early as November 2007 but wasn't put into operation due to security and provision problems. On February 20, 2014, the Energy Ministers of Kyrgyzstan, Tajikistan, Afghanistan and Pakistan signed the inter-governmental agreement on CASA-1000 project in Washington, D.C. According to feasibility study reports, the CASA-1000 project is related to 1000 megawatt of high-pressure transmission line that as long as 759 kms with an estimated investment of 1 billion USD. As to the financing of the project, the World Bank and the Islamic Development Bank will contribute to 40% and 20% of financing. And ADB and the Arab Bank are inclined to join the project financing. The project, according to the agreement, is supposed to be accomplished in 2018.

[22] TAPI is a natural gas pipeline project that connects Turkmenistan, Afghanistan, Pakistan, and India. The conception has been brought forth with by the US in the 1990s. It was designed to transport natural gas recovered in Turkmenistan to Pakistan and India through Afghanistan. In 2010, presidents of Turkmenistan, Afghanistan, Pakistan, and India signed a cooperative agreement to work together to push forward the construction of the TAPI natural gas pipeline.

[23] Jyoti Prasad Das: "India's 'Connect Central Asia' Policy", October 29, 2012, http://www.foreignpolicyjournal.com/2012/10/29/indias-connect-central-asia-policy/#. UzqYgBHNu70.

fact, such non-traditional security elements as the acquisition of energy and resources, commercial and trade opportunities, and terrorist threats and China's rising influence on Central Asia are five decisive factors for India to release the CCAP plan. The US provides with India favorable conditions to carry out CCAP via NSRP, in return expecting that India can play a critical role in its NSRP. Nonetheless, NSRP needs the support and cooperation from Pakistan, which worries India most. To reduce the risks of being dependent on NSRP, India conceived the idea of activating the "North–South Transport Corridor"[24] that passed Iran to connect with Central Asian countries. Besides, India looks for cooperation with Russia on TAPI projects and tries to talk Russia into building an oil pipeline that connects the two countries and is parallel to TAPI so as to realize the goal of purchasing oil from Russia.[25] The plans are big but hard to put into practice due to constraints of costs, geopolitics, and financing. And there are only three paths for India's energy management projects. The first one is IPI that should pass Iran and Pakistan. The second is TAPI that needs to pass Afghanistan and Pakistan. The last one is the oil pipeline from Russia to India but it has to pass China. The first two paths are confronted with the problem and dilemma of relations with Pakistan and the third one has to go through disputed areas between India and China.[26]

---

[24] The idea of building "North–South Transport Corridor" was originally coined in 2000. By 2012, sixteen countries have participated in the project, including all Central Asian countries. The main function of this corridor is to connect ports on western cost of India and Bandar Abbas and Chah Bahar in Iran. Goods will be transported by railway to a Iranian port in the Caspian Sea and then to Central Asian countries, Russia and North Europe through either sea shipping or land routes on Azerbaijan. Given that Myanmar and Thailand are connected to India by both land and sea, the plan is expected to boost trade in Southeast Asia and Europe.
[25] "Plan to route crude from Russia in pipeline", *Financial Express*, January 15, 2014, http://archive.financialexpress.com/news/plan-to-route-crude-from-russia-in-pipeline/1218372.
[26] C. Raja Mohan: "The Great Game Folio: Russian Pipeline", Carnegie Endowment for International Peace, July 16, 2014, http://carnegieendowment.org/2014/07/16/great-game-folio-russian-pipeline.

The third is the MIEC under the framework of India's Look East Policy (LEP). The Mekong-India Economic Corridor (MIEC) is a notion derived from the Southern Economic Corridor (SEC) under the framework of Mekong Subregional cooperation, as well as an important constituent in the Bay of Bengal Initiative for Multisectoral Technical and Economic Cooperation (BIMSTEC) in 2004 and a part of the Asian Highway Network and Pan-Asian Railway initiative by the United Nations Economic and Social Commission for Asia and Pacific (UNESCAP). The MIEC is a comprehensive network that includes land and sea transportation which extends the SEC westwards to connect with the emerging markets in Myanmar and Southeast Asia through India. The corridor includes such nations as India, Myanmar, Thailand, the Laos, Cambodia, and Vietnam. The Indian government actively promoted the research on the MIEC and took it as an important constituent of the LEP and the policy of economic integration with ASEAN countries. India fastened the implementation of the MIEC after reaching the CEPF with ASEAN by the end of 2012. However, although India and ASEAN postponed signing the FTA on service trade and investment, the Indian Ministry of Foreign Affairs is studying on the MIEC which excludes China.

The fourth is India's Project Mausam. In face of China's growing ability and influence over the region of Indian Ocean, Modi's government has been ready to initiate a major diplomatic strategy, namely the Project Mausam. Project Mausam is a plan of trans-Indian Ocean sea voyage and cultural landscape, covering the Indian Ocean region in the broad sense from East Africa, Arabia, the subcontinent of India, Sri Lanka all the way to Southeast Asia. As South Asian scholars conclude, Project Mausam not only absorbs Indian culture and also contains serious strategic design, aiming at restore old sea routes, enhancing cultural connection of peripheral countries around the Indian Ocean, and competing China's 21st Century Maritime Silk Road by making use of its old relations. Although the Indian government hasn't mentioned details of the plan publicly, its intention of expanding its impact over the region psychologically, culturally and strategically is obvious.[27]

5. Conclusions

The Belt and Road Initiative and the two Corridors are strategic decision of China, being of profound significance to tightening economic and trade ties of China with Central Asia, South Asian countries and Eurasian countries, deepening regional exchanges and cooperation, planning China's development domestically and internationally as a whole, safeguarding neighboring environment, expanding Western Development and the space of openness. As the pivot of Maritime Silk Road and vital link in the middle of the Belt and Road, South Asia is the key region for China to promote grand strategy.

China is endowed with several major opportunities during promoting the Belt and Road Initiative and two Economic Corridors in South Asia.

Firstly, China has willingness and ability. China put its neighboring diplomacy of "amity, sincerity, mutual benefit, and inclusiveness" into actions, hoping to be on friendly terms with South Asian countries and contributing to the development of the region. By taking the wings of the Belt and the Road, China is committed to achieve economic takeoff together with South Asian countries. Through the two Economic Corridors, China wishes to invite 3 billion people on two sides of Himalayas to share with China peace, friendship, stability and prosperity.[28] Besides, China is actively preparing for the establishment of the AIIB and Silk Road Funds to facilitate the implementation of the Belt and Road

---

[27] Akhilesh Pillalamarri: "Project Mausam: India's Answer to China's 'Maritime Silk Road'", September 18, 2014. Retrieved from http://thediplomat.com/2014/09/project-mausam-indias-answer-to-chinas-maritime-silk-road/.

[28] Chinese President Xi Jinping delivers speech at Indian Council of World Affairs. December 1, 2015. Retrieved from http://english.cntv.cn/2014/09/19/VIDE 1411095370882449.shtml.

and to offer financial support for infrastructure construction of countries involved.

Secondly, South Asian countries have needs. The Belt and Road Initiative and economic corridors fit perfectly with national development strategies of relevant South Asian countries. China's capability, in the eyes of South Asian countries, has no match in terms of large infrastructure construction. South Asia is badly in need of improvement and construction of infrastructure facilities, and attracting foreign investment on infrastructure to pull up economy and social development. China, on the other hand, owns considerable foreign exchange reserves and excessive output capacity, thus showing impetus and demands for investing over-seas. By now, China has invited South Asian countries including China to join in the construction of the AIIB. At the fifth Multilateral Consultations on AIIB preparation, twenty one countries till September 2014 that had decided to or were willing to be the initial members of the AIIB reached a consensus on the final draft of AIIB Preparation Memo, including five countries in South Asia as India, Pakistan, Bangladesh, Sri Lanka, and Nepal.

Thirdly, it is possible that India will participate in the 21st Century Maritime Silk Road. India's willingness for cooperation is the biggest uncertainty China is faced with in implementing and promoting its Initiative, although Modi's government is at least adopting a double-rail policy which strengthens economical connection with China and counterbalances China's growing strength.[29] Indian Prime Minister Modi described the vision of India–China relations as "Inch towards Miles",[30] for which reason some Indian scholars believe that India should take part in and

---

[29] "India and Japan Pursue Closer Ties to Counter China", WSJ, September 1, 2014, http://online.wsj.com/articles/indias-prime-minister-narendra-modi-wants-closer-ties-with-japan-to-counter-china-1409555754.

[30] Literally, "Inch toward Miles" means the changes of length. However, 'Inch' indicates "India–China" and Miles refer to "millennium of exceptional synergy". See "INCH" towards MILES: Modi's China mantra", The Times of India, September 17, 2014, retrieved from http://timesofindia.indiatimes.com/india/INCH-towards-MILES-Modis-China-mantra/articleshow/42670778.cms.

exert its influence on the Road initiative.[31] Besides, as to join the AIIB, India didn't respond actively initially. But China is now definitely taking India as a potential partner in an interconnected neighboring political and economic network.[32] In this regard, Indian officials declared that, "we need funds and the right of speech in an organization, based on which logics we should join in the AIIB."[33] In October 2014, India made its standpoint more clearly, "India has its own concerns but it should join in … We are discussing on concerned issues. Hopefully they can be solved soon."[34] Besides, the support to the Road Initiative of South Asian countries as Maldives, Sri Lanka and Bangladesh poses pressure on India. In order to avoid being isolated and marginalized, India has to respond to the initiative positively.

Fourthly, the NSRP of the US and the connection plans India is planning or implementing set their targets in national and regional development, stability and prosperity, which accord with the aims of China's initiative. Besides, China's initiative is complementary to connection plans of South Asian countries instead of replacing others. As for the NSRP, there are only a few countries like Kazakhstan in South Asia that are in support of the plan while most of the countries and scholars are having low expectations towards it. Particularly, as the influence of China and Russia on Central Asia keeps growing in the framework of SCO, Afghanistan and Central Asian countries are looking forward to the Silk Road Economic Belt.

---

[31] C. Raja Mohan: "Silk route to Beijing", *The Indian Express*, September 15, 2014, http://indianexpress.com/article/opinion/columns/silk-route-to-beijing/.

[32] Atul Aneja: "China invites India to join Asian Infrastructure Investment Bank", *The Hindu*, June 30, 2014, http://www.thehindu.com/todays-paper/tp-national/china-invites-india-to-join-asian-infrastructure-investment-bank/article6161311.ece.

[33] "India Considering Joining New Regional Infrastructure Bank", *The Wall Street Journal*, August 27, 2014, http://online.wsj.com/articles/india-considering-joining-new-regional-infrastructure-bank-1409149842.

[34] "India likely to join Asian infrastructure bank", *The Times of India*, October 6, 2014, http://timesofindia.indiatimes.com/business/india-business/India-likely-to-join-Asian-infrastructure-bank/articleshow/44455632.cms.

Fifthly, South Asia is a key area to promote the Belt and Road while India a big power in that region. Therefore, India is of significance for China to promote its initiatives. India is willing to and needs to be a part of it. However, India's participation does not mean the remove of its misgivings and concerns. At present, India, although being less competitive in trade and economics, is in a relatively advantageous position in security field due to geopolitical and political factors. Besides, India is eager to enhance cooperation with the US, Japan, parts of ASEAN countries, and neighboring South Asian countries in economy, politics, and security. The reason why Modi's government amended India's relation with its neighbors as Nepal, Bangladesh, and Bhutan is to establish an advantageous position in South Asia. Moreover, its diplomatic focus leans towards the US, Japan and Australia is partially counterbalancing China.

Lastly, South Asia is the key area and joint point for the 21st Century Maritime Silk Road. The region as a whole is indispensable for the initiative without doubt, while India's absence in the initiative will not hold back the implementation of the initiative. Different to passages on land, the construction of passages for the Maritime Silk Road is possible by "Leap frog promotion". Nevertheless, India's participation will surely increase the confidence in other countries and erase their worries and concern, thus contributing to a deeper and wider cooperation under the framework of the Maritime Silk Road.

To sum up, the nature of big power relations are competition and cooperation, so is China–India relation. From the perspective of the dimension of current economic development, China has advantages in economy, but China's initiative on interconnection in South Asia will boost China's infrastructure construction and pull its economy. As to political dimension, China has regarded India as an important partner in the international society and looked for partnership of development for peace and prosperity, although India still has worries towards how China will influence the region of Indian Ocean with its initiative. The worries include factors of traditional foreign policy, of ethnic psychology, and realistic ones as current cooperative mechanism in dominant region. India's final solution and policy to respond to China's initiatives will depend on the answers to how to acquire economic profits from participating in the Road initiative, to how to constrain China's influence in the region and at the same time to fortify the roles of and dominate SAARC, Indian Ocean–Alliance Regional Cooperation (IO–ARC), and multilateral maritime security mechanism in the Indian Ocean such as Indian Ocean Naval Symposium (IONS).

Chapter 10

Central Asian Countries and the Silk Road Economic Belt

Baoyi

Russia and Middle Asia Research Institute
Chinese Academy of Social Sciences
larisabao@163.com

The Silk Road Economic Belt blueprint covering more than 40 countries and 3 billion populations across the Eurasia is a brand new regional cooperation model. Up till now, no President Xi's speech or official document offer detailed explanation for the strategic positioning or major content. The goal of the blueprint is to include countries like Russia and those in the Middle Asia in active conversation and in establishing an interregional comparative advantage, a community of shared interest and destiny, thus achieving common progress. Today, the Asia Investment Bank and Asia Fund Plan under the frame of Silk Road Economic Belt have received positive responses from Central Asian countries.

1. What is Silk Road Economic Belt?

Silk Road Economic Belt is a strategic concept of economic geography. Starting from Central Asia, the Belt builds a trans-Eurasia transportation line based on ancient Silk Road. It serves as an axis.

Countries and cities with economic advantages along the axis will act as an engine to pull up the economic conditions of regions around them. By linking dot to dot and line to line, the comprehensive regional cooperation will be formed gradually.[1] President Xi brought up five goals for building the Belt, which are policy communication, road connection, smooth flow of goods, free circulation of currencies and common aspiration of peoples. Specifically speaking, the Belt aims at promoting economic cooperation, realizing infrastructure connectivity, easy trade and investment, convenient currency exchange and settlement with local currencies, as well as laying social foundation for economic development. In the short term, the Belt may not contribute a lot to China's economic and international trade aggregate, while in the long run, it will facilitate the building of a transportation path from the Pacific Ocean to the Baltic, and the realization of road connection and free trade and investment. The Belt is expected to grow into a region of rapid development, exporting goods of a stronger competitive edge with relatively low logistical and transportation cost. To China, cities and regions along the Belt will become its new engines of economic growth.[2] As the beginning of the Silk Road, the western region of China is expected to spring many economic growth points that will boost the cause of western development up onto a new stage. The Belt is the new diplomatic strategy of China towards Eurasia, including not only Central Asia, but also South and West Asia and Europe.

The Silk Road Economic Belt is a cultural link. The Silk Road is a cultural concept as the historical witness of cultural exchanges between East and West. Communication and integration of Chinese and Western material and cultural products have formed a solid

---

[1]"Present Xi Gave Important Speech on Building Silk Road Economic Belt Collectively", July 9, 2013. Retrieved from http://news.xinhuanet.com/world/2013-09/07/c_117272280.htm.

[2]Cao Yun: "4 Strategic Goals of Silk Road Economic Belt", *Chinese Social Sciences Weekly*, January 10, 2014. Retrieved from http://www.cssn.cn/skyskl/skyskl_qyjj/201401/t20140110_940419.shtml.

foundation for exchanges and cooperation among countries and regions along the Silk Road, providing a prerequisite for cultural identity. As a cultural brand with rich cultural and historical connotations and symbolic meaning, Silk Road can be easily accepted and recognized among Central Asian countries and those along this Road. The tradition of cultural exchanges has laid foundation for humanity cooperation, which will help China to reshape its image in this area.

The Silk Road Economic Belt is also a Chinese style of integration. The increasing interdependency in political security and economic development calls for regional integration. Central Asia is an age-old wrestling ring for external parties. Since its independence, major powers including the US and Russia have been selling their integration plans to it. The New Silk Road Plan, led by the US, centers on Afghanistan, connecting India, Pakistan and South Asian countries with the five Central Asian countries. Russia promotes an integration process for Commonwealth of Independent States, led by Collective Security Treaty Organization and Customs Union. Japan brought up an economic and energy cooperation mechanism between Japan and Central Asian countries named "The Silk Road", while Turkey raised Turks Integration. The contention of major powers forces Central Asian countries to make either single or multiple choices. Hence, the Silk Road Economic Belt is defined as a Chinese way of integration by Western media. In fact, it differs from other integration plans by its inclusive nature. It is by no means a tool and platform for China to mark out its own sphere of influence.

Moreover, different from Shanghai Cooperation Organization, the Belt is not a regional cooperation organization with interior structure or framework. It promotes the construction of a community of shared interest and destiny in accordance with China's new outlook of regional development and security. This trans-regional cooperation mode does not feature leadership of major powers nor regional segmentation. It encourages participation and win–win cooperation of multiple parties. Sun Weidong, Chinese Minister to Kazakhstan pointed it out that the building of Silk Road Economic

Belt is more a common goal of the entire region than a single country's mission as it will not only benefits participants but advances multilateral cooperation. Transport facilities are taken as the focus of construction and economic growth as the major objective. By building the Belt, China intends to eliminate trade barriers, spur economic growth, improve quality of trades, unlock investment potential in other countries, and boost the regional economic cooperation to a new level.[3]

2. Interest Requests of Central Asian Countries from Silk Road Economic Belt

Silk Road Economic Belt is also considered as the longest economic corridor with most potential in the world, on which a significant contrast could be witnessed between the ends, namely Chinese Eastern coastal region and Western Europe with advanced economy, and the middle, namely an economic sag area of Chinese Western region and Central Asia with underdeveloped economy. As continental countries, Central Asian countries lack estuaries, which lead to incomplete infrastructure and liaison with the outside world. Tajikistan and Kyrgyzstan even suffer insufficient natural resources, holding back their economic development. To realize transportation and trade facilitation and to form coupling effects on economic development are urgent needs of Central Asian countries. Hence, the five goals of Silk Road Economic Belt, especially the initiative of cooperating in connectivity have received active responds from Central Asian countries along the Belt.

Kazakhstan, with its rocketing oil economy and growth potentials, has become a major economy in Central Asia. Recently, it has also expanded political influence in the region through presence on political platforms including World Congress of Religions, Conference on Interaction and Confidence Building Measures in Asia and Shanghai Cooperation Organization. All oil and natural

---

[3] "Kazakhstan: We should build Silk Road Economic Belt Free Trade Zone", *International Affairs Southern Metropolis Daily*, May 25, 2014.

gas pipelines from Central Asia to China go through Kazakhstan. The country plays an indispensable role in Silk Road Economic Belt. It can, as what China expects it to be, be a competent pivot point with its economic aggregate and influence. The country positions itself as the gate and bridge on the Belt through which China reaches the Caspian Sea and Russia directly and Asia-Pacific region connects to Europe. It looks forward to turning its geographic disadvantages into geo-economic advantages, seeking a new way for economic growth and shaking off its reliance on energy export through international transportation and logistical economy. Kazakhstan government fully agreed on the Silk Road Economic Belt initiative and had high hopes for cooperation in transportation, in particular, regarding which the government raised series of implementation schemes. Hanneche Sultanov, Senator of Kazakhstan Parliament and former Kazakhstan Ambassador to China, indicated that "the initiative would tap economic and trade potentials between China and Kazakhstan, which is beneficiary to Kazakhstan and even the entire Central Asia". He also expressed that Nursultan Nazarbayev, Kazakhstan President, supports the initiative, considering infrastructure construction highly important to the Belt. For example, the international transportation corridor program from Chinese Western region to Western Europe would expand commodity exchanges between China and Kazakhstan, create more jobs and promote infrastructure construction in cities along the Belt.[4] Genis Kasimbek, Transportation Minister of Kazakhstan pointed out that transportation cooperation is the priority and foundation of building Silk Road Economic Belt and "Kazakhstan is ready to collaborate with China in completing large-scale programs". In June 2014, Elgin Malbecof, Deputy Chief of Railway Director, Ministry of Transportation of Kazakhstan, said that "Kazakhstan is an essential bridge connecting the East and the West; the Belt initiative is the revival of ancient Silk Road". Transit railways provide major

---

[4] "Kazakhstan Attaching Huge Hope to Silk Road Economic Belt", *Economic Daily News*, June 13, 2014, http://finance.sina.com.cn/roll/20140613/062019399860.shtml.

capital support for the rapid growth of Kazakhstan economy, reducing its reliance on Russia. The country expects to strengthen the construction railways, drive ways and airline network in Central Asia by making full use of China's technologies and funds. In the President's State of Union address for 2015 released in November 2014, Nazarbayev stressed that Kazakhstan would initiate a new economic policy of the Bright Road in 2015 in order to improve infrastructure construction, especially in transportation. It is clear that the country determines to cooperate with China and make something of the Belt initiative.

The foreign minister of Kazakhstan indicated that Silk Road Economic Belt generally agrees with the initiative of Kazakhstan-New Silk Road promoted by President Nazarbayev at the 25th Meeting of the Council of Foreign Investors held in May 2012. Nazarbayev suggested that "Kazakhstan should revive its historical role and become the biggest business and transit hub of Central Asian region, a distinctive bridge between Europe and Asia".[5] The country is capable of developing strong transportation and logistics services with its geographical advantage, sound economic growth and investment climate, as well as its identity as a Customs Union member. By the new Silk Road plan, Kazakhstan aims at developing transportation and logistical infrastructure so as to become a main transport artery connecting Asia-Pacific region and Europe. The project of New Silk Road is based on the "principle of 5S" — Speed, Service, Cost, Safety and Stability.[6] Specifically speaking, the project includes integration of transport infrastructure, railway construction and economic development along the railways by 2020,[7] as well as the building of a united transportation and logistics corporate with Russia and Belarus. Combined with

---

[5] "Closing Speech of the President of the Republic of Kazakhstan N.A. Nazarbayev at the 25th Meeting of the Council of Foreign Investors", May 22, 2012, http://www.kazlogistics.kz/en/useful/orders_president/detail.php?id=1516.

[6] C stands for the initiative letter of high speed, service, value, maintenance and stable in Russian. The Economic Corridor of New Silk Road, http://www.kazlogistics.kz/ru/media_center/interview/detail.php?id=577.

[7] The revival of Silk Road and the change of global trade route, June 8, 2014.

the suggestion of China–Kazakhstan Trade Corridor brought up by President Xi, Kazakhstan initiated a Silk Road Economic Corridor between the two countries.[8]

Another reason why the Silk Road Economic Belt is so attractive to Central Asian countries like Kazakhstan is that it paves the way for inland countries in Central Asia to sell their goods overseas. At the opening ceremony of China–Kazakhstan Lianyun Port Logistics Station Project in May 2014, officials of Kazakhstan pointed out that the Station is not only Kazakhstan's biggest logistics base in China but will also become an international economic platform for the five countries in Central Asia. Many proposals in the Silk Road Economic Belt such as "stressing on transportation interconnection" and "improving trans-regional transport system so as to form a transport network that connects East, West, and South Asian regions" under the framework of Shanghai Cooperation Organization, accord with the development goals of the New Silk Road project of Kazakhstan.

As to trade and investment facilitation, Kazakhstan advocates improving investment environment and building a free trade area (FTA) along the new Silk Road. On May 23, 2014, the Minister of Economic Integration of Kazakhstan (Ministry of Economic Integration of Kazakhstan) welcomes foreign companies to invest in Kazakhstan with promises of maximum convenience and suggests build free trade zones with countries along Silk Road Economic Belt.[9] Kazakhstan values integrated traffic lanes for the reason that they create more space for trades along Silk Road and optimize the allocation of businesses and factors of production in the region. The Minister pointed out that the Silk Road Economic Belt will promote the economic and trade integration in Central Asia and bring along opportunities of historic significance from which countries involved will benefit.

---

[8] New Silk Road economic corridor, http://www.kazlogistics.kz/ru/media_center/interview/detail.php?id=577.
[9] "Kazakhstan: Build Silk Road Economic Belt Free Trade Zone," *International Affairs Nanfang Daily*, May 25th, 2014.

Cooperation in trade and economy between China and Kazakhstan is increasingly closer, fruitful and of strategic significance. During co-constructing the Belt, the two countries gain more possibilities for cooperation in trade, economy and investment, in energy industry in particular. Meanwhile, Kazakhstan is trying to simplify related investment red tape and upgrade commercial environment to attract more investment from countries including China.[10] At the same time, Kazakhstan stresses the value of energy diplomacy and utilizes energy as the tool to balance interests among superpowers, to attract foreign investment, and to intensify economic connection with external world. The Silk Road Economic Belt will give Kazakhstan access to large amount of foreign investment and advanced technologies, in virtue of which its economy will enter into a post-energy era. In this regard, the Belt provides a platform for energy cooperation and spurs the implementation of its energy strategy.[11] At present China's investment mainly focuses on energy and raw material industries and Chinese companies have become the biggest energy investors. Kazakhstan looks forward to more Chinese investment in non-energy field. In August 2014, Kazakhstan's first Executive Deputy Director of President's Fund indicated that China invests intensely on energy, light, and catering industries while there is still large room for infrastructure investment. The complementary nature of economic and trade cooperation between China and Kazakhstan hasn't been fully used and investment environment along the Belt is yet to be improved.[12]

Among Central Asian countries, Uzbekistan who has almost the same political influence with Kazakhstan, shows support to the Silk Road Economic Belt initiative. Uzbekistan has

---

[10] Kazakhstan Hopes High on Silk Road Economic Belt, *Economic Daily*, June 13, 2014. http://finance.sina.com.cn/roll/20140613/062019399860.shtml.

[11] *China and Kazakhstan Building Silk Road Economic Belt*, http://www.chinastock.com.cn/yhwz_about.do?methodCall=getDetailInfo&docId=4459415.

[12] *China-Kazakhstan Experts Discussing Silk Road Economic Belt: Project Implementation Realizes Industry Connection*, September 7, 2014, http://www.chinesetoday.com/en/article/919680.

been seeing itself as the "Bazantine" of Central Asia. Its sense of cultural superiority comes from the important role it played in ancient Silk Road. Samarkand, Bukhara, and Khiva of Uzbekistan are all famous historical cities and stops that all passengers along the ancient Silk Road had to pass through. Natural resource in the country is abundant and its agriculture economy is basically self-sufficient. It always take an independent stand in its policies towards foreign affairs. After independence, Kazakhstan grew dramatically and replaced Uzbekistan as the leader of Central Asia, discouraging the latter. The Authoritarian management and unique foreign policy of President Karimov leave the country constantly tangled among the geopolitical game of superpowers like Russia and the US, therefore losing more political support. The factors above restrain its economy from sustainable development.

Silk Road Economic Belt offers Uzbekistan an opportunity to revitalize national culture, to resume national confidence and to find new economic development spot. China has been in good long-term relationship with the country and even escalated the partnership to a strategic one in 2012. Up till 2013, China has become the biggest investor and the second largest trade partner in Uzbekistan. In May 2014, President Xi suggested that the two countries make a five-year plan for their cooperation under the framework of the Silk Road Economic Belt to facilitate cooperation in economy and trade, energy and telecommunication, and to speed up the laying of China–Mid Asia natural gas pipeline.[13] Uzbekistan highly values its strategic partnership with China. The two have established cooperative relationship in various fields such as economy and trade, transportation and energy and both are working together on the construction of trans-national railways like China–Kyrgyzstan–Uzbekistan railway.

---

[13] President Xi Proposes to Restore the Great Silk Road with Uzbekistan, May 25, 2014, http://www.uznews.net/ru/world/26429-si-czinpin-predlozhil-uzbekistanu-soobscha-vosstanavlivat-velikij-shelkovyj-put.

Different from other resource exporters, Kyrgyzstan and Kazakhstan trade much with China their agricultural and livestock products and other reproducible ones that take larger proportion in their national economy. Abdul Daev, Foreign Minister of Kyrgyzstan, when elaborating the possible trade complementary structure and the investment advantages of Kyrgyzstan, pointed out that agricultural, livestock and some chemical and textile products may be main part of goods exported to China in the future.[14] Sally Jef, Economic Minister of Kyrgyzstan believed that China–Kyrgyzstan cooperation could go deeper and larger, "hopefully, with China's help, the export trade volume will be enhanced." At the same time, he expressed his expectation of advancing Kyrgyzstan's industrial economy with the aid of China's Belt initiative.

In general, the five Central Asian countries expect more in-depth cooperation in industries than increment of trade and investment. Kazakhstan is the most active one of the five. It makes transportation network and infrastructure construction as the focus of future cooperation and investment and become the first Central Asian country to join Asian Infrastructure Investment Bank.

Of course, negative propaganda against the Silk Road Economic Belt is unavoidable. Most of Central Asian citizens know little about China and the third party never stops anti-China propaganda in the region, leading to misunderstanding of the China's foreign policies. After President Xi brought up the initiative of Silk Road Economic Belt, China Threat Theory came along as well. Having had a prejudice against China's economic and migrant issues, Central Asian countries worry that the Belt might bring about unfavorable results. As media in some countries assert, the Silk Road Economic Belt showcases the diplomatic ambition and even "soft invasion" of Chinese government. The economic development of China thus is always linked with "resource exploitation", "output-based development", and "environment deterioration".

---

[14]*Kyrgyzstan Foreign Minister: Silk Road Economic Belt Promising.* February 1, 2014, CRI, http://news.cnr.cn/special/sczl/zxxx/201402/t20140201_514779009.shtml.

There is also an opinion in Central Asia that the closer the economic relation with China, the more they rely on Chinese economy and eventually they will become either the markets of Chinese products or energy or raw material sources for China. The opinion and bias reflect the disagreement of Central Asian countries to Chinese economic model. Therefore, some Central Asian countries take the FTA proposed by China with a grain of salt as they are afraid of loosing momentum of national industrialization once the FTA opens the gate for large flow of foreign goods.

3. Favorable and Unfavorable Elements for the Belt

In the long run, the Silk Road Economic Belt has a broad cooperation prospect. Central Asian countries along the Belt have long been in communication and cooperation with China, laying a solid foundation building the Belt. Meanwhile, due to geopolitical environment and social transition that Central Asian countries are experiencing, there are still many contradictions and problems in social, political, and economic development as well as in their external relations, which consequently incurs challenges and difficulties for China to deepen cooperation with Central Asian countries.

Firstly, there is a strong foundation for the cooperation between China and Central Asia. Over the past 20 years since the independence of the five Central Asian countries, China have long maintained a good political relations with them, and bilateral political relations is constantly upgraded. Currently, China has established strategic partnerships with Kazakhstan and Uzbekistan, the two major Central Asian countries, and established overall peace and political trust in the region. At the same time, China is the biggest trade partner and investor for almost all the Central Asian countries. For instance, China is the biggest investment source for Uzbekistan and Tajikistan, the second biggest investor for Kyrgyzstan, the biggest trade partner for Kazakhstan and Turkmenistan, and the second biggest trade partner for Uzbekistan and Kyrgyzstan. Those data indicate that there is certain complementariness in the economic development and growth of the five Central Asian countries with China. Besides, China shares a border of more than 3,300 km with three Central Asian countries, and China's four oil and natural gas pipelines cover all Central Asian countries. Therefore, Central Asian countries are stakeholders that share a common destiny with China, be it for the sake of national security or people's livelihood.

Secondly, most Central Asian countries are either developing countries or in transition period. Given their relatively backward economy, they are eager to become economically independent from big powers and find a way out of economic bottleneck through financial and technological support. Although all Central Asian countries have realized that integration will be the best solution, and there already exist some cooperation mechanisms of regional integration, an effective and integrated regional economic cooperation has yet to be established. Kazakhstan has never given up its conception of integration since independence, and brought forward many proposals for the integration of Central Asia. Moreover, Kazakhstan launched the initiative of three unions in Central Asia, i.e. water and energy union, transportation and communication union, and agricultural production union, to woo Uzbekistan, but it turned out to be fruitless. Up till now, Kazakhstan has joined Eurasian Integration initiated by Russia and become a Eurasian Economic Union (EEU) member. Kyrgyzstan and Tajikistan consider joining EEU as their priority in regional cooperation. Nevertheless the EEU is overtly exclusive and its looming political intention doesn't agree with Kazakhstan. From 2013 to 2014 in particular, Russia's tough stance in dealing with Ukraine issue and its disrespect to the sovereignty of the former Commonwealth of Independent States exposed its ambition to realize political integration in the post-soviet space via EEU, making Central Asian countries, including Kazakhstan very cautious about Russia's integration proposal.

As Ukraine crisis developed and oil price dropped due to Western countries' sanctions against Russia, Russia's economy has suffered a sharp decline. Since Central Asian countries are highly dependent on Russia's economy, they were most directly impacted, be it big energy exporters like Kazakhstan, Turkmenistan and Uzbekistan, or labor exporters like Kyrgyzstan and Tajikistan. In 2014, all Central Asian countries showed a relatively positive attitude towards the Silk Road Economic Belt Initiative. In November 2014, the President of Kazakhstan released the 2015 State of Union address ahead of schedule where he proposed the new economic policy of Bright Road, and appropriated $24 billion to support the development of small and medium-sized businesses and of major transportation and logistics routes, to establish special economic zones, to improve infrastructure in energy industry, to optimize economic structure, and to enhance people's living conditions and social welfare. In terms of transportation, Nazarbayev was inclined to connect the planning of domestic transportation with the Silk Road Economic Belt. In this regard, he put forward a series of large-scale infrastructure construction and upgrading plans, and urged the completion of transportation construction projects that connect the country with western Europe and western China. The President's State of Union address names the new economic policy as "the engine for future national economic growth", and considers it "a comprehensive step" for Kazakhstan to realize its goal of "becoming the top 30 of the world's most developed countries". Kassymbek, Minister of Transport and Communication would like to talk with China about headquartering the Silk Road Revitalization Program in Astana or Alma-Ata. Besides, Kazakhstan is also a participant of Asian Infrastructure Investment Bank as well as an active advocate for Shanghai Cooperation Organization Development Bank. Generally speaking, the Silk Road Economic Belt has received broad recognition among most Central Asian countries for the reason that its development philosophies of mutual equality, voluntary participation, peaceful coexistence, and mutual benefit and win–win results are in accordance with their needs for financial and technical support and effective regional cooperation, as well as goals of economic independence and development.

Most favorable elements come from interior demand and appeal for development of Central Asian countries, while unfavorable elements, which are more complicated, from both inside and outside the region.

First element is Russia. Russia has been traditionally exerting its influence over Central Asia, so its power and range of influence on the region should be taken seriously for Russia's attitude towards the Silk Road Economic Belt will immediately affect that of Central Asian countries. In 2012, Putin proposed a four-step strategy to realize Eurasian integration, i.e. a Customs Union, a unified economic space, an Eurasian Economic Union, and finally a Eurasian Union.[15] In the meantime, Russia's control and influence over Central Asia is exclusive, being against China as well. Russia's intention to reunite the former Commonwealth of the Independent States can be seen from its recent political behavior on those states. Therefore, the implementation Silk Road Economic Belt will inevitably been affected by Russia, and contradictions between China and Russia are foreseeable if China promotes regional economic and transportation integration in Central Asia. Nevertheless, being a historically major participator of the Silk Road, Russia's national interests are closely related to the Road as well. Hence, it would be better if China start the creation of a community of shared destiny in Eurasia by building one with Russia. In most cases, cooperation between China and Russia in Central Asia are externally impelled rather than self-motivated. Economic sanctions of the West against Russia, military withdrawal of the US and NATO from Afghanistan, terrorist activities and religious extremist forces in Central Asia will provide opportunities for the two countries to join hands in Central Asia.

Secondly, non-traditional security factors will continue trouble Central Asia. Despite that the American and NATO troops began to withdraw in a large scale from Afghanistan in 2014, local situation remained under control, and major countries in Central Asia such as Kazakhstan and Uzbekistan kept stable. So military conflicts in

---

[15] Zhao Huasheng: "China and US has the Potential to Cooperate Under the "New Sick Road" Initiative", *Oriental Morning* Post (*Shanghai Economic Review*), May 7, 2014, Retrieved from http://news.ifeng.com/a/20140506/40166435_0.shtml.

Afghanistan were not sever. Threat to Central Asia mainly comes from non-traditional field. Central Asia is the pathway for drug trafficking from Afghanistan. In order to smoothen the "drug trafficking transport corridor", international criminal groups often conspire with extremist forces and terrorists, who raise funds by drug trafficking, and help the former to disturb border control.[16] Religious extremism together with drug trafficking, is destroying border stability of Central Asia and posing a serious threat to the security systems of this region.

When it comes to political development, Central Asian countries are not uniform, but more and more diverse. In this regard, Central Asian countries could be divided into two groups. Resource export oriented countries, including Kazakhstan, Uzbekistan and Turkmenistan, are politically stable due to involvement of big powers' interests. Nonetheless, Kazakhstan and Uzbekistan are into a entering gerontocracy and new regimes need to be selected, which may lead to political vacuum during post-authoritarian period. Although both countries carried out political reforms in order to guarantee a smooth transition to new presidency and stable political situation in post-authoritarian era, many issues regarding the transition are still uncertain and unpredictable. On the other hand, Turkmenistan, with a relatively stable regime, has no need to change neither national leaders nor domestic political authorities. But the country still suffers relatively low living standard and in the meantime the government makes high welfare policies to buy domestic supports, the contrast between which decides that the country relies heavily on the high income via exporting natural gas.[17] That is a common practice for energy-based countries to maintain political stability, which indicates the fragility of their regime systems. Tajikistan and Kyrgyzstan, with relatively less resources, are confronted with unstable economic growth and

---

[16] Sun Zhuangzhi: "Hot spots and trend analysis of Central Asia security", *Journal of Xinjiang Normal University* (*Philosophy and Social Sciences*), 2011(02), Retrieved from http://www.faobserver.com/NewsInfo.aspx?id=6516.

[17] *Ibid.*

weak national defense. They even had to seek assistance from Russia with border control. Given that, Central Asian countries are still in need of in-depth independence. In a word, unstable national political authority and decreasing recognition for secular regime generally result in instabilities, providing shelter for religious extremism, terrorism and national separatism, as well as losing control on drug dealing, smuggling, and other organized crimes.

Finally, the strategic positioning of China on its existence and development would also impede the building of Silk Road Economic Belt to some degree. The initiative, upon its promotion, has been analyzed as an and continuation of China's previous strategies like "western development", "rise of central China", "going global of enterprises" and so on. Its strategical goals was to solve domestic issues regarding regional development, economic growth pattern, and industrial restructuring in the first place so as to maintain a high-speed economic growth and to absorb surplus domestic productivity. The connectivity to Europe and Asia ensures energy security and other strategic plans of China. Since countries along the Silk Road have their own plans and tempos for development and economic growth, not all countries would like to "stride forward" with China when the latter advertises its ambitious programs. Moreover, the environment issue in China's development pattern has become the new focus of China Threat Theory following immigration problem. Sustainable development and environmental friendliness are mentioned for many times in Russia and Central Asian countries' development strategies and plans. In comparison, the Silk Road Economic Belt advocates the pattern of government providing services and support for enterprises to develop. With enterprises playing a leading role on the stage government has set up, there are possibilities that they break their commitments to environmental protection in order to pursue profits even though they have made promises of introducing programs and industrial chains that are environmentally friendly and in accord with local demands.

In summary, the Silk Road Economic Belt meets the interest appeal for economic development and development ideal of regional cooperation of Central Asian countries, thus receiving positive responses. It is necessary for China to balance short-term and long-term benefits and partial and overall interests, and to combine the needs of national economic growth with diplomatic benefits outside China when building the Belt. While creating the community of shared interest, China should also make commitment to establishing a community of shared destiny by winning popular support, reducing concerns and reinforcing political mutual trust, in order to shape the image of a responsible power and divert public opinion from "China Threat Theory".

The Belt and Road Initiative and Hot Issues

Chapter 11

The Political Risk Analysis on China's Direct Investment Environment of the Belt and Road Initiative

Piao Zhuhua*, Liu Xiaomeng†, and Teng Zhuoyou‡

GrandView
*pzhuhua@yeah.net
†liuxiaomeng@grandviewcn.com
‡tengzhuoyou@grandviewcn.com

Since the Belt and Road Initiative was proposed for the first time by President Xi in 2013, Chinese governments at both central and local levels have put ideas into actions through top-level design. In 2013, China's foreign direct investment reached 90.17 billion USD. Under such circumstances, the initiatives were expected to accelerate the pace of going out for Chinese enterprises and to create new round of chances in markets. Nevertheless, risks are unavoidable. The present paper reveals political risks which Chinese enterprises are to encounter when going out and analyzes relevant cases. It suggests that companies take into full consideration recipient countries' political, economic and social situations in combination of their strategic goals when going out.

1. The Belt and Road Strategy and New Trends in Investment

In the fall of 2013, President Xi put forth with the Silk Road Economic Belt and the 21st Century Maritime Silk Road respectively during his visits in Kazakhstan and Indonesia, emphasizing that nations involved should work together to build communities of shared interests and shared destiny.

Despite that the State Council has not issued any specific policy with regard to the Belt and Road strategy, governments of different levels in China have been making intense preparation for top-level design and putting ideas into practice since President proposed it. During the NPC and CPPCC[1] in 2014, Premier Li Keqiang pointed out in the Report on the Work of the Government that to fasten the planning and construction of the Road and the Belt would be the central task for the year. In the fall of the same year, the State Council re-simplified examination and approving procedures for investment projects and even removed approval procedure for almost all overseas investment projects (with very few exceptions).

The Belt and Road strategy offers opportunities to Chinese enterprises, and challenges in the meantime. An enterprise can make use of this chance to expand its overseas business. But it has to be alert to many risks resulting from political, economic, and social conditions in the host country. Thus, the present paper suggests that enterprises should make comprehensive and serious inspection on the investment climate in a host country and watch out for any risks from political instability, corruption and legal systems in the host country and from deteriorative bilateral political relations of the host country and the home country.

President Xi made a proposal of building the Silk Road Economic Belt together with Kazakhstan in his speech in Nazarbayev University on September 7, 2013. That was also the first time that the Chinese government has put forth with specific plans with regard to Eurasian Economic Integration. On October 3rd of the

---

[1] NPC & CPPCC refer to the National People's Congress and Chinese People's Political Consultative Conference.

same year when he made a speech in the Parliament of Indonesia, President Xi brought forward the idea of constructing the 21st Century Maritime Silk Road. Henceforth, the Silk Road Economic Belt and the 21st Century Maritime Silk Road are called in short "the Belt and the Road". Geographically, the Belt and the Road cover the large area of Eurasia including Southeast Asia, South Asia, Central Asia, West Asia, North Africa, Central and Eastern Europe.

1.1. Background

The raise of the Belt and Road Initiative by China is a historical choice. To begin with, the initiatives are a result of evolvement of global political and economic situations. The lift of economic position of Eurasia called for changes in geopolitical and economic strategies of China. Recent years witnessed the rise of Asia, global economic center moving eastwards, revival of Europe from global financial crisis, and closer ties between the two parts of Eurasia. Under such circumstances, the Belt and Road Initiative is expected to effectively enhance the relevance and consistency of Asia and Europe and to form an auto-cycle economic circle[2] in Eurasia based on infrastructure construction.

Secondly, the initiatives are necessary for China to create a favorable environment for developing new strategies so far as the new cooperative trend in Asia is concerned. Protectionism prevailed across the world these years due to financial crisis. Doha Round negotiations merely made any progress. China and other new emerging economies resorted to multilateral and bilateral trading agreements (RTAs).[3] As the biggest economy in Asia, China gained financial support from the AIB for its Belt and Road Initiative. Hopefully the initiatives will contribute to a new regional cooperative mechanism that is far better than the current one in terms of both depth and range.

---

[2] Sun Xingjie: Geopolitics of the Silk Road, *The Economist*, 2014 (112).
[3] Chen Shumei and Quan Yi: TPP, RCEP Negotiations and Asia-Pacific Economic Integration Process, *Asia-Pacific Economic Review*, 2013 (2).

Thirdly, the enthusiasm towards overseas investment in the emerging market marked the changes in global pattern of investment governance, facilitating the rise and acceleration of foreign investment from China. There was a rapid growth trend in foreign investment by new economies after global financial crisis. In 2013, the BRICS ranked top twelve globally among major countries (regions) regarding overseas investment stock. Specifically, China ranked the seventh, Russia tenth, Brazil the eleventh and India the twelfth.[4]

Fourthly, the initiatives are responding to China's rising up which demands industrious upgrade, continuous adjustment to domestic industrial structures, and expended reform in broader market. For the past few years, China has joined the league of middle-income countries. Given increasing domestic economy and accelerating foreign investment, China is speeding up its pace of going out, which is necessary for the country to avoid falling into the trap of "middle income". From January to October in 2014, investors from China have directly invested on 4977 overseas enterprises in 154 countries and regions around the globe, accumulating up to 503.15 billion RMB (81.88 billion USD), 17.8% of increase compared to former year.[5] Moreover, serious oversupply is shown in current capacity of traditional industries and foreign exchange reserve. In 2013, the utilization rate of industrious capacity across China was less than 80%, touching the bottom in the last four years. The severe supply of capacity results in waste of social resources and low allocative efficiency, which hinders industry upgrading. In the case of foreign exchange, the national balance in foreign exchange reserve of China was 382,000 million USD by the end of 2013, exceeding what the real economy needed and thus

---

[4] Ministry of Commerce, National Bureau of Statistics, and State Administration of Foreign Exchange of China. *Statistic Bulletin on Direct Foreign Investment of China* in 2013.

[5] The Ministry of Commerce of China: Statistic of China's Non-Financial Direct Foreign Investment from January to October 2014. Retrieved from http://hzs.mofcom.gov.cn/article/date/201411/20141100802447.shtml. November 16, 2014.

leading to inflation. Under such circumstances, foreign exchange reserve can be used to push forward the infrastructure construction of countries involved in the Belt and Road Initiative and to insist Chinese enterprises in their going abroad. Besides, despite that China's economic aggregate has been going upwards, structural contradictions in the case of development in east and west China never disappear. In this case, the Belt will drive the economic growth in west China by a large margin.

1.2. Diplomatic propeller

President Xi Jinping has been popularizing and advocating China's neighborhood diplomacy — amity, sincerity, mutual benefit, and inclusiveness — whenever he pays visits to other nations or attends big events since he brought forward the Belt and Road strategy, in pursuit of support from countries along the Belt and the Road and other beneficiary nations. During that period, the Belt and Road strategy came to be distinct.

In a macroscopic view, the Belt and Road Initiative is to be linked up with the development strategies of countries along the Belt and the Road through pushing forward interconnection construction.

According to the Joint press communiqué of the dialogue meeting on promoting interconnection partnership where President Xi and the leaders of Bangladesh, Cambodia and Laos participated on November 8, 2014, infrastructure construction is the basis and priority of interconnection. At the 22nd Asia-Pacific Economic Cooperation (APEC) Economic Leaders' Meeting on November 11th of the same year, President Xi laid stress on the strategic role interconnection plays in the Belt and Road Initiative and pointed out that interconnection cooperation is the core of the Belt and Road Initiative.[6]

---

[6] APEC Authorized Publication: President Xi Jinping Presided over the 22nd APEC Economic Leaders' Meeting and Made a Speech. Retrieved from http://news.xinhuanet.com/world/2014-11/11/c_1113206623.htm. November 29, 2015.

As far as countries along the Belt and the Road and beneficiary countries are concerned, "one nation, one policy" acts as the pivot in building the Belt and Road community of shared destiny. During his visits to Tajikistan, Maldives, Sri Lanka, and India in mid-September, President Xi emphasized that the Belt and Road should be linked up in full with the development plans of relevant countries and China's competitive industries should be geared to the geographical characteristics and development needs of the four countries.

One of the notable achievements that the Belt and Road strategy has made is the construction of the Asian Infrastructure Investment Bank (AIIB). As most of the countries along the Belt and the Road are in their primary stage of industrialization, infrastructure construction in those countries is beset with fund shortage, which to some extent impedes the promotion of interconnection. The AIIB thereby functions as a fund provider for the Belt and Road strategy, as well as a propeller for the construction of exemplary projects such as Eurasian Continental Bridge, Bangladesh-China-India-Myanmar (BCIM) Economic Corridor, and China-Pakistan Economic Corridor (CPEC). Moreover, the establishment of AIIB marked that China has transformed from the stage of product output to that of capital export.

1.3. Domestic recognition

The State Council, the National Development and Reform Commission (NDRC), the State Administration of Foreign Exchange (SAFE) of China have been making specific plans since President Xi proposed the Belt and Road Initiative to push forward the initiatives from strategic phase to pragmatic one. In the end of 2013, the 3rd Plenary Session of the 18th Communist Party of China (CPC) Central Committee passed *Decisions of the Central Committee of CPC on Major Issues Regarding Deepening Reform in an All-Round Way* which clearly indicates that China should "quicken the construction of infrastructure interconnection with neighboring countries and regions and promote the establishment of the Belt and the Road so as to form a new pattern of being open to the world in an all-round way (Paragraph 26)".[7] In December 2013, the NDRC and the Ministry of Foreign Affairs (MFA) co-hosted the symposium on promoting construction of the Belt and Road, where nine provinces in West China including Sichuan Province, and five coastal provinces including Jiangsu Province expressed their suggestions to help pin down guiding work ideas. During the NPC and CPPCC held in 2014, the Report on the Work of the Government, reported by Premier Li Keqiang, officially enlisted "cracking on with the planning and construction of the Belt and the Road" as one of the key tasks next year.

On October 8, 2014, the State Council decided to re-revise the catalogue of investment projects need approval by the government. Almost all foreign investment projects are exempted from going through government approval procedures with a few exceptions.[8] At the same time, an overall plan for the Belt and Road strategy made by concerted efforts of the NDRC, MFA, Ministry of Commerce, and involving sectors is expected to be issue officially by the end of 2015, followed by specific plans and supporting policies.

What is more, provinces and municipalities are striving for being a part of the Belt and Road economic zone. The provincial government of Xinjiang Uygur Autonomous Region in Northwest China, for example, set up a leading group for the construction of the Silk Road,[9] aiming at becoming a "core connection area" by making use of its geological advantages. Shaanxi determined to function as the biggest transit center of logistics along the Silk Road

---

[7] *Decisions of the Central Committee of CPC on Major Issues Regarding Deepening Reform in an All-Round Way.* Retrieved from http://www.gov.cn/jrzg/2013-11/15/content_2528179.htm. November 17, 2014.

[8] Retrieved from http://www.gov.cn/xinwen/2014-10/09/content_2761574.htm. November 17, 2014.

[9] Retrieved from http://www.scio.gov.cn/ztk/wh/slxy/31208/document/1386669/1386669.htm. November 17, 2014.

Economic Belt that could carry on with industries transferred from east China and connect mainland China with the Asian Continental Bridge.[10] In Southwest and Southeast China, Yunnan Province, Guangxi Province and Fujian Province, by virtue of their geological connection with Southeast Asian countries, were busy building a grand interconnection channel and a new platform for economic and trade cooperation along the Belt.[11] In Northeast China, Heilongjiang Province focused on the channel involving Russia in order to contribute to the east path of the Silk Road Economic Belt and to become a crucial constituent of the cross-shaped external economic corridor.[12]

From the intense actions and planning on the construction of the Belt and Road from the central government of China down to local ones, we can expect a big leap, in both quality and quantity, in the investment from China to countries along the Belt and the Road.

2. Investments of China in Nations along the Road and the Belt

2.1. Nations along the belt and the road

The Belt and Road countries cover nations that are related or involved in the Silk Road Economic Belt and 21st Century Maritime

---

[10] "Build Shaanxi Province into new starting point of new Silk Road". Retrieved from http://photo.china.com.cn/news/2014-05/22/content_32457355.htm, November 17, 2014.

[11] "New Silk Road ignites investment boom in Xinjiang Uygur Autonomous Region and Fujian Province". Retrieved from http://news.xinhuanet.com/fortune/2014-09/11/c_126974333.htm, September 11, 2014. "Six measures of Guangxi Province to build Maritime Silk Road". Retrieved from http://news.163.com/14/0917/07/A6B0AP1600014Q4P.html. September 17, 2014. "Build Yunan into strategic junction of One Belt and One Road". Retrieved from http://www.mofcom.gov.cn/article/resume/n/201411/20141100790382.shtml. November 10, 2014.

[12] "Heilongjiang Province aims at Silk Road economic belt center in eastern China". Retrieved from http://www.scio.gov.cn/ztk/wh/slxy/31208/Document/1386197/1386197.htm, November 17, 2014.

Silk Road. Currently, there are several points of view in regard to the scope of the Belt and Road countries.

2.1.1. *Ancient Road Theory*[13]

The Ancient Road Theory, set against historical background, endow the Belt and Road with the significance of carrying on the historical friendship of China with countries involved. In this case, Belt and Road countries refer to those that the ancient road went through. Support for the theory mainly comes from local officials and local scholars in answer to the strategic needs of the country and in pursuit of a major role in the cause of the Belt and Road Initiative. Basically, theory holders will resort to application for the world heritage, various kinds of exhibitions, and history-related symposiums.

2.1.2. *Linking up of existing corridors*

This viewpoint advocates the linking up of current corridors between China and other countries and expanding the influence of the Belt and Road by taking advantage of available accomplishments. Major economic corridors the China initiated before the official proposal of the Belt and Road strategy are China–Pakistan Economic Corridor which Premier Li Keqiang put forth with during his visit to Pakistan in May 2013, BCIM Economic Corridor as a consensus reached between China and India during Premier Li's visit to India during the same period, and the Nanning Singapore Economic Corridor between Nanning of Guangxi Province of China and Singapore.

Actually, the concept of the Belt and the Road is never as simple as an ancient path of tea and commodity trades or the connection of main lines of transportation. It is far more than a "belt" and a "road" in their literal meanings. Instead, the concept embodies almost the whole Eurasian continent. The Belt refers to the terrestrial economic belt going

---

[13]Retrieved from http://yn.yunnan.cn/html/2014-03/06/content_3109912.htm, http://yn.yunnan.cn/html/2014-03/28/content_3149430.htm, http://sn.people.com.cn/n/2014/0819/c226647-22033563.html, and http://stock.hexun.com/2014-06-23/165945095.html. November 17, 2014.

from the Central Asia, West Asia, and Persian Gulf to the Mediterranean. The Road is an offshore economic belt covers the area from Southwest China to South Asia, from Southeast China to Southeast Asia and South Asia, and goes through the Strait of Malacca to the Indian Ocean and further to Europe. However, neither covers East Asia.

Generally, the Belt and Road ranges from Western Europe to the west and the eastern coast of Africa to the south (Fig. 1). This extensive region includes more than sixty countries and regions in Southeast Asia, South Asia, Central Asia, West Asia, North Africa, and Central and Eastern Europe. All those countries with China excluded have an overall population of 3.08 billion and Gross Domestic Product (GDP) of 12.8 trillion USD, occupying 44% and 17% of the world's total respectively. Thus, it is the most

Figure 1:   Countries along the Belt and Road
Source: GrandView.

economically dynamic region in the world. Besides, only six of them accomplished GDP of over 500 billion USD. Most of them are still newly emerging market and developing countries with strong potentials and promising prospects. The Belt and Road will become the economic corridor of the longest span and the highest potential across the world upon its realization.

The countries along the Belt and Road are hot investment target countries, being in accordance with the trend of investment from developed countries in Europe and America. By the end of 2013, more than a half, forty three to be exactly, of them has reached over 10 billion USD of Foreign Direct Investment (FDI) absorption stock, of which Singapore, Russia, Poland, Indonesia, India, Saudi Arabia, Thailand, Turkey, Malaysia, Czekh, Hungary, and the United Arad Emirates (sorted by amount of stock) acquired an absorption stock of over 100 billion USD (Fig. 2).

These years, countries have taken active steps to invite foreign investment but with little performance. The financial crisis in 2008 is tagged for this as it damaged the economy of traditional investors, or developed countries, severely and foreign investment inclined to shrink.

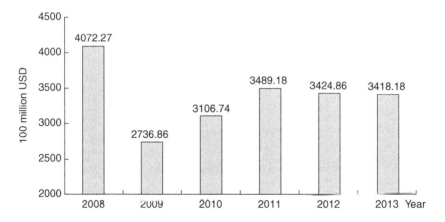

Figure 2:   FDI flow absorbed by countries along the Belt and Road from 2008 to 2013

Sources: UNCTAD and GrandView.

2.2. Overview of China's investment in nations along the road and the belt

Recent years witnessed acceleration in FDI flow absorption by countries along the Belt and Road (Fig. 3). China's investment on those countries has been rocketing since 2008, reaching up to 12.634 billion USD in 2013, an increase of more than fourfold compared to that in 2008. However, the amount of investment remains little in comparison of the total FDI obtained by those countries, accounting for merely 3.7% of the latter. By the end of 2013, the stock of FDI from China to countries along the Belt and Road runs up to 57.417 billion USD,[14] 1.3% of total FDI stock of those countries. Thus, to enlarge investment to those countries is a pivot on the cause of realizing the Belt and Road strategy.

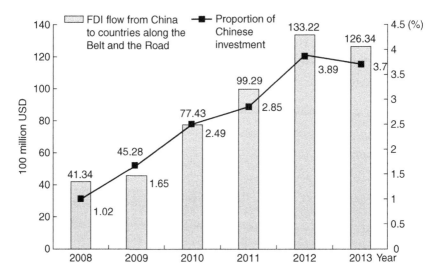

Figure 3:   FDI flow from China to Countries along the Belt and Road from 2008 to 2013

Sources: 2013 Statistical Bulletin of China's Outward Foreign Direct Investment and GrandView.

---

[14] Ministry of Commerce, National Bureau of Statistics, and State Administration of Foreign Exchange. *2013 Statistical Bulletin of China's Outward Foreign Direct Investment.*

Among the top twenty target countries and regions of China's FDI in 2013, ten are countries along the Belt and Road. Obviously the countries along the Belt and Road occupy an important place in China's FDI list.

By the end of 2013, there are 38 countries along the Belt and Road absorbing a FDI stock of over 10,000 million USD from China, among which Singapore, Russia, Kazakhstan, Indonesia, Myanmar, Mongolia, Iran, Cambodia, Laos, Thailand, India, Pakistan, Vietnam, Saudi Arabia, Malaysia, and the United Arab Emirates (sorted in order of stock amount) obtain more than 1 billion USD. Besides, it is not hard to discern by comparing Tables 3 and 1 that China's investment targets still focus on its neighbors so far. The cases of Central Asia and Central and Eastern Europe are the most conspicuous examples. Up till the end of 2013, only Kazakhstan and Turkmenistan among Central Asian countries had large FDI stock while the direct investment from China on five countries in Central Asia remained relatively large. In contrast, countries in Central and Eastern Europe that obtained large FDI stock were as many as fifteen in 2013 and in the meantime only eight were taken as key investment targets by China.

Main target industries of China's FDI on countries along the Belt and Road up till the end of 2013 are lease and commercial service, finance, wholesale and retail, mining, transportation, storage, and postal service. Investment on lease and commercial service in both Asia and Europe is on the top of the investment target list, thereby facilitating China's investment on infrastructure construction (Table 2).

3. Environmental and Political Risks to China's Investment

3.1. Political risks

The "going out" of Chinese enterprises is the main propeller for the Belt and Road strategy. Therefore it is crucial for those companies to investigate the host countries' investment environment in an all-round and prudential way before "going out".

Table 1: Countries along the Belt and Road that Received over 10,000 Million USD of FDI Stock from China by the End of 2013

No.	South Asia	Sum (Unit: 100 m USD)	Southeast Asia	Sum (Unit: 100 m USD)	West Asia & North Africa	Sum (Unit: 100 m USD)	Middle and Eastern Europe	Sum (Unit: 100 m USD)
1	India	24.47	Singapore	147.51	Iran	28.51	Russia	75.82
2	Pakistan	23.43	Indonesia	46.57	Saudi Arabia	17.47	Hungary	5.32
3	Sri Lanka	2.93	Myanmar	35.7	The United Arab Emirates	15.15	Georgia	5.32
	Bangladesh	1.59	Cambodia	28.49	Turkey	6.42	Estonia	3.31
4	East Asia, Central Asia		Laos	27.71	Yemen	5.49	Poland	2.58
5	Kazakhstan,	69.57	Thailand	24.72	Egypt	5.11	Czech	2.05
6	Mongolia	33.54	Vietnam	21.67	Afghanistan	4.88	Bulgaria	1.5
7	Kyrgyzstan	8.86	Malaysia	16.68	Iraq	3.17	Romania	1.45
8	Tajikistan	5.99	The Philippines	6.92	Qatar	2.54		
9	Turkmenistan	2.53						
10	Uzbekistan	1.98						
11	Belarus	1.16						
12								

Sources: 2013 Statistical Bulletin of China's Outward Foreign Direct Investment, GrandView.

Table 2: Distribution of Target Industries of China's Direct Investment on Countries along the Belt and Road

Region	Industries	Investment stock (100 m USD)	Proportion (%)
Asia	Leasing and business services	1398.2	31.2
	Finance	838.1	18.7
	Wholesale and retailing	709.8	15.9
	Mining	571.7	12.8
	Transportation, warehousing and storage, and postal service	277.2	6.2
	Total	**3795.0**	**84.8**
Europe	Leasing and business services	113.1	21.3
	Manufacture	108.6	20.4
	Mining	93.3	17.6
	Finance	89.0	16.7
	Wholesale and retailing	45.1	8.5
	Total	**449.1**	**84.5**

Sources: 2013 *Statistical Bulletin of China's Outward Foreign Direct Investment*, GrandView.

Theoretical research indicates that three aspects are needed considering for the good of foreign investment, namely conditions of enterprises *per se*, factors in the mother countries of enterprises, and elements in investment receiving countries, or host countries. As to elements in a host country, economic and political situations, social stability and so on, according to reports on international commercial investment and case studies, should be estimated before investment. Literatures show a focus of research regarding FDI on the advantages and bottle neck of development from an economic perspective. Specifically, the economy size (GDP and per capita GDP), economic stability (inflation rate and stability of foreign exchange), economic potential (economic growth rate, infrastructure level, and technology), and the openness of economy (bilateral volume of trade, revenue, customs, and trade barrier) are to be taken into account to estimate whether it is eligible for investment.

Nevertheless, the indicators mentioned above do not suffice to interpret the absorption of FDI of countries along the Belt and Road according to the analysis of FDI from China and other countries in a series of years. As global economic integration increasingly improves, the negative effect that political risks could possibly exert on international economic cooperation is bound to be paid special attention by FDI investors. The theory of Simon Jeffrey regards political risk as a phenomenon that will pose negative influence on foreign business operation and foreign capital from either the interior or the external of a host country and by means of government and social action policies.[15]

Furthermore, political risks, according to literatures in the GrandView think tank, are categorized as interior risks and exterior ones. Interior political risks include instable political situations, adjustment of supervision policies, corruption of government officials, crimes, and the environment for practicing laws. Exterior political risks virtually refer to the deterioration of diplomatic relations between mother country and host country (with the length since the establishment of diplomatic relation and numbers of high-level mutual visits as main indicators). In most cases, interior political risks can be extended and transformed into exterior ones, and at the same time, exterior political risks are likely to affect interior political stability of a host country due to fluctuation effect. Moreover, some non-political factors such as property/asset transfer, environmental protection, and employee–employer relations can be politicalized.

3.2. Political risks need evading in China's investment in other countries

First is the risk of political stability, resulting from political unset, ethnic and religious collision, and internal strife triggered by interest conflicts inside a host country.

---

[15] Simon Jeffrey D: "Political risk as assessment: Past trends and future prospects", *Columbia Journal of World Business* (1982).

More often than not, such countries, in face of regime change and sharp ethnic conflicts, fail to secure their government policies, especially policies in regard to foreign investors, which results in discouragement to investors that could hardly restore in a short term. In 2013, the political turmoil in the Middle East directly affected FDI and enterprises were implicated in it. The disorder is partially due to instable social relations. Specifically speaking, the considerable and over-concentrated oil earnings for a long period of time have bred internal corruption and furthermore led to severe social conflicts. What was worse, clashes among religious groups undermined regime stability in that region. Under such circumstances, governments soon lost capacity of controlling economic and social risks. Contracted projects by Chinese enterprises in those countries were thus under serious threat. Some Chinese companies suffered shut down, and defaulted payment, and lose of contact with customers.

Literatures and enterprise survey in terms of international investment consider political turbulence as a relatively important element that affects FDI. The political risk index from International Country Risk Guide (ICRG) is usually taken internationally as a comprehensive index to measure systems of a host country from twelve aspects such as government stability, social and economic conditions, investment environment, internal conflicts, external ones, corruption, military and politics, and administrative system. Zhang (2014)[16] proves through empirical tests that the ICRG indexes of 1% of host countries will cause changes in 4.05% of Outward Foreign Direct Investment (OFDI) of China. Ramasamy (2012)[17] concluded that 1% of changes in political stability will give rise to 0.26% of flow changes in OFDI of Chinese enterprises by hypothesis tests on influence on Chinese enterprise's FDI move. Moreover, the Warsaw University launched an investigation on

---

[16]Zhang J: "System-related elements, resource finding, and location choices of China's FDI", *Industrial Technology & Economy*, December 2013 (239).

[17]Bala Ramasamy and Matthew Yeung and Sylvie Laforet: "China's outward foreign direct investment: Location choice and firm ownership *"Journal of World Business* (2012).

foreign enterprises of different sizes in CIS states, which shows that political stability has been a key factor that foreign entrepreneurs consider during investment, especially in Kyrgyzstan.

Second is corruption. Investors have to pay more due to the corruption of officials in a host country instead of doing business by simply following international conventions and market rules. If it goes like this in the long run, government in the host country will pay back with its credibility.

Research concludes that corruption will lead to tremendous waste of money and labor, distort foreign direct investment, squander skills of enterprises, and even undermine economic efficiency and growth. The severer corruption is in a host country, the higher uncertainty the FDI is to be faced with. There are exceptions, according to discoveries by some researchers, that corruption facilitates economic growth.[18] Nevertheless, the bulk believes that corruption accounts for flight of capital caused by high transaction costs and uncertainty.

Market economy, upon its establishment in Kazakhstan, brought about negative effect of market economy because of rapid privatization. Political power was free in market operation, leading to economic corruption, in energy-related fields in particular. By contrast, Singapore has been rated as the country of least corruption in Asia for several consecutive years according to Global Perceptions Index (GPI) by Transparency International and its work in anti-corruption is widely acknowledged across the world. Higher GPI creates benign environment for investment, contributing to the second top position of the country in terms of the Index of Economic Freedom. Moreover, investigations on the investment environment in the Philippines carried out by the ERDI of Asian Development Bank show that corruption is the very first

---

[18]Leff N: "Economic development through bureaucratic corruption", *American Behavioral Scientist*, 1094, 8(2), pp. 8–14; Leff (1964) holds that corruption promotes investment through a special mechanism, that is foreign enterprises avoid paying for bureaucracy and bribe the host government in order to save the loss from inefficiency of the government.

issue that entrepreneurs are cared about before making investment in the country.

In recent years, transnational enterprises have stridden in investment in countries which are experiencing economic transformation. For instance, the Central and Eastern Europe and CIS countries have attracted large amount of investment from transnational enterprises during the liberalization of economy, and the same goes to China and East Asia. Although many companies have succeeded in internationalization, many more are confronted with troubles of different kinds. The CASE in Poland probes into how business environment in CIS states (Ukraine, Moldova, Georgia, Kyrgyzstan) affected FDI investors. Objectives of this research are three types of investors with various motives, which are market demander, resource or labor demander, and profit demander. CASE found out by a great deal of enterprise surveys that corruption issue in a host country is the key element that enterprisers, regardless of types, consider before staring business there.

Third is the law system, which is a broad concept that includes rule of laws, strength of supervision, and law practices in terms of business contracts of an enterprise.

These years, the risk from law system is prominent in cases of merger and acquisition by Chinese enterprises in foreign countries.

If a host country is lack of sound legal system, foreign enterprises will have to face frequent harassment and fine by local governments or sectors, which incurs loss in enterprise capital. In the meantime, enterprises which fail to abide by the legal norms or operate improperly during mergers are likely to be involved in lawsuit with the risk of losing the case. Thus, enterprises pay much attention to the legal system of a host country when making investment decisions. A host country is expected to assure foreign enterprises that it has absolute control over domestic key industries, and therefore it will examine merger and acquisition by FDI investors with high seriousness. For example, the USA passed a law on strengthening safety check on merger and acquisition by foreign capital in 2007 and refined it in 2008. The law, in particular, extended the time and stepped up efforts to investigate state-owned enterprises under government control. Groh[19] (2009) finds out through studies of 127 countries which absorb FDI that legal system is of 26.8% of importance to a country to attract FDI, being as crucial as economic environment and infrastructure are.

Fourth is number of visits of government leaders, which together with the time span of the establishment of diplomatic relations is the baseline of measuring how diplomatic relations between a host and a mother country especially when a mother country is considering investment in the host country.

Generally speaking, the increase of mutual visits of government leaders helps add FDI between the two countries and FDI will be affected when bilateral relations go worse or come to a stop. A host country often deems foreign enterprises as informal overseas organizations of other countries. Thus, it inclines to vent discontent on foreign-owned enterprises by expropriating, imposing strict supervision and heavy duties, and lifting entrance barrier. At the same time, the FDI cannot be withdrawn in time when diplomatic relations deteriorate as in most cases it is used as a long-term fixed investment, thereby causing huge loss to enterprises.

In Thailand, for example, regular investment of overseas enterprises and consumption of its citizens have suffered a lot since the explosion of large-scale anti-government protests in 2013. Under such circumstance, lots of short-term overseas capital sought flight out to elude political risks and a large amount of FDI enterprises withdrew investment. In contrast, as China–Thailand relations have always been sound and high-level mutual visits kept normal and stable regardless of political fluctuation in Thailand, Chinese enterprises in Thailand trusted the Thailand government and did not withdraw their investment. Zhang *et al.*[20]

---

[19] Alexander Peter Groh and Matthias Wich: "A composite measure to determine a host country's attractiveness for foreign direct investment", *Working Paper* (2009).
[20] Jianhong Zhang, Jiangang Jiang and Chaohong Zhou: "Diplomacy and investment — the case of China", *International Journal of Emerging Markets*, 9(2), pp. 216–235 (2014).

(2014) made an empirical research of China's investment in 131 countries and concluded that mutual visits of leaders is significantly and positively correlated with China's FDI in a host country. To be specific, 1% of changes in mutual leader visits arouse 4.1% of China's OFDI flow changes. In this case, frequency of mutual leader visits is a relatively important factor needs considering when China's FDI is analyzed.

More often than not, Chinese enterprises are confronted with the political risks mentioned above when they are making direct investment overseas. Interior political risks are an integration of various aspects like corruption, political instability, and changes in policies and laws. Any factor alone is not sufficient to get a comprehensive and complete understanding of problems an enterprise is beset with.

4. China's Investment in the Belt and Road Initiative: Case Study

Case One: Political instability of a host country

Chinese enterprises will be in a disadvantageous position when a host country suffers political turbulence. Sometimes, their business goes abnormal and profits come down, and even in extreme cases their investment capital is swept off totally that they lose confidence of investment. Since the very beginning of Ukraine crisis, the interference of the US, EU, and Russia adds uncertainty to its politics. The intense political situations exert direct influence on the resolve of foreign investment. Enterprises are apt to avoid potential political risks. Enterprises dealing in exports with Wenzhou, China were affected by the unrest politics. According to statistics provided by Wenzhou Customs, exports from Wenzhou to Ukraine in January 2014 reached 170 million RMB, 30% of decrease compared to the same period in the former year. Enterprise owners explain that Ukraine customers cannot pay on time under such political circumstance so that they cannot send out their goods to them.

Case Two: Changes and adjustments to industry policies or laws and regulations in a host country

Despite of relative sound and stable political situations in Mongolia, policies regarding mining industry in Mongolia have been capricious for the last few years. China's direct investment to Mongolia drops down largely for that reason. Mongolia, as a country with abundant mineral resources, attracts many investors from the globe. China's investment in Mongolia focuses on mining industry, 72% of which is for geological investigation and exploration as well as petroleum recovery.[21] However, Mongolian government kept adjusting laws and policies related to mine industry to safeguard its own interests and the changes were too frequent to maintain the trust and confidence of foreign investors. In the 1990s, Mongolian government promised to provide a fair and stable legal environment for overseas investors in order to attract foreign capital. In 2001, it released a catalogue of key industries (including mining industry) that invite foreign investment, boosting investment on mining to the peak.[22] However, Mongolian government kept tightening up its control over mineral resources. In July 2006, the Ulsyn Ikh Khural of Mongolia amended the Law of Mineral Resources of 1997 and listed 15 grand mines as state-owned strategic mining fields. For the past decade, the government has made several pro-and-fro adjustments to the Law,[23] resulting in low continuity of policies and damage to investment confidence of foreign investors.

---

[21] Tumen Q and Wang Y: "Current situations, problems, and countermeasures regarding China–Mongolia economic and trade cooperation", *Journal of Finance and Economic Theory*, 2013 (4).

[22] At that time, Mongolia did not impose any bar on mine recovery. Everybody was allowed to register for mining without any proof materials. Anyone could get an exploitation permit by simply providing locations of the mine, filling out a form, and handing over a commission charge of 200 plus RMB.

[23] In August 2009, Mongolia Parliament amended the Law of Mineral Resources which reduced taxes on mine exploration and attracted a large amount of Chinese investors. But before long, the favorable conditions was overturned by a Presidential decree in April 2010 which ceased infinitely to issue new exploitation permits and called off the transfer of mine prospecting claim and mine recovery claim.

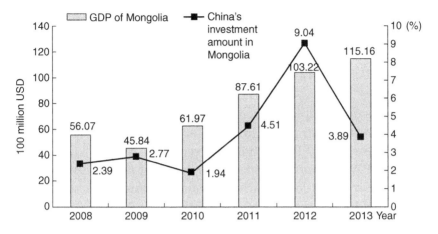

Figure 4:   Mongolia's GDP and China's FDI flow to Mongolia (2008–2013)

Sources: IMF, *2013 Statistical Bulletin of China's Outward Foreign Direct Investment*, and GrandView.

China's direct investment to Mongolia has rocketed since 2010 while investment amount dropped down sharply in 2013 by 57% to the former year. Apart from less attractive investment environment due to poor economic conditions, the Law of Coordination of Foreign Investment in Strategic Fields[24] taken effect in 2012 mainly accounts for the decrease for foreign investors began to worry that the Mongolian government was using this law to constrain their business (Fig. 4). In October 2013, Mongolia abolished the law and passed a new Law of Investment in order to stimulate its economy. Despite of its good intent of cutting down restrictions over foreign investment, FDI amount dropped in a large scale instead of increasing as is shown in the statistics[25] of the first quarter in 2014. Obviously, capricious changes to investment-related policies make investors

---

[24] Mining industry, finance and media, information and telecommunication are listed as three strategic sectors by Mongolia. The law stipulates at the same time that foreign investors must get approval from the Mongolian government and parliament if their shares in those sectors exceed 49% and total investment amount is over around 76 million USD.

[25] In the first quarter of 2014, foreign investment in Mongolia reached 2.904 million USD, decreasing by 65.2% compared to 5.518 million USD of the same period in 2013.

more prudent and recovery of market confidence is bound to take time.

Case Three: swings in bilateral relations of China with host countries

The worsening diplomatic relations between China and a host country pose direct threat to the safety of FDI of Chinese companies. These years, fluctuations of relations between China and some ASEAN countries impeded investment from China in these nations. For example, as maritime issues became acute, severe anti-China incidents have occurred to Vietnam.

The large-scale anti-China riots in Vietnam caused severe damages to the interests of enterprises in mainland China and Taiwan of China, and even casualties of Chinese staff. According to the information provided by the Economic and Commercial Counselor's Office of Chinese Embassy in Vietnam, Vietnamese government released several regulations regarding investment to set limits to FDI from China in the second half of 2014.[26] In addition, the audit department under the Ministry of Science and Technology of Vietnam practiced administrative interference into case processing of DH-981 Incident in May 2014 and trademark disputes, aggravating strained relations between the two countries.

Figure 5 shows that China put more investment on the Philippines in 2009 but has lessened its investment ever since 2011. In sharp contrast, GDP of the Philippines is going up all the way through. Reasons accounting for this phenomenon are multiple. China finds it hard to cater for the industrial structure of the Philippines; in other words, economy in the Philippines is dominated by service industries while Chinese investment pattern hasn't developed to that level yet. More importantly, the diplomatic relations between China and the Philippines go worse. Huangyan Island incident has resulted in a stand-out in South China Sea of the longest duration, widest sphere of influence, and the highest severity throughout history.

---

[26] For example, anti-dumping duty is imposed on stainless steel cold-rolled sheets imported from mainland China. Another example is that the trademarks of some Chinese enterprises in Vietnam are taken over maliciously.

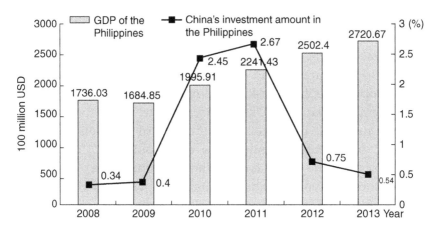

Figure 5:   GDP of the Philippines and China's FDI flow in the Philippines (2008–2013)

Sources: IMF, 2013 Statistical Bulletin of China's Outward Foreign Direct Investment, and GrandView.

5. Conclusions

Political situations in the countries along the Belt and the Road in 2014 were not quite peaceful. In Southeast Asia, some countries suffered instable politics and social turmoil. Economically, the rates of unemployment and of inflation were high in the Philippines. Large-scale anti-China riots occurred to Vietnam due to conflicts in islands and reefs in South China Sea and disputes over sea sovereignty between the two nations. In Central Asia, the three forces were still active. The arc belt of religious extremism and terrorism going through the Middle East, South Asia and Central Asia to Xinjiang Uygur Autonomous Region of China is going to take shape. Terrorist and extremist organizations were ready to make troubles despite the high-pressure measures taken by Central Asian countries against extremist religious forces. And evil activities by three forces would possibly peak.[27] In South Asia, Afghanistan remained in the vacuum stage with poor safety conditions after the

---

[27] Sun L and Wu H: Yellow Book of Central Aisa: Annual Report on Development of Central Asia. *China: Social Sciences Academic Press* 2014.

withdrawal of NATO armies. Pakistan, the pivot country of southern line of the Belt and Road, was struggling to restore its legal order which was disturbed by the issue of Balochistan separatists, of the underworld in Karachi, and of Punjabi extremism.[28] In Central and East Europe, geopolitical risks could not be removed in a short-term as problems in relation to Ukraine accumulate.

In a nutshell, the smooth promotion of the Belt and Road strategy, on the one hand, relies on "going out" of Chinese enterprises; on the other hand, whether companies "going out" can be sound, favorable and profitable depends on the strategic support from the mother country, clearly identified strategies for the company, and stable economic and political conditions in host countries, of which the estimation of investment environment in a host country is the most important elements against the background of a promising future for the Belt and Road initiatives. Particularly, evaluation of the political environment of a host country is the priority of priorities. Any neglect of political risk evaluation is likely to result in loss of properties and even casualties, causing damages to an enterprise as much as it affects the whole foreign investment activities in the long run. Of course, only by judging the investment conditions in a host country from multiple aspects like politics, economy, and society can the estimation be comprehensive.

---

[28] Mao S: "Why is Negotiation between Pakistan and Taliban hard to have any results?". Retrieved from http://www.zaobao.com/special/report/politic/attack/story20140424-335892. November 17, 2014.

Chapter 12

The Non-Traditional Security Issues in Realizing the Belt and Road Initiative

Li Zhifei

National Institute of International Strategy
Chinese Academy of Social Sciences
lizf@cass.org.cn

The Belt and Road has been upgraded and positioned as a neighboring strategic idea. There are not a few non-traditional security problems during implementing the idea, covering fields like terrorism, energy safety, transnational crimes, maritime research and rescue, and the safety of water resources and environment. At present, non-traditional safety issues have become safety-related elements that are critical to forge ahead with the Belt and Road strategy in a smooth and sound manner. Objectively, it calls for integration of domestic resources, supply of necessary regional public products, and a network-based guarantee mechanism for security cooperation to address non-traditional safety issues. In the long run, solving and responding to non-traditional security problems will facilitate cooperative frameworks established by countries along the Belt and Road, boost economy and common safety, strengthen China's strategic influence, and reach the goals of the Belt and Road Initiative.

President Xi Jinping proposed that neighboring countries join hands with China to build the Silk Road Economic Belt and the 21st Century Maritime Silk Road when he visited Kazakhstan and Indonesia in September and October 2013 successively. At the Peripheral Diplomacy Work Conference of the same year, two initiatives were officially integrated together to be China's neighboring strategic idea and were included in the *Decisions of the Central Committee of CPC on Major Issues Regarding Deepening Reform in an All-Round Way* as a national strategy.

The Belt and Road is a path that upholds continuous interconnection and win–win cooperation. It virtually aims at promoting bilateral and regional cooperation with countries along the Belt and the Road in an all-round way through innovating cooperative modes and connecting the dots and lines to get the whole, so as to improve international relations and geopolitical stability and to realize peace, development and win–win across the world.[1] The construction of the Belt and Road involves lots of non-traditional security issues and the features of being transnational and overflowing bind relevant countries in a position of common destiny. Thus, it is decisive to the success of the construction of the Belt and Road whether these non-traditional security issues can be solved properly and efficiently.

1. Five Non-traditional Security Issues to the Belt and Road Initiative

According to the Belt and Road route map published by Xinhua News Agency of China, there includes economic corridors on land between China and Pakistan, among Bangladesh, China, India, and Myanmar, and among China, Mongolia and Russia, and New Eurasian Continental Bridge, as well as key coastal port cities dotted along the Maritime Silk Road. The route map covers a

---

[1] Xiao L: "Overall planning of land and sea for the construction of the Belt and Road Initiative." *Pacific Journal*. 2014 (2).

population of around 4.4 billion, taking up 63% of the globe. Countries involved demonstrate economic aggregate of about 21 trillion USD, 29% of the world economic aggregate. The Belt and Road is the "grand passage for China to carry out economic, trading, and cultural exchanges with Central Asia, Southeast Asia, South Asia, West Asia, East Africa, and Europe".[2] Thus, it is rather crucial to keep interconnection made possible by this passage continuous. Nowadays, the passage is faced with five categories of non-traditional security issues.

1.1. Terrorism

Terrorist threats have been aggravating in countries and regions along the Belt and the Road since 9/11 attacks. Terrorist activities in various forms are too frequent to be taken as a key safety issue that puts national safety and regional stability in danger. There are mainly two types of terrorism, namely maritime terrorism and on land, on the way of constructing the Belt and the Road.

1.1.1. *Maritime terrorism*

Maritime terrorism is prevalent in Southeast Asia where the well-known Islamic separatist organizations are active, such as Jemaah Islamiyah of Malaysia and Abu Sayyaf of the Philippines. In addition, some pirate organizations, according to the investigation of International Maritime Organization (IMO), collude with local rulers and stay in contact with local warlord and political movements, which conversely are related to terrorism.[3]

As the Council for Security Cooperation in the Asia-Pacific (CSCAP) defines, terrorist activities at sea refer to "the undertaking

---

[2] "Xi Pledges $40b for Silk Road fund", *China Daily*. Retrieved from http://www.chinadaily.com.cn/china/2014-11/09/content_18888916.htm. December 2, 2015.
[3] Catherine Raymond: "Piracy in Southeast Asia: New Trends, Issues, and Responses" (*Working Paper*, Institute of Defence and Strategic Studies Singapore, October 2005), p. 7.

of terrorist acts and activities within the maritime environment, using or against vessels or fixed platforms at sea or in port, or against any one of their passengers or personnel, against coastal facilities or settlements, including tourist resorts, port areas and port towns or cities".[4] Nowadays, al-Qaeda has shifted its targets to those at sea. In their points of view, the tankers and facilities for oil recovery represent far more than targets of attacks but the regime which they want to overthrow and the rich western nations which invest on Gulf states. The typical case is that the M·STAR tanker of Mitsui of Japan was confronted with the attacks by the Abdullah Azzam Brigades, an armed organization affiliated with al-Qaeda near the Strait of Hormuz in 2010.

The hazards caused by maritime terrorism can be tremendous, including considerable economic loss of the victimized countries and more importantly immeasurable catastrophe for human beings. Any inflammable and explosive items like a bottle of lique-fied petroleum gas (LPG) kidnapped by maritime terrorists could be portable bombs for port attacks. A tanker carrying with 600 tons of LPG can explode into a huge fire ball of 1,200 diameters that could ruin all matters and living things within the range of its diameter and cause massive disasters and casualties. In addition, terrorists are likely to detonate or attack pivot ports and vessels coming in and out, which will trigger contamination of radioactive substance from vessel leakage and result in large amounts of industrial waste for many countries across the Strait of Malacca will have to change courses.[5] Once maritime terrorism occurs, the whole region would be under the shadow of mental stress and political impacts; energy transportation lines would become

---

[4]Council for Security Cooperation in the Asia-Pacific. "Defining Maritime Terrorism", Retrieved from http://www.maritimeterrorism.com/definitions/ December 5, 2015.

[5]Michael Richardson: *A Time Bomb for Global Trade: Maritime Related Terrorism in an Age of Weapons of Mass Destruction* (Singapore: Institute of Southeast Asian Studies, 2004), pp. 112–14. Ben Sheppard, "Maritime Security Measures," *Jane's Intelligence Review*, Jane's Information Group, March 1, 2003.

weaker; finance and energy market will be ripped apart; and potential investors will be frightened away.[6]

1.1.2. *Onshore terrorism*

Onshore terrorism, compared to maritime one, covers more and wider countries and regions. According to the report on global terrorism index released by the Institute for Economics and Peace, 18,000 people were killed in terrorist attacks around the world in 2013, increasing by 60% compared to 2012. And the report points out four terrorist organizations that are posing threats to the world are active in Iraq, the "Islamic State" in Iran, Boko Haram in Nigeria, Taliban and al-Qaeda in Afghanistan.[7]

South Asia has always been the hard-hit area of terrorism. Terrorism is posing great threat to the safety of the region and countries within. Statistics show that there are about 176 terrorist, separatist, and extremist organizations exercising dangerous acts in India, and 52 extremist organizations in Pakistan, of which 16 are of domestic origins and 32 international. Apart from the Liberation Tigers of Tamil Eelam (LTTE), there are 36 organizations with the aim of establishing Tamil state having been shown or organized activities in Sri Lanka.[8] Besides, terrorists in South Asia have accumulated to 58844 from 2005 to November 23, 2014, and there are 976 terrorists in India in 2014 and 4745 in Pakistan.[9] In addition, violent attacks undertaken by terrorists have caused a large number of casualties among the innocent. Statistics demonstrate that at least 13,485 people died from various kinds of terrorist violence in Pakistan from 2003 to 2008. The Asymmetric War that lasts for over

---

[6] Bronson Percival: "Indonesia and the US: Shared Interests in Maritime Security," US–Indonesia Society, June 2005, pp. 7–15.
[7] Institute for Economics and Peace. *2014 Global Terrorism Index*. Retrieved from http://economicsandpeace.org/reports/. December 5, 2015.
[8] Zhang J: "Contemporary situations of terrorist activities in South Asia", Retrieved from http://qk.cass.cn/nyyj/zdlj/200907/t20090709_10983.htm.
[9] Statistic source: http://www.satp.org/satporgtp/southasia/datasheets/Fatalities.html.

two decades in Sri Lanka is to blame for the death of more than 60,000 people and thousands of hundreds of people who had to flee their homes.[10]

Terrorism in Central Asia is dominated by religious extremist terrorism. In other words, it includes Islamic fundamentalism of extremity or terror, terrorism of ethnic separatism, and terrorism that combines religious extremism and ethnic separation.[11] These terrorist forces frequently show up in eastern Tajikisan, southern Kyrgyzstan, and Fergana Valley in Uzbekistan, For example, Islamic Movement in Uzbekistan has plotted to assassinate President, kidnapped innocent people, launching suicide attacks. The Eastern Turkistan Islamic Movement (ETIM), al-Qaeda, and Taliban and the like are organizing long-term training, offering financial support for the East Turkistan separatist organizations in Xinjiang Uygur Autonomous Region of China, and shielding them with arms to facilitate their frequent violent and terrorist activities.

In general, terrorism in countries along the Belt and Road includes both new type of terrorism of extreme religion represented by the al-Qaeda and tradition type rooted in conflicts of traditional ethnic groups and ideologies like in South Asia. These terrorist organizations interrelate with each other, so the arc belt of religious extremism and terrorism from Middle East, to South Asia, Central Asia, and to Xinjiang Uygur Autonomous Region of China is going to form, pushing terrorism and extremism in Central Asia to a new round of peak period in the near future.[12] Once terrorist activities is going out of control, they will definitely threaten the security of economy, personnel, and trade passages, effect regional

---

[10] Zhang J: "Contemporary situations of terrorist activities in South Asia", Retrieved from http://qk.cass.cn/nyyj/zdtj/200907/t20090709_10983.htm.

[11] Ma Y and Wang J: "On origins of terrorism in Central Asia", *World Economics and Politics*, 2003(2).

[12] Su C: "Current religious extremist forces and terrorism in Central Asia", Retrieved from http://www.shekebao.com.cn/shekebao/2012skb/lilun/u1ai7810.html.

stability, and undermine the construction of the Belt and Road. Besides, Uygur terrorists are found in Vietnam and Indonesia trying to get trained in Southeast Asian countries. At the same time, Kazakhstan and other countries, be in concern of the overflow of terrorists in Xinjiang of China, set strict limits on visa application, which inevitably will influence trades and mobility of staff during constructing the Belt and Road.

1.2. Energy security

Theodore W. Schultz, the renowned economist, once remarked, "Energy is irreplaceable." The Belt and the Road reach the economic circle of Central Asia, Russia, and Europe to the west, South Asia, West Asia, and Africa to southwest, and Asia-Pacific economic circle to the east. It covers many energy-abundant zones except North America. Thus energy safety, especially the safety of energy passages and supply, is another important non-traditional security issue.

Central Asia in the economical circle of Central Asia, Russia, and Europe, is known as the "strategic energy base of the 21st Century". There are dozens of basins full of oil and natural gas, including Caspian Sea Basin, Volga–Ural Basin, Afghanistan–Tajikistan Basin, Fergana Basin, Chu–Saleisu Basin, Turgay Basin, and West Siberia Basin, etc. If the energy zones in Central Asia are connected with energy consumption areas, the strategic directions can be divided into westward, eastward, and southward. The westward connection involves the petroleum and natural gas pipelines from Russia to Europe and the export passages from Central Asia to Europe. The eastward connection includes the line from Central Asia to markets in East Asia and Northeast Asia through China. And the southward connection is mainly from Iran to the outside world by sea routes.[13] Russia and the US are in severe disagreement and fierce competition regarding the construction of

---

[13] Jiang X: "Geopolitics related to Central Asia oil and China's onshore safe energy passages", *Northeast Asia Forum*, 2007 (3), pp. 62–64.

these passages, especially those to the European market. Russia suggests that the passages heading for European markets go through Russian pipelines, while the US holds that those passages should go from Azerbaijan to Ceyhan on the coast of the Mediterranean Sea through Georgia. As to the eastern line, the US has been holding back oil in Central Asia from going eastwards into China and further to markets in East Asia and Northeast Asia through China. The disputes between US and Russia directly affected the development, exploitation and export of petroleum in Central Asia, which concerns the safety of China's energy transit passages as well as the safe utilization of energy of some countries along the Belt and Road.

South Asia is lack of petroleum resources with even distribution. According to statistics, the volume of oil reserves in South Asia merely takes up 0.5% of the total of the world, thus the region grows increasingly dependent on petroleum import. In particular, 70% of oil demands in India are imported from overseas countries. The petroleum resources in South Asia are mainly located in the Middle East. But as Middle East is suffering turbulence and frequent military conflicts, the access to petroleum resources for South Asian countries are instable and unsafe, thus affecting economic safety of these nations.[14] Moreover, since South Asia is the place where petroleum pipelines pass, the security situations of that region is in direct relation to the security index of imported energy in China. Thus, to carry out cooperation regarding energy safety with South Asia is one of the main content in the construction of the Belt and the Road.

1.3. Transnational crimes

Transnational crimes take various forms, of which piracy and drug trafficking dominate in the process of building the Belt and the Road.

---

[14] Wu F: "Energy safety: Common problems in face of China and India", *South Asian Studies Quarterly*, 2006 (2), p. 50.

Piracy is the most important embodiment of transnational crimes at sea and the biggest threat to the freedom and safety to sea voyages. The Maritime Silk Road goes through the South China Sea and the Strait of Malacca. The region that piracy often strikes is somewhere around Mangkai Island and Anambas archipelago of Indonesia, the busiest sea route for international trades for many vessels are passing here to reach the Strait of Malacca. Another sea area is the Sulu Sea and Sulawesi Sea that adjacent to three nations namely Malaysia, the Philippines, and Indonesia. Large tankers that are not able to pass the Strait of Malacca often take this route, heading for Java Sea through Makassar Strait and eventually reaching the Indian Ocean through Sunda Strait.[15] The piracy problem in South China Sea and the Strait of Malacca has already started to pose threats to national safety and trading interests of China. At present, over 80% of international trades in China are relied on the route of South China Sea and the Strait of Malacca.

As many as thirty two vessels being attacked by pirates of the total four hundred and six cases in the world in 2009 were Chinese vessels. According to the statistics released by the IMO, the first quarter of the year 2010 witnessed thirty piracy incidents occurred to South China Sea (including the sea area of Southeast Asia), only second to the thirty nine cases in African sea areas including Somali, Gulf of Aden, and West Africa waters. Piracy incidents that happened in South China Sea have been increasing in number for the past few years. IMO statistics for 2010 show that number of piracy attacks in that area (including the Strait of Malacca and sea area of Southeast Asia) is next only to that in Somali and the Gulf of Aden. What is worse, many areas in South China Sea are "vacuum" and thus turned into the paradise for pirates.[16] Moreover, IMO statistics demonstrate that piracy targeting at small cruises in Southeast Asian sea areas are climbing

---

[15] "South China Sea is the target next to Somali of pirate attacks, China suffers a lot". Retrieved from http://news.xinhuanet.com/mil/2010-07/05/content_13810713.htm.

[16] Bronson Percival: "Indonesia and the United States: Shared Interests in Maritime Security," United States–Indonesia Society, June 2005, p. 6.

up. Indonesia, Malaysia and Singapore Strait became the sea area of the most pirate attacks and hijackings around the world. Piracy attacks in Southeast area kept in a high level. Sixty four incidents occurred in the first half of the year 2014, occupying 56% of all piracy incidents across the world. And in the sea area of Indonesia there were forty incidents, being 85% of all in sea area of Southeast Asia.[17]

Piracy not only endangers the safety of staff and assets of countries which use the South China Sea and Strait of Malacca, but also directly affect global economy through prolonged duration of transportation, added insurance fees and mounted risks of vessel's being stolen. Besides, piracy will cause damages to vessels and lead to the leakage of goods or oil that will do harm to the maritime environment.[18]

Nowadays, over 70% of pirates are and vessel robberies occur in international seas, mainly in Southeast Asian seas. Maritime crimes including piracy bring along lots of hidden dangers. Statistics indicate that the loss in international trades in the southern end of South China Sea area is as high as 16 billion USD each year. Moreover, smuggling and drug trafficking at sea are rampant. Heroin produced in Myanmar is usually trafficked into Thailand, Vietnam, China, and India through sea routes. In 2006, police forces in Guangdong, Shenzhen, and Hong Kong joined hands in tracking down a big case of trafficking heroin via sea lanes from other countries, seizing heroin weighted at over 100 kg. This was the biggest international maritime drug trafficking uncovered by Chinese police force for the past few years. What is foreseeable is that illegal activities at sea will continue to rise given that China is reaching up onto a higher level of development with closer relations with other countries by sea and more convenience and higher frequency of staff going to and fro the country.

---

[17] "IMO report: Pirate acts in Southeast Asia grows to be rampant", *China Ocean News*, September 2, 2014. A4 edition.
[18] Mark J. Valencia: "Security Issues in the Malacca Strait: Whose Security and Why it Matters", *Vanderbilt Journal of Transnational Law*, January 2007, p. 6.

1.4. Maritime search & rescue and aids

Maritime search & rescue (SAR) and aids refer to activities undertaken to search for and rescue victims at sea by using rescue working groups and equipment. There are four hundred vessels and ships falling into dangers in the world each year. Fishing boats encounter dangers on South China Sea every year, and even passenger cruises or ships inevitably grounded or broke down unexpectedly every now and then on the lanes of China and ASEAN countries. Thus, the smooth transportation at sea calls for international collaboration in maritime SAR.

Malaysia Airlines flight MH370 went missing on March 8, 2014, after taking off from Kuala Lumpur airport bound for Beijing. Twenty six countries including China, Malaysia, Vietnam, Singapore, Thailand, the Philippines, the US, Australia, the UK, and New Zealand joined the search and rescue. The international maritime SAR raised the attention to itself as a non-traditional safety issue. The incident exposed several problems during the construction of Maritime Silk Road in future.

Coordination in SAR at seas is embodied in the linkage of multiple subjects and areas involved in the action. Overlaps are inevitable for the roles of subjects participated vary. In order to avoid operational conflicts and increase working efficiency, subjects should agree to a reasonable coordinative plan.[19] The ASEAN Regional Forum (ARF) held on August 1, 2014 issued a Statement on Strengthening Coordination and Cooperation on Maritime and Aeronautical Search and Rescue. The statement calls for enhanced SAR coordination and cooperation at bilateral and multilateral levels, including dialogues and coordination in ARF. There are two main problems remaining despite the efforts have made in promoting maritime SAR coordination and cooperation within ASEAN.[20]

---

[19] "Cooperation mechanism for international maritime search and rescue is called for", *Beijing Daily*, March 19, 2014.

[20] *The ASEAN Regional Forum Statement on Strengthening Coordination and Cooperation on Maritime and Aeronautical Search and Rescue.* Retrieved from http://english.gov.cn/archive/2015/04/02/content_281475081921656.htm. December 5, 2015.

First is the guarantee of provisions on SAR. Maritime SAR is a non-profit and international action with huge expenditures that it is impossible for an individual or a general company could ever afford. Since the subjects of maritime SAR are sovereign states, the source of provisions of course comes from government finance. But many countries cannot afford SAR due to poor economic conditions. Therefore, provisions, if not guaranteed, will be a major obstacle for the institutionalization of maritime SAR.

China announced to establish China–ASEAN Maritime Cooperation Fund valued at 3 billion RMB in November 2011, listing maritime SAR as one of the key cooperation fields between China and ASEAN.[21] President Xi Jinping delivered a speech when he visited Indonesia in October 2013, when he called for strengthening maritime cooperation with ASEAN members, making the best use of the Fund, and developing maritime partnership for cooperation as so to join hand in building the 21st Century Maritime Silk Road.[22] The Fund gradually turned into a platform of comprehensive maritime cooperation aiming at the 21st Century Maritime Silk Road. Under such circumstances, how to distribute and use the fund properly so as to efficiently improve the joint SAR capacity of both China and ASEAN becomes the critical question in relation to the construction of the Belt and the Road.

The second problem is the coordination of maritime SAR. As a task with strong comprehensiveness, maritime SAR calls for coordination among participants and actions in the air, on lands, and at sea, and between astronomy and geology, and between the public and the military forces. More often than not, maritime SAR can be international. Therefore, efficient coordination in aspects of information exchanges and technological support should be strengthened to assure smooth and productive operations. Unfortunately,

---

[21] Wen Jiabao Remarks: China will Allocate 3 billion RMB to Support the China–ASEAN Maritime Cooperation Fund. Retrieved from http://www.chinanews.com/gn/2011/11-18/3470532.shtml.

[22] President Xi Delivered a Speech at the Indonesian Parliament. Retrieved from http://www.chinanews.com/gn/2013/10-03/5344133.shtml.

the cooperation and coordination in such aspect between China and relevant countries need to be further enhanced.[23]

For now, the international society has already established a fundamental legal system in regard to international maritime SAR, which consists of the International Convention for the Safety of Life at Sea (SOLAS 1974/88), the International Convention on Maritime Search and Rescue (SAR 1979) and the International Convention on Search and Rescue. However, many countries refused to join in the conventions due to different levels of economy, gas in SAR technologies and frequent disputes on sovereignty of lands and seas. Thus, coordination at the level of international laws are absent when carrying out maritime SAR, which constraint the activeness of operations to a great extent.

1.5. Water and environment security

Being influenced by climate change, countries along the Belt and the Road are confronted with the issue of water supply and safety. Statistics show that precipitation in Southeast Asia has been decreasing for the past 100 years.[24] The water resources per capita in India slumped from 2451 m^3 in 1990 to 1389–1498 m^3 in 2025, thereby India entering into the list of countries with water shortage.[25] Available water amount per capita will be less than half of that in 2001 by 2025. India is confronted with increasingly austere crisis of water shortage.[26] In Central Asia, glaciers on Pamirs and snow mountains in Tianshan Mountainous area are disappearing. It is forecasted that the water in this region will reduce by a third

---

[23] "Cooperation mechanism for international maritime search and rescue is called for", *Beijing Daily*, March 19, 2014.

[24] Intergovernmental Panel on Climate Change (IPCC), Working Group II Contribution to the IPCC Fifth Assessment Report, Climate Change 2014: Impacts, Adaptation, and Vulnerability. http://www.ipcc.ch/report/ar5/wg2/.

[25] Chen Z: "Relations among population, economy and water resources", *Haihe Water Resources*, 2002(2), p. 1.

[26] "Water shortages: Some Asian and African countries suffer the most". Retrieved from http://info.water.hc360.com/2010/03/250840178820.shtml.

15–20 years later, the whole region ending up with catastrophic water shortage.[27]

Besides, the warming weather will accelerate the disappearing of glaciers on Tibetan Plateau. Rivers in Southeast Asia and South Asia which rely on the ice melt water supply will be put in the danger of the lessening of available water resource. Geoff Dabelko, a project manager in environment and safety projects of the Woodrow Wilson International Center for Scholars (WWICS), indicates that the slowing down of ice melt water from glacier ablation on the Tibetan Plateau will put almost 2 billion residents in China, India, Pakistan, Bangladesh, and Bhutan in the tough situations of water shortage.[28]

At the same time, environment contamination along the Belt and Road is relatively prominent. Take maritime pollution as an example. In general, maritime pollution consists of contamination from petroleum, toxic or hazard chemical matters, radioactive matters, solid rubbish, organics, and oxygen deficit in seawater. It will cause grievous harms to marine organisms and human health.[29] Of all those pollutants, oil leakage is a super killer of marine environment. The petroleum leakage incident of Vietnam in South China Sea in 2011 resulted in large sphere pollution of sea area.

The SAR for flight MH370 in 2014 uncovered the severity of marine rubbish pollution. The Australian Maritime Safety Authority announced that four highly suspected objects in the sea area of Indian Ocean on March 30 and considered them as the "most hopeful clues for now". But the four orange floating objects were identified as fishing gears used by fishermen shortly one day later, blowing out the flame of hope. Scholars on marine research pointed out that "searching wreckage on the surface of the sea is very hard

---

[27] Li D: "Water resources disputes in Central Asia: Causes and current situation", *International Data Information*, 2009(9), p. 26.
[28] "Glacier shrinkage on Tibetan Plateau: water shortage will befall Asia ", http://www.hbzhan.com/news/detail/8144.html.
[29] Sea in rages: Non-traditional security threats at seas from the perspective of the Indian Ocean tsunami, http://worldview.dayoo.com/gb/content/2005-02/01/content_1930835.htm.

for there is full of marine rubbishes that were originally containers falling down from merchant ships and life garbage of human beings". These marine rubbishes retarded normal pace of SAR operation.[30] In addition, they are also posing a threat to the safety of sea voyage and to the virtuous circling of maritime ecological system, being unfavorable for the development of maritime economy. Thus, how to deal with rubbishes on the sea is another key question needs to be answered during interconnection of relevant countries.

2. Features of Non-traditional Security Issues and Threats to the Construction of the Road and the Belt

Problems regarding non-traditional security along the Belt and Road come one after another. Multiple non-traditional safety issues are interwoven with each other. Generally speaking, there are three main characteristics as to these issues.

2.1. Diversified and interwoven threats

Non-traditional security issues related to the Belt and Road not only include terrorism and transnational crimes, but also cover water resource safety, environment safety, and energy safety. These issues coexist and are all posing threats to the security of interconnection and the national security of China and countries along the Belt and the Road. Besides, they are interwoven with each other, presenting a feature of complexity. For example, the rate rise of trafficking in Central Asia must be closely related to terrorist organizations. Taliban, al-Qaeda, and three forces are controlling over drug plant zones and farmers who plant opium so that they will acquire sufficient funds through collecting high opium taxes for purchasing arms, paying the recruited soldiers, and organizing

---

[30] Australian experts: sea rubbishes retard search for the missing MH370, http://www.chinanews.com/gj/2014/04-02/6022665.shtml.

international terrorist acts. A typical case is that the Uzbekistan Islamic Movement played a critical role in trafficking drugs from Afghanistan to Europe through Central Asia.[31] Thus, the interwoven non-traditional security issues as the drug-terrorism mode as a representative pose greater threat to the region and the country. And the threats have all kinds of ties with the society, politics, economy and culture of the country, making the disposal process longer, harder and with more comprehensiveness.

2.2. Regional and international trends in threats

The threats from non-traditional security issues are transregional beyond borders of nations. Take maritime non-traditional security threats as an example. Those threats in various forms as well as illegal behaviors on the sea are likely to occur not only in inland waters and territorial seas, but also possibly in adjacent international seas. There are cases when they occur in not only the sea areas of one nation or region but also most likely in adjoining sea areas that belong to neighboring countries or regions. Moreover, the threats and crimes will do harm to the security of not only a single nation or region, but also probably some relevant ones.

2.3. Difficulties in building early warning and prevention mechanism

The research and observation on non-traditional security issues are hard for these issues are compound and multilateral, geopolitics is complicated, and geological locations are special. The high-level technologies and grand costs demanded by early warning system, in particular, make it even harder to establish forecasting and early warning and to prevent the threats.

Generally speaking, the non-traditional security issues along the Belt and Road are of different types with an obvious trend of

---

[31] Zhang B and Gao Y: "Transnational drug crime and three forces around Xijiang Province", *Journal of Xinjiang Vocational University*, 2011(2).

pan-internationalization and more and more direct relations with the economic safety and stability of nations, regions and beyond. Especially, the increasing fierce terrorism, exacerbated energy and environment safety, and the refractory transnational crimes have been transformed into chronic diseases and bottleneck for regional issues and national safety. Therefore, the role non-traditional security issues plays during the cause of constructing the Belt and Road remain prominent and resolving these issues is of great realistic meaning.

3. Addressing Non-traditional Security Issues while Constructing the Belt and the Road

The construction of the Belt and Road, as a continuous process, involves many aspects like economy, politics, and safety. Non-traditional security issues which are transnational, public and overflowing can never be solved by single power of any country or organization but through bilateral and regional cooperation. Thus, there are three aspects need to be paid special attention regarding how to deal with non-traditional problems during the construction of the Belt and Road in the future.

3.1. Provide necessary public products

Non-traditional security issues are public issues in nature, so those along the Belt and Road are of regional public problems, whose generation and development can be effectively solved and constraint only by supplying sufficient public products. Neighboring region is the zone where China depends strategically on its way of rejuvenation.[32] The proposal of the Belt and Road strategy fundamentally aims at

---

[32]See the speech made by Zhang Xunling, researcher of the Presidium of the Chinese Academy of Social Sciences (CASS) Academic Divisions and head of the Academic Division of International Studies, at the "Current Situations, Challenges and Countermeasures of the 21st Century Maritime Silk Road" conference held by the Center for Regional Security Study of CASS.

a better management and plan of neighboring environment given today's changes in geopolitical situations and the formation of regional new order and rules in favor of China's national security. Thus, China is supposed to full play its role as a responsible regional big power in solving public issues like non-traditional security problems. To be specific, China should holds the active advantageous position and exercises leadership in setting up the regional management mechanism so as to make countries along the Belt and the Road fully enjoy the benefits China's development brings along and experience the new concepts of joint construction, sharing, win–win, and cooperation that China advocates, thereby raising strategic trust of those countries on China and lifting China's influence over the region.

Currently, China has clearly identified that the Belt and the Road are open. At the eighth conference of CPC central finance leading group held on November 4, 2014, President Xi pointed out that the construction of the Road and Belt should be promoted by cooperating with countries involved based on the principle of mutual benefit and win–win result so as to favor the development of those nations. He further indicated at the Dialogue on Strengthening Connectivity Partnership in November of the same year that the Road and Belt initiative derives from, depend on, and will benefit Asia. China is ready to provide its neighbors in Asia with more public products through interconnection and invite them to take the ride on the train of China's development. China initiates and cooperates with other countries to build the AIIB and establishes the Silk Road Fund valued at 40 billion USD[33] for the use of interconnection construction of infrastructure like railways, highways, aviation, and water carriage. Deep down, these measures taken by the Chinese government are active support and supply of public products needed to construct the Belt and the Road. They will greatly stimulate the enthusiasm of countries involved so as to promote the construction of the Belt and the Road.

---

[33] Xi Pledges $40b for Silk Road fund. Retrieved from http://www.chinadaily.com.cn/china/2014-11/09/content_18888916.htm. December 2, 2015.

3.2. Facilitate network-based guarantee mechanism for safety cooperation

In terms of regional non-traditional security issues, the consensus of cooperative responses to those issues has been reached among most countries and various bilateral and multilateral cooperative mechanisms established. For instance, multilateral dialogues and cooperative mechanisms have been practiced among countries along the Maritime Silk Road that goes from Quanzhou of China, through South China Sea, the Strait of Malacca, Andaman Sea, the Bay of Bengal, Indian Ocean, Arabian Sea, the Persian Gulf, the Gulf of Aden, and the Red Sea, and to the Indian Ocean. ARF has held symposiums on regional maritime security cooperation for several times since maritime security was mentioned for the first time on the Second ARF Foreign Ministers' Meeting in 1995. Under the framework of signed agreements, China and ASEAN countries carry out a series of acts in terms of maritime security cooperation and establish China–ASEAN Maritime consultation mechanism. In November, ten ASEAN countries: Japan, China, South Korea, India, Bangladesh, and Sri Lanka reached an agreement on the Regional Cooperation Agreement on Combating Piracy and Armed Robbery against Ships in Asia (ReCAAP) and founded an Information Sharing Center (ISC) in Singapore. Moreover, Malaysia, Singapore, Australia, New Zealand, and the UK formed the Five Power Defence Arrangements (FPDA), and eighteen states including Australia, China, France, Indonesia, Japan, New Zealand, Malaysia, Thailand, the USA, Vietnam, and India constitute the West Pacific Naval Symposium (WPNS). The FPDA has launched various kinds of military exercises among navy and land and air forces to deal with non-traditional security problems like terrorism since the September 11 incident.

Apart from multilateral cooperation, China has also established a list of bilateral cooperative mechanisms with countries along the Belt and the Road. The representative example is the strategic partnership agreement signed between China and Indonesia in April 2005 which targets at enhancing maritime cooperation and joining hands to combat piracy and drug trafficking. What is more, China offers financial aid valued at around 650 billion rupiah to Indonesia for building a marine police station called Malacca in Duman of Riau and equipping the station with wharf facilities, fast patrol boats, helicopters, military telecommunication equipment, and other facilities. The station is expected to take part in the security protection acts in the Strait of Malacca.

Therefore, in order to deal with non-traditional security issues in the future, countries involved in the Belt and the Road should make full use of current bilateral and multilateral mechanisms and existing efficient platforms for regional cooperation. At the same time, they should, taking into consideration new situations and demands, explore new mechanisms and boost the formation of the cooperative mechanism on network-based guarantee of security so as to realize a pattern of solving and preventing non-traditional security issues in three-dimensional way that connects dots, lines, and planes.

3.3. Clear channels for domestic communication, coordination and collaboration and start efficient public diplomacy

Non-traditional security issues are usually specialties demanding. Departments of foreign affairs and security are not enough to deal with them. In many cases, it calls for the coordination of several departments in China such as the Ministry of Commerce, Ministry of Finance, National Development Reform Commission (NDRC), Ministry of Environment, Ministry of Public Security, and Oceanic Administration, so on so forth. The first step before seeking for cooperation and coordination with other countries is to sort out domestic departments that should be involved in building the coordination mechanism with the department of foreign affairs. Only by doing this forces can be concentrated to be ready for international cooperation. Besides, government sectors of China are supposed to work together on forming a complete and unified mechanism for emergency management to improve crisis management. In addition, crisis management organs to deal with specific issues should be established as far as information collection, policy making, situation evaluation, and post-crisis management are concerned and the highest consultative institutions and comprehensive crisis management to facilitate national crisis control should also be formed.

Besides, China's diplomacy, as an important approach to safeguard national security, should pay much attention to the research of non-traditional security threats, to systemically sorting out and studying the non-traditional security issues existing along the Belt and Road, to getting a clear understanding of the relationship between non-traditional security issues and the construction of the Belt and Road, and to diversifying solutions to those issues.

4. Conclusions

The production and existence of non-traditional security issues pose a threat to the countries along the Belt and the Road that any single country's prosperity would bring blooms to all others and its loses harms to all others, too. In this case, the safety issues will push forward the construction of natural basis for communities of common interests and of shared destines between China and its neighbors, and promotes greatly the cooperation among participants. At present, the issues will challenge the safety conditions for constructing the Belt and Road to different degrees, although the common interest-oriented choices will boost the form of stability framework based on non-traditional security cooperation among nations along the Belt and the Road, specifically advancing mutual trust through dialogues, solving disputes through peaceful negotiations, and realizing common safety via cooperation. At the same time, China's strategic influence is strengthened and international image improved, which is the top one significance of promoting the Belt and Road Initiative.

Chapter 13

21ˢᵗ Century Maritime Silk Road Construction and the Situations of South China Sea

Xue Li

Institute of World Economics and Politics, Chinese Academy of Social Sciences
xueli@163.com

The situation in the South China Sea in 2014 showed the following features: Conflicts or frictions mainly happened in the middle of the year; the Philippines was the main initiator and most incidents took place in the Second Thomas Shoal; progress has been made in the consultations on Code of Conduct in South China Sea; there occurred "cold politics and hot economy" phenomenon in China–Philippine relations, as well as in China–Vietnam relations; China's South China Sea policy has been adjusted to active control.

HD-981 has finished its experimental drilling in Xisha waters, which objectively played a protective effect on the large-scale blowing sand and land reclamation project in Spratly Islands (Nansha Islands) such as Johnson South Reef etc., but the side effects caused by the HD-981 Incident cannot be ignored. The Philippines' complaint against China might be accepted. The Belt and Road Initiative is a medium-term strategy China made for large surrounding area of America's "Asia-Pacific Rebalance". In this case, the implementation of this strategy calls for urgent solving of the South China Sea issues. Maybe China will deal with the South China Sea issues by the following principles: strengthening the presence in the South China Sea and obtaining legitimate interests without affecting the China–ASEAN relations.

Different from the relatively quiet situation in 2013, the situation in the South China Sea was not a bed of roses in 2014. Although the overall situation was not as tense as in 2012, impact of individual events on relations among some countries became severer. In the latter half of the year, the tense in South China Sea generally eased as "ironing out differences and promoting cooperation" has become a policy option for most of the directly concerned parties in the South China Sea disputes. China's policy choice, which of course depends upon its consideration of neighboring strategy, was one of the influential factors to this change. So, will China's exerting influence on the South China Sea become a new normal? If the answer is yes, are there any proper limits for carrying out this policy? This paper is going to explore the answers. The first part of this article outlines the main features of the South China Sea situation in 2014. The second part analyses the key events, and the third part analyses the relations between the Belt and Road Initiative and the South China Sea issues.

1. Featured Situations in South China Sea in 2014

In the past year (to be exact, 11 months), related events with the South China Sea were: the arbitration Philippines filed has made progress; the Philippine marine police in civilian clothes arrested Chinese fishermen at Half Moon Shoal; the Philippines and China had several frictions at Second Thomas Shoal; HD-981 Incident occurred in Xisha waters; in mid-July, the United States offered three suggestions on freezing the South China Sea action and then the Philippines made a three-step plan to resolve the South China Sea disputes mid-August, China put forward twin-track idea to deal with the South China Sea disputes; in November, China agreed to actively carry out consultations in order to reach an early consensus on Code of Conduct in South China Sea. These events showed the following features.

1.1. Second Thomas Shoal: the new key point for China–Philippine conflict

Three out of four frictions between China and the Philippines in the Second Thomas Shoal waters. On March 9, 2014, two Philippine cargo ships reached the Second Thomas Shoal waters with construction materials such as reinforced concrete on board. Besides repairing "stranded" tank landing ships, these building materials could also be used to build temporary structures on the reef. This was the second time after May 2013 that the Philippines had transported construction materials to the Second Thomas Shoal. China couldn't tolerate this kind of status-changing behavior, and sent a public service ship to expel the ships. On March 29, the Philippines sent a fishing boat carrying soldiers, food and other supplies to the Second Thomas Shoal, and invited some Western reporters to "observe" the action. Chinese Coast Guard ship in this area tried to expel the "fishing boat" from Chinese waters. After two hours, these shallow-draft ships reached the shallows. Chinese Coast Guard ship stopped taking further actions for fear of being stranded. The Western reporters on board covered the confrontation.[1] The Philippine Air Force declared that they found five Chinese ships near the Second Thomas Shoal, including the research ship "Xiang Yang Hong 10", "Jianghu V" frigate and three

---

[1] The author believes that China Coast Guard ships did not continue to take actions to expel the Philippine "fishing boats", because they believed that the shallow draft ships were not equipped with construction materials, only with some supplies for the "stranded" old warships. See "the Philippines excitedly broke China Coast Guard two-hour blockade landing on the Second Thomas Shoal," March 31, 2013, Huanqiu, http://world.huanqiu.com/exclusive/2014-03/4940895.html.

Coast Guard ships, when they air-dropped supplies to the "stranded" old warships in the Second Thomas Shoal on May 3.

1.2. The Philippines as a major trouble source

Among the member states of ASEAN, Brunei and Malaysia keep relatively stable and friendly relations with China. The Philippines and Vietnam are the member states of ASEAN who had new disputes with China, the former being the main trouble source; In the disputed events between China and the Philippines, the Philippines was still the active initiator, while China was the responding party. The Philippines submitted 4,000 pages of memorial to the arbitral tribunal "UNCLOS" on March 30, 2014. The Philippines arrested Chinese fishermen in Half Moon Shoal and started frictions in Second Thomas Shoal.

1.3. Tough middle months and easy starts and ends

The first two months of 2014 were relatively peaceful. Three frictions occurred in the Second Thomas Shoal between China and the Philippines, two of which were at the end of March and early May. The Philippines arrested 11 Chinese fishermen in Half Moon Shoal on May 6. HD-981 Incident occurred in early May, and continued until mid-July. The United States made a number of reactions to the HD-981 Incident, the Senate passed the bill 421 on July 10.[2] On July 11, Deputy Assistant Secretary Flowserve, who was responsible for Asian and Pacific Affairs, proposed three recommendations on specific freezing actions in the South China Sea.[3] The Philippines

---

[2] The main contents are: the US requests China to evacuate "Offshore Oil 981" rig and escort ships from the South China Sea, restoring the original status of the South China Sea, urging China to control the implementation of the declaration of the East China Sea Air Defense Identification Zone.

[3] The main contents are: the parties shall stop the actions of capturing the reefs, setting up outposts, changing the landform status and unilateral actions against other countries.

subsequently proposed a three-step plan to resolve the South China Sea disputes.[4] On August 4, the Philippines declared that this plan had gained support from Vietnam, Indonesia, and Brunei. China announced on August 6 that it has finished its field survey and site selection work for lighthouse construction in five Paracel Islands (Xisha Islands), namely the North Reef, Lingyang Reef, Jinqing Island, Nansha Island, and Gaojianshi Reef.[5] The plan proposed by the Philippines did not get the consensus of ASEAN member countries in ASEAN and East Asia Foreign Ministers Conference Series held from August 8 to 11. China also believed that the Philippines' arbitration practice meant it had jumped to the third step and the plan was more in name than reality. In response, Foreign Minister Wang Yi proposed "twin-track thinking" to deal with the South China Sea issues in the press conference after China–ASEAN Foreign Ministers' Meeting on August 9. By the end of August, CPV Politburo member Le Hongying paid a visit to China as special envoy of the General Secretary. In November, Prime Minister Li Keqiang proposed to make 2015 China–ASEAN maritime cooperation year. Thus it can be seen that, since mid-August, the momentum of cooperation among Claimants has prevailed. It is worth mentioning that the "twin-track thinking" was released. Its main contents are: the disputes should be solved peacefully by directly concerned parties through friendly consultations and negotiations. China and ASEAN countries should jointly safeguard peace and stability in the South China Sea. This shows that China no longer sticks to the stance that "Nansha

---

[4] The main contents are: the first step is to suspend tension exacerbating activities in the South China Sea in the short term; The second step is to implement "Declaration on Conduct of Parties in the South China Sea" comprehensively and effectively and complete the Code of Conduct in South China Sea as soon as possible in the medium term; The third step is to eventually settle the disputes by settlement mechanism under international law.

[5] *South China Sea maritime security center has completed Lighthouse(pile) site selection in five Paracel Islands (Xisha Islands)*, August 6, 2014, *People's Daily*, http://world.people.com.cn/n/2014/0806/c1002-25412948.html.

disputes should only be solved through bilateral negotiations, non-Claimants of ASEAN cannot participate", trying to use "moderate regionalization" to prevent "comprehensive internationalization" of the South China Sea disputes.

1.4. "Powerful punches back to active adjustment and control"

China denies the Philippines' presence via placing "stranded old warship" on the Second Thomas Shoal. So the eight Nansha reefs mentioned by Hua Chunying do not include the Second Thomas Shoal. China has strengthened its administration of the Second Thomas Shoal in recent years by increasing cruise frequency, monitoring the actions of the Philippines, especially constructing activities. Apparently, China has demonstrated a positive attitude to deal with the disputes, but its overall operation is reactive with obvious restraint. However, in the HD-981 Incident, China became the active doer and controlling party all through from the beginning to the surprisingly early end. This change was significant. The great repercussions caused by this incident was up to China's expectation. Comments on this event will be detailed later.

1.5. "Cold politics and hot economy" occurred among parties in disputes

Trade between the Philippines and China followed the legacy of high growth rate in the previous three years. Bilateral trade totaled $10.3 billion from January to July in 2014, with an increase of 19%. China has become the second largest trading partner of the Philippines after Japan. In April, China was the largest trading partner of the Philippines. China was also the Philippines' largest source of imports, with an increase of about 20% by the end of July. From January to August in 2014, total imports and exports between China and the Philippines grew 15%, and the growth rate ranked second in the ASEAN countries. At the same time, two-way investment between China and the Philippines was on the rise. More and more Chinese enterprises increased investment in manufacturing, services, and information and communication industries in the Philippines. In the first half of the year, Philippine government approved investment from China amounted to $214 million, far higher than the year before.[6]

Situation between China and Vietnam was similar. China has been Vietnam's first largest trading partner for ten consecutive years. From January to August in 2014, bilateral trade amounted to $5000310.4 billion, 25.9% over the the year of 2013. On August, it was $685375.7 billion, increasing by 22.2%.[7] There is no statistics of investment between China and Vietnam in 2014 yet, but the high growth momentum in trades of goods and services is apparent.

1.5.1. *Consultation on the code of conduct in south China sea made progress*

The sixth Senior Officials Meeting and the ninth meeting of the Joint Working Group on *Declaration on the Conduct of Parties in the South China Sea (Declaration for short)* held in Suzhou, China in September 2013 authorized the Joint Working Group to make consultations on the code of conduct, and agreed to set up a subcommittee of prestigious experts. The tenth meeting of the Joint Working Group was held in Singapore on March 18, 2014 to implement the *Declaration*, continuing consultations on relevant issues. In April, the seventh Senior Officials Meeting was held in Thailand, where China and ASEAN countries made candid and extensive communication on the Code of Conduct in South China Sea and discussed the establishment of a joint maritime search and rescue platform. In early June, on the ASEAN Regional Forum Senior Officials Meeting in Myanmar, Chinese Vice Foreign Minister Liu Zhenmin advocated

---

[6]Lu Xiaodong: With China–Philippine trade rising in recent years, Philippine officials are optimistic about China-Philippine trade and development, November 4, 2014, Xinhua, http://news.xinhuanet.com/world/2014-11/04/c_127176392.htm.
[7]Customs Statistics Report, November 23, 2014, Chinese Customs official website: http: //www.customs.gov.cn/publish/portal0/tab68101/.

that all the member states should fully and effectively implement the *Declaration*, and steadily push forward the consultation on the Code of Conduct in South China Sea. At the same time, Liu opposed any attempt of involving extraregional countries in the disputes or unilateral and ill-considered recourse to international arbitration. In August, Chinese Foreign Minister Wang Yi proposed the "twin-track thinking" to deal with the South China Sea disputes, showing that China agreed ASEAN to play a role in solving South China Sea disputes. In November, Chinese Prime Minister Li Keqiang said in his speech at the ASEAN summit that China would like to actively join the consultations on and to complete as early as possible the Code of Conduct in the South China Sea on the basis of consensus, which has achieved early harvest. China agreed to establish a joint maritime search and rescue hotline platform with member states' maritime sectors, and set up hotline with foreign ministries to cope with emergencies in the sea. The Parties talked about the establishment of exchange and cooperation mechanisms among littoral countries of the South China Sea. While seeking to resolve the disputes, China advocated joint development, which is also a pragmatic and effective approach to reserve differences.[8] This shows that although China's stance on promoting the code of conduct under the framework of the *Declaration* has not been changed, China agreed on ASEAN's playing a greater role in maintaining peace and stability in the South China Sea, and accelerating the completion of the Code of Conduct in South China Sea rather than further stressing on "rational expectations".

2. Cases Analysis

Among South China Sea-related events mentioned above, The HD-981 Incident and the Philippines' arbitration are the most sensational. The former seems to mark the change in China's South China Sea policy. The latter is likely to have a profound impact on

---

[8] "Li Keqiang's speech on the ninth East Asia Summit (full text)," November 14, 2014, Xinhua, http://news.xinhuanet.com/2014-11/14/c_1113240192.htm.

settlement of the South China Sea disputes. The case of the Philippines arresting Chinese fishermen is also worth mentioning.

2.1. HD-981 Incident

China National Petroleum Corporation (CNPC) started the project of drilling two exploration wells in the south of Triton Island on May 2 this year, and completed the drilling operation of the first well on May 27. The second well drilling operation started on May 28 and finished on July 15. "981" Rig was transferred to Lingshui waters in Hainan to continue its work on the 16ᵗʰ. This whole process was a month earlier than originally announced.

It should be noted that this was not China's first exploration activity in the south of Triton Island. In addition to the well-known American Christopher Stone Company Wanan — North case, China also tried similar exploration activities in Xisha waters in 2011, which were suspended due to the strong obstruction of Vietnam. In May, Vietnam attempted to repeat the experience once, but China has changed countermeasures by ensuring the smooth conduct of experimental drilling and completing the task ahead of schedule.

HD-981 Incident undoubtedly was the most eye-catching issue in the South China Sea in 2014, and could become an annual landmark event. The dispute lasted more than two months, but the beginning and ending parts, where China took an active role, were unexpected. So, why did China act in this way? Why did China finish the project early? What effects and impact did the event generate?

In 2012, China's strategy to the South China Sea and East China Sea disputes policy is "try peaceful means before resorting to force, and the counter-attack if necessary has to be strong". This strategy protects China from breaching moral norms and lets its opponents pay for their whistle. But in the HD-981 Incident, China apparently didn't use this strategy.

Mainstream opinions in and outside China hold that Europe and America made weak response to the turbulent situation in Crimea, showing its "paper tiger" nature, which has been taken by

China as a chance to promote its oil and gas development in Xisha waters; Obama visited Japan, Philippines, and Australia to sell its Asia-Pacific Rebalance strategy, while China tried to show its disinterest; troubled by corruption cases, CNPC wanted to make a difference, at the meantime oil and gas development in Xisha waters reached to the experimental stage; Under the circumstance that anti-corruption action encountered great resistance, the drilling operation which required coordination of many sectors not only showed China's power to others, but also helped unite the central authority so as to advance anti-corruption.

In most cases, a big decision is a result of several causes. Views summarized above have revealed some aspects of the problem, but may have missed one point. China's action in the HD-981 Incident might aims at diverting the world's attention to the blowing sand reclamation operations on the five reefs, namely Johnson South Reef, Huayang Reef, Hughes Reef, Nanxun Reef and Eldad Reef. China had accelerated the speed of blowing sand reclamation since March. By August, there had been a number of buildings and trees on the Johnson South Reef, and the port was also under construction.[9]

If, as the media said, the Johnson South Reef will be turned into a 2 km^2 island,[10] and the Fiery Cross Reef a 5 km^2 island with airports, ports, radar stations, troops and other facilities,[11] China's presence in Spratly Islands (Nansha Islands) will definitely be reinforced, which is more significant than oil and gas exploration in the waters. To make such a massive project proceed smoothly,

---

[9] "Philippine media: China's reclamation work in Johnson South Reef has been transferred to the green phase" August 29, 2014, Xinhua, http://news.xinhuanet.com/world/2014-08/29/c_126933408.htm.

[10] "Foreign media: China made reclamation in the Johnson South Reef and pushed the South China Sea base 850 kilometers forward," September 3, 2014, Xinhua, http://news.xinhuanet.com/yzyd/local/20140903/c_1112344614.htm.

[11] "The story behind China's eagerness to build the South China Sea islands and commencement of operation on reefs Taiwan Taiping Island" June 25, 2014, Xinhua, http://news.xinhuanet.com/mil/2014-06/25/c_126669459.htm?prolongation=1.

appropriate cover operations were necessary. The plain truth is that this action failed to hold global attention. Philippines' protests in May and the interview took by a correspondent from British Broadcasting Corporation in early September, etc., were nothing but a flash.

Regarding China's early withdrawal of drilling platforms, there are several possible reasons. First of all, the scheduled drilling sampling and other tasks have been completed. Secondly, Typhoon Rammasun was approaching. Thirdly, China was getting prepared for the ASEAN Forum in August by easing the tense in the South China Sea disputes so as to promote cooperation with ASEAN, improve relations with Vietnam, and show the U.S. proper courtesy.[12]

Through this action, China achieved the strategic objectives of "oil and gas development in the south of the Triton Island," and periodical technical objectives of "experimental drilling of oil and gas resources in the south of the Triton Island", taking a solid first step to exploit oil and gas resources officially in the south of Triton Island even the whole Nansha waters in the future.

On the downside, firstly, it triggered a strong reaction of Vietnam. China and Vietnam launched a fierce confrontation in the waters around the platform which lasted more than two months. Vietnam riots against foreign industries (mainly Chinese mainland and Taiwan enterprises), with hundreds of Chinese casualties and many industries and equipment destroyed. Bilateral relations became strained, significantly stirring public opposition between the two peoples. Secondly, China had insisted that there was no dispute in Xisha islands, but the incident showed to the world the other way around. Thirdly, the incident made ASEAN member countries further involve in the South China Sea issues that ASEAN issued a foreign ministers' statement and expressed concern over the situation in the South China Sea for the first time. Fourthly, the

---

[12] Xue Li: "Why China withdrawed 981 rig early?", "Financial Times" (Chinese network), July 21, 2014.

United State took a tougher stance on the South China Sea disputes and its interference in the issues became overt. US Defense Minister publicly criticized China in the Shangri-La Dialogue Conference. US Senate passed a resolution to request China to withdraw the drilling platform, and the State Department officials proposed three recommendations on freezing the South China Sea action. Moreover, in October, the United States lifted the ban of the sale of lethal weapon in the reason of "helping Vietnam enhance maritime security". Fifth, Vietnam and Malaysia sped up the progress of the block bidding.

Nevertheless, China will not loose control over this issue, as it has been dealing with the South China Sea disputes under the framework of China–ASEAN relations, and now also by considering its Belt and Road Initiative. China will continue to strengthen its existence in the South China Sea (especially the Nansha islands) through a number of measures, including the necessary experimental drilling, but in a more tactical way.

2.2. The Philippines-China Arbitration

In January 2013 the Philippines claimed to form an arbitration tribunal based on UNCLOS and Annex VII to settle disputes with China over maritime jurisdiction in the South China Sea. According to the No. 1 Procedural Order of the Court of Arbitration, on March 30, 2014, the Philippines submitted nearly 4,000 pages of memorial.[13] If China responded, in accordance with general international arbitration procedures, China should submit Counter-Memorial by the end of October 2014. Then there are 8–10 months for the Philippines to file a reply and for China to submit rejoinder. However, on March 30, Chinese Foreign Ministry spokesman Hong Lei said that China still refused to accept international arbitration. In the statement to the United Nations in August 2006, China excluded the approach of resolving reefs sovereignty and

---

[13] Song Yanhui: "On the jurisdiction of the arbitral tribunal over the case of the Philippines v China, from the "DOC" "International Law", 2014 (2), p. 6.

sea demarcation disputes through international arbitration, declared that the Philippines' practice violated "Declaration on Conduct of Parties in the South China Sea", and urged the Philippines return to bilateral negotiation to resolve the disputes.[14] Of course, China is unlikely to change its position to participate in the arbitration although it has the right. The PCA may give a verdict on whether it has jurisdiction to adjudicate the case in 2015. International jurisprudential scholars believe that the PCA tends to give positive answer on its jurisdiction over the arbitration, but in the meantime it will only support part of the request of the Philippines.

The impact of this case is multifaceted. Firstly, it set an example for other countries, telling that they can copy the Philippines if there were any disputes with China. For example, Vietnam declared on many occasions that it would take international legal actions to deal with conflicts with China. It filed a lawsuit in its own on May 26 alleging that Chinese vessels crashed and sank a Vietnamese fishing boat in Xisha waters.[15] Once China decides to implement the policy "the unilateral open policy leveraging multilateral joint development in the Nansha waters, "suing China" could become a common practice for ASEAN claimants. Secondly, although China has the right not to accept arbitration, it may give an impression to the world that "China does not comply with the international rules", influencing China's efforts of peaceful rise and international image of "a responsible power". Thirdly, among the requests made by the Philippines, the most crucial one is the request of calling the "nine-dotted line" invalid. Once PCA accepts this one, China's fuzzy strategies on the issue of

---

[14]"Foreign Ministry spokesman Hong Lei met the press over the arbitration the Philippines filed," March 30, 2014, Retrived from http://news.xinhuanet.com/world/2014-03/30/c_1110013644.htm.

[15]The Chinese side stressed that Vietnamese vessel capsized by itself in the process of interfering in China's drilling platform operations, China rescued drowning Vietnamese fishermen, see "Vietnamese fishing boat strongly interfered Chinese drilling platform and capsized", May 28, 2014, Xinhua, http://news.xinhuanet.com/mil/2014-05/28/c_126555797.htm.

"nine-dotted line" could be unsustainable, and the legitimacy of the nine-dotted line will be seriously weakened. ASEAN claimants who had doubts in the oil and gas exploration in the "nine-dotted line", will carry out large-scale joint exploitation within the line, which will drag China into passive dilemma.

In addition, this case objectively stimulated academic research enthusiasm; the South China Sea issues have once again after the 1990s become a major research focus for scholars in fields of international jurisprudence, strategic research and Chinese issues studies. Many international conferences have been held in ASEAN member states, which deepened academic understanding towards the South China Sea disputes. Most of overseas scholars support or sympathize with the Philippines, while only a few think negotiation between the two countries is a better choice. Chinese scholars also held different views on this issue. Most scholars, especially those in international jurisprudence, believed that China has good reason of not responding. But some argued that total ignorance does not meet the national interests of China and China should have at least participated in the arbitration when PCA decided whether it had the right of jurisdiction, as this would not affect China's official stance. Besides, observations show that the Philippines was abusing complaint proceedings, because most of its requests were non-actionable.

2.3. The incident of Chinese fisherman's being arrested by Philippine police

On May 6, Philippine maritime police seized a Chinese fishing boat and arrested 11 fishermen near Half Moon Shoal on the grounds that they found 350 endangered sea turtles on board. A Philippine boat which was transferring sea turtles to the Chinese boat was also seized. The Philippines released two underage fishermen on May 8, and accused the other nine Chinese people of "environmental crimes" regardless of China's negotiations and warning. In accordance with the Philippine law, the maximum sentence of this crime is

20 years, with a fine of 1 million pesos.[16] Since then the Philippine local court repeatedly delayed the trial, for they "could not find qualified translators". No subsequent message was heard until mid-November.

As Chinese Foreign Ministry spokesman Hua Chunying disclosed in the end of April 2013, the Half Moon Shoal is not among the eight Nansha reefs illegally occupied by the Philippines.[17] Half Moon Cay is located between the above reefs and Palawan, which the Philippines call "Kalayaan Islands". However, these reefs are all within the "nine-dotted line". It is obvious that this area belongs to the disputed waters. The Philippines and China had a rough understanding of how to deal with similar cases in the disputed waters. Usual practice was fine and release of seized people, and the sentence, if there had to be any, was not heavy.[18]

But this time around, the Philippines dispatched maritime police in civilian clothes on a fishing boat, arrested people on board after fired into the air, and then insisted on prosecution.[19] The reason of "protection of endangered animals" morally supported their behavior, but it cannot explain why local authority "dealt with issues in internationally disputed waters by domestic law". What was worse, the incident even occurred before the 24ᵗʰ ASEAN Summit which was going to be held on April 11. Given these, China has every reason to believe that the Philippines wanted to

---

[16] "The Philippines forced the prosecution of Chinese fishermen who refused Philippine survey", April 13, 2014, Retrieved from http://world.huanqiu.com/exclusive/2014-05/4993487.html.

[17] The eight reefs are: Nanshan Island, Flat Island, Thitu Island, Loaita Island, Northeast Cay, West York Island, Commodore Reef and Loaita Nan. See "8 Chinese reefs occupied by the Philippines", April 27, 2013, Retrived from http://news.xinhuanet.com/mil/2013-04/27/c_124640962.htm.

[18] Tao Tao: "Chinese fishermen detained mostly because of fishing, Youth Reference", December 7, 2011, 8ᵗʰ edition.

[19] Zhao Yingquan, Guo Xinfeng: "Fishermen told the experience of being arrested by the Philippine maritime police", May 16, 2014, retrieved from http://news.xinhuanet.com/2014-05/16/c_1110716511.htm.

magnify and politicalize the issue. We couldn't help wondering that whether the Philippines would like to see its fishermen who did the similar be treated in the same way.

In addition, in early August, Palawan district court of the Philippines announced the arrested 12 Chinese fishermen in April 2013 guilty of "illegal fishing", with a sentence from 6 to 12 years in prison and a fine of $100,000 per person, fishing boat confiscated. The Philippines also said it would continue to hear their behavior of holding protected pangolin, destroying 4,000 m² of reef in the Tubbataha Reef. The Sulu Sea where the incident happened belongs to the Philippines, so the Philippines was entitled to judge according to domestic law. However, the judgment was so heavy, highlighting the Philippines' intention to express its tough stance on the South China Sea issues. An obvious contrast is that the US minesweeper was stranded and caused huge damage to Tubbataha Reef in January 2013, and the Philippines only gave a fine instead of filing a lawsuit.[20]

3. South China Sea Issue and the Belt and Road Initiative

The Belt and Road Initiative, as a product of the times, gradually shows its characteristics as a medium-term international strategy made by the new Chinese government, in which the South China Sea plays an important role.

3.1. Background

As China takes increasingly position in global economy and politics in the 21st Century, especially after the global financial crisis in 2008, China has been seen as the next superpower. Thus, after its wish to establish "G2" or "Chimerica" failed, the US turned to

---

[20]"The Philippines tries to express its tough stance on the South China Sea disputes through heavy sentences of Chinese fishermen", August 6, 2014, retrieved from http://news.xinhuanet.com/mil/2014-08/06/c_126839670.htm.

"pivot to Asia", and adjusted to "Asia-Pacific Rebalance" in 2013. Objectively speaking, rebalancing policy was the traditional Anglo-Saxon regional strategy, in contrast to the containment strategy to Soviet Union during the Cold War. But from a security and economic point of view, China is the main target of the US rebalancing strategy.

Domestically, the negative effects of the "four trillion plan" launched in November 2008 on China's economy become prominent: a lot of excess capacity, lifting non-performing loan ratio, slow economic restructuring and huge foreign exchange reserves growth.[21] Taking the slow economic recovery in Europe and America, saturated market and trade protectionism into account, China needs to cultivate and develop another market except the European and American market in order to keep foreign trade growth, transfer excess production capacity and reduce foreign exchange reserves. To implement these plans in neighboring countries, allowing them to further share the fruits of China's economic growth is undoubtedly a win–win choice that should be given top priority. In diplomacy and security areas, China also need to break the US' Asia-Pacific rebalancing strategy, to build China's own secure space and mechanism, advisably starting from its neighboring countries.

Therefore, after a period of deliberation, President Xi Jinping proposed the building of Silk Road Economic Belt that will involve nearly 3 billion people during his visit to Kazakhstan in early September 2013. Shortly after when he visited Indonesia in early October, he proposed to build 21st Century Maritime Silk Road with the ASEAN countries. An unprecedented neighboring diplomatic forum were held at the end of October, confirming strategic objectives, working ideas and implementation plan over the next 10

---

[21] Excessive foreign exchange reserves is not a good thing, Premier Li Keqiang admitted that "excessive foreign exchange reserves has become a great burden." See "The central bank reduced foreign exchange reserves overseas investments may accelerate", October 17, 2014, *People's Daily*, http://gx.people.com.cn/finance/n/2014/1017/c352207-22637657.html.

years of diplomacy with neighboring countries, which could already be observed in China's diplomatic actions in 2014.

Therefore, the Belt and Road Initiative is a medium-term strategy for its neighboring area in the broad sense so that China, as a regional power, can get rid of the constraint of the Asia-Pacific Rebalance, and hence form a large regional economic and political security network, where the economy is the center of the field, and the neighboring area in the narrow sense the focus of the region.

3.2. Political and economic effects of the Belt and Road Initiative

From the economic perspective, with the rapid development of economy and comprehensive national strength, China needs to design for its own the international economic and diplomatic environment for the next stage of development. "Promoting reform through opening-up" has proven to be an effective way, but China needs to find a new breakthrough. However, China–US, China–Japanese economic relations have little room to improve, while the room for improvement of economic relations between China and Russia is not small, although Russia's total economy is limited. In this case, there are two directions for China to expand its economy and diplomacy: on land, the direction is mainly westward expansion, through the Silk Road Economic Belt construction, driving in Central Asia, the Caucasus and the Middle East West Asia, going through the whole Europe; on the ocean, the direction is mainly southward expansion, through the construction of the Maritime Silk Road, driving ASEAN, further connecting South Asia and the Middle East, with Africa, Latin America and Europe as three terminals of the "Maritime Silk Road". As the gateway to Europe, the "Maritime Silk Road" is used to make up for a major thoroughfare on the Eurasian land. "Maritime Silk Road" literally means a road of peace, security, cooperation and common prosperity, which will

lead the countries along the Road towards comprehensive cooperation through economic cooperation, and help alleviate some
countries' doubts on China's implementation of the "string of
pearls" strategy.

From the political and security perspective, China's maritime
neighboring countries refer to Korea, Japan, and littoral countries of
the South China Sea. There is little possibility of a significant
improvement in the political and security relations between China
and Japan in the coming years, and the room for China and South
Korea to enhance political and security relations is also limited, so
littoral countries of the South China Sea have become the primary
targets of China' construction of the 21st Century Maritime Silk
Road. ASEAN countries are very likely to resume their position as a
hub in ancient Silk Road. After all, in the past 20 years, ASEAN has
been the place where China practices its multilateral diplomacy and
new security concept. The China–ASEAN Free Trade Area is one of
the fruits of this endeavor.

3.3. ASEAN and South China Sea issue from the perspective of the Belt and Road Initiative

In theory, the Belt and the Road are respectively located on western
and eastern parts of China, which are complementary. If the Road
construction turns out to be difficult, China can focus on the construction of the Belt, which has a huge room for growth, and can
better play a leading role. However, maritime trade dominates
China's foreign trade, which cannot be replaced by land-borne
trade. The ending terminal of the Road is not limited to Eurasia,
but the world's major economies. Beside, with rapid economic
development in Southeast Asia, ASEAN is China's third largest
trading partner. The depth and breadth of economic cooperation
between China and Southeast Asian countries cannot be replaced
by the Silk Road Economic Belt.

Situations in politics, security, and economy determine that
ASEAN countries are not only where China starts its Road

initiative, but as well a vital key to the success of this initiative. The South China Sea dispute is a vulnerable point in China–ASEAN relations, and also the most concerned security issue of ASEAN. Thus, the settlement of the South China Sea disputes is urgent. China of course should expand presence in the South China Sea to defend its sovereignty and maritime interests. However, the South China Sea issue is not the core interest of China, but only a part of China–ASEAN relations. Thus, "strengthening the presence in the South China Sea and gaining legitimate interests without affecting bilateral relations" should be the principle for China to handle the South China Sea disputes.

4. Conclusions

The year 2014 witnessed major incidents in the South China Sea. The incidents mainly occurred in the middle of the year with less tensity than those in 2012. The Philippines is the initiator of most events. Second Thomas Shoal is the place where most events happened. The consultation on Code of Conduct in South China Sea has made some progress. China–Philippines relations and China–Vietnam relations featured "cold politics and hot economy". China launched and finished an experimental drilling project in the south of Triton Island. China had both gain and lose in the HD-981 Incident. Objectively speaking, the HD-981 Incident secured the operation of the large-scale blowing sand and land reclamation action on Spratly Islands (Nansha Islands). In the meanwhile, the Philippines-China arbitration might be accepted by PCA and China may get unfavorable verdict. The incident of Chinese fisherman's being arrested and put on trial by the Philippines showed the Philippines' tough attitude towards China.

The Belt and Road Initiative is a medium-term strategy of China for its neighboring region, aiming at peacefully breaking the constraint of America's "Asia-Pacific Rebalance". ASEAN is the first hub in the 21st Century Maritime Silk Road. Given the depth and breadth of cooperation between China and Southeast Asia, ASEAN is replaceable. At present, the South China Sea issue is an obstacle for cooperation and common concern of both parties. Thus, a proper settlement of the issue is currently urgent, all through which the principle of "strengthening the presence in the South China Sea and gaining legitimate interests without affecting bilateral relations" should be followed.

Index

Lightning Source UK Ltd.
Milton Keynes UK
UKOW05n1323151216
290109UK00001B/15/P

9 789813 140202